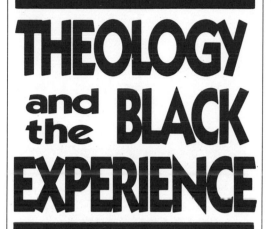

# THEOLOGY and the BLACK EXPERIENCE

The Lutheran
Heritage Interpreted
by African &
African-American
Theologians

Edited by

## Albert Pero and Ambrose Moyo

**AUGSBURG** Publishing House • Minneapolis

**THEOLOGY AND THE BLACK EXPERIENCE**
**The Lutheran Heritage Interpreted by African and African-American**
**Theologians**

### Library of Congress Cataloging-in-Publication Data

Theology and the Black experience: the Lutheran heritage interpreted
  by African and African-American theologians / edited by Albert Pero
  and Ambrose Moyo.
     p.    cm.
  Papers presented at the Conference of International Black
Lutherans held at the University of Zimbabwe in Sept. 1986.
  Bibliography: p.
  ISBN 0-8066-2353-5
    1. Lutheran Church—Doctrines—Congresses. 2. Afro-American
Lutherans—Congresses. I. Pero, Albert, 1935– . II. Moyo,
Ambrose, 1943– . III. Conference of International Black Lutherans
(1986 : University of Zimbabwe)
BX8065.2.T48 1988
284.1'08996—dc19   *# 18589824*        88-7778
                                       CIP

Manufactured in the U.S.A.          APH 10-6284

1   2   3   4   5   6   7   8   9   0   1   2   3   4   5   6   7   8   9

# CONTENTS

# ACKNOWLEDGMENTS

On behalf of all those who have contributed essays to this book and all the participants at the historic conference on the "Lutheran Heritage and the Black Experience in Africa and North America," we would like to express our thanks to all those who have contributed toward the success of the conference and the realization of our dream. In particular we wish to mention the two institutions that cosponsored the conference, namely, the Lutheran School of Theology at Chicago, and the University of Zimbabwe through the Department of Religious Studies, Classics, and Philosophy. Our thanks also go to the Evangelical Lutheran Church in Zimbabwe, which hosted the conference at the University of Zimbabwe; to the Lutheran World Federation through its Advisory Committee on Theological Education in Africa, the Protestant Association for World Mission (Evangelisches Missionswerk), the Lutheran Church in America, and the American Lutheran Church for providing the necessary financial support. It is our hope that the essays published here will provide a perspective that has been missing within Lutheranism and also a basis for further discussions within our multicultural context.

AMBROSE MOYO and ALBERT PERO

# PREFACE

The essays in this book were originally presented at the Conference of International Black Lutherans held in Harare at the University of Zimbabwe in September 1986 on the theme: "The Lutheran Heritage and the Black Experience in Africa and in North America." As editors of this material, we have attempted to maintain the substantive content and intention of the authors. These essays reflect the fact that a significant event is often precipitated by a particular problem, issue, or malady. In this case the issue under discussion can be stated in the form of a question: Is Lutheranism large enough to house more than one cultural tradition? The issue can be stated in a different way: "Following the example of Paul, the Church became Jewish with the Jewish world and Greek with the Greek world. However, it has not become Asian with the Asians, black with the blacks, Native American with the Native Americans, Hispanic with the Hispanics. Viewed as a whole, the Church of Jesus Christ has remained a European-American church." Must we as Africans and African-Americans become European-Americans to become Christians? The essays in this volume are an attempt to answer the question: What does it mean to be Lutheran and black?

It is our contention that there can be no people without a culture. Any destruction of a people's culture is a destruction of the people themselves and will result in an identity crisis. As Africans and African-Americans we have suffered greatly from the missionary and the white American efforts to destroy our cultural identity, but despite all that, we have maintained distinct African and African-American cultural perspectives which have contributed to forms of Christian spirituality and practice that are different from those of the white Americans or Europeans from whom we have received our Lutheran heritage. These essays intend to affirm the contribution of Africans and African-Americans to the Lutheran heritage and show how we can also claim it for ourselves.

The theological perspective on being black and Lutheran points to the critical necessity of understanding Christian unity in cultural diversity. It also raises the question of universality and contextuality in the theological enterprise. The appearance of this subject comes from our experiences with God both within and apart from Lutheranism. Its presence is due to the failure of Christian theologians to relate the gospel of Christ to the pain and suffering of being black in racist or tribal societies which include Lutherans. This book arises from a long, historical struggle of black Christian people in general and Lutherans in particular, who have tried to develop a theology where unity in diversity is celebrated within a culturally inclusive church. The book argues that the context of the African and African-American churches must become a major point of departure for theological reflection on the black Christian experience. The result will be a discovery of the gifts that black people offer to the ecumenical Christian table.

At Harare we offered some answers to the critical question of our Lord Jesus Christ: "Who do you [Lutherans] say that I am?" These essays are an attempt to answer that question from distinctively African and African-American perspectives.

Finally, this book is the outcome of a dream which emanates from *(a)* the many years of Pete Pero's work and participation in "The Black Theology Project," which made him wonder what the implications of a theological analysis of Lutheranism from the perspective of African Lutheran theologians in diaspora would be; and *(b)* Ambrose Moyo's research interests in relating African theology to black theology in America through dialog. The process was initiated when Ambrose Moyo came to Chicago at the beginning of 1984 on a three-month study leave, where he visited black churches and met with leading church people in the city. After several meetings in which we shared our dreams and research interests, the two of us realized that we had access to resources to bring together African and African-American theologians at a conference. There is a high level of excitement for our future conferences and about subsequent research we plan to do and share with you, our colleagues and partners in Christ.

We herewith offer this book and the "Harare Message of Black Lutherans" (the full text of which appears as an appendix to this book and represents the views of all the participants at the Harare conference) to the international Lutheran family and to the church catholic for discussion and response.

AMBROSE MOYO and ALBERT PERO

# 1

# JUSTIFICATION BY FAITH AND ITS SOCIAL IMPLICATIONS

## RICHARD J. PERRY

*Lift ev'ry voice and sing*
*Till earth and heaven ring,*
*Ring with the harmonies of liberty.*
*Let our rejoicing rise high as the list'ning skies;*
*Let it resound loud as the rolling sea.*
*Sing a song full of the faith that the dark past has taught us;*
*Sing a song full of the hope that the present has brought us;*
*Facing the rising sun of our new day begun,*
*Let us march on, till victory is won.*

*Stony the road we trod,*
*Bitter the chast'ning rod,*
*Felt in the days when hope unborn had died;*
*Yet, with a steady beat, have not our weary feet*
*Come to the place for which our parents sighed?*
*We have come over a way that with tears has been watered;*
*We have come, treading our path through the blood of the*
*    slaughtered,*
*Out from the gloomy past, till now we stand at last*
*Where the white gleam of our bright star is cast.*

*God of our weary years,*
*God of our silent tears,*
*Thou who hast brought us thus far on the way;*
*Thou who hast by thy might led us into the light:*
*Keep us forever in the path, we pray.*
*Lest our feet stray from the places,*

*Our God, where we met thee;*
*Lest, our hearts drunk with the wine of the world, we forget thee;*
*Shadowed beneath thy hand may we forever stand,*
*True to our God, true to our native land.*[1]

■

This study offers an African-American understanding of justification by faith through grace and its social implications. I think it helpful and relevant in a book by black Lutherans to use the "black national anthem," "Lift Ev'ry Voice and Sing," to provide some insights and guidance into these issues out of the black experience. This will be a basis by which I will attempt to address four critical questions:

1. What is justification?
2. What is an African-American Lutheran understanding of justification?
3. What are some African-American responses to justification?
4. What contributions may African-American Lutherans make toward understanding the social implications of Article 4 of the *Augsburg Confession?*

A basic assumption of this study is that an African-American perspective on justification is rooted in the cultural expressions of and actions of faith by African-American people. In other words, the social implications of African-American faith are confessed in and through the synthesis of our thought and action which is hammered out in the context of oppression.

At the very beginning, let me state that I will be using an African-American hermeneutic. That means unfolding our past and listening to the voices of our forerunners to ascertain what African-Americans said, did, and still believe. Henry Mitchell has explained this African-American principle of interpretation: "The Black hermeneutic seek(s) to look into the message of the Black past and see what the Black (Mothers and) Fathers could be saying to Black people today."[2] Mitchell cites two rules: "The first is that one must declare the Gospel in the language and culture of the people—the vernacular" and "The second hermeneutical principle is that the Gospel must speak to the contemporary [person] and [his/her] needs."[3] Taking the cue from Mitchell, we turn to the testimonies, songs, sermons, prayers, and actions of African-Americans in the past to see the social implications the doctrine of justification may have had for them and can have for us. This principle of interpretation bridges the gaps African-American Lutherans experience between their contemporary needs and their black identities, so in this essay I will hold up several spirituals and conversion experiences, together with resulting actions among some who knew that they were justified by God's grace through faith. Doing that will, I think, show that justification by faith does have social implications.

## 1.  Justification: A Lutheran Perspective

*Lift ev'ry voice and sing*
*Till earth and heaven ring,*
*Ring with the harmonies of liberty. . . .*

One persistent and present debate today among Lutherans concerns what meaning, if any, justification by faith through grace has for people in the 20th and 21st centuries. Is that doctrine too archaic for persons in a highly technological and scientific world? What is this doctrine to which Lutherans cling so tenaciously in the midst of people who struggle for economic, political, and social justice?

The Lutheran understanding of justification came as a result of Luther's struggle to find a gracious God. Luther had accepted the late medieval church's method for gaining salvation. However, he did not experience wholeness and salvation through the prescribed method. Works righteousness failed to quench his thirst for forgiveness from sin and for freedom. His breakthrough occurred in the Wittenberg tower when he was able to name his problem:

> I had indeed been captivated with an extraordinary ardor for understanding Paul in the Epistle to the Romans. But up till then it was not the cold blood about the heart, but a single word in Chapter 1 (:17), "In it the righteousness of God is revealed," that had stood in my way. For I hated that word "righteousness of God," which, according to the use and custom of all the teachers, I had been taught to understand philosphically regarding the formal or active righteousness, as they called it, with which God is righteous and punishes the unrighteous sinner.[4]

The law was surrounding Luther. Doing what other human beings required in the quest for salvation made Luther feel that he could never be justified before God. When the gospel broke through, he was led to see that God justifies sinners freely through grace by faith in Jesus. As he observed society from his new stance, Luther saw ways in which works righteousness operated in the lives of those around him. Buying indulgences became more important for some than trusting God in Christ. More important, however, Luther realized the nonscriptural methods used by popes and other church authorities and what they required of believers. So he acted. Luther was seeking "to rescue forgiveness from fundraising. He was trying to restore the original good news of free grace, or God's unconditional acceptance."[5] Luther proposed to argue in his *Theses*, "For the graces of indulgences are concerned only with the penalties of sacramental satisfaction established by [humankind]," and later preached that such measures were forms of the nonsaving "active righteousness" which contrasted with the saving "passive righteousness."[6] Luther discovered and continued to deepen the biblical understanding that justification before God came as God's act of grace, and that grace is appropriated by faith (*fides*) in God's promise to forgive sins and to make the person just. While this may heighten the person's understanding that she or he is both sinner and a saint (*simul justus et peccator*), it also continues to point the saint/sinner to the unconditionality of God's act of justification. The impact of the message forces sinners to look away from themselves and to look up to God as the center of the universe.

While the gift of justification came to be described in different ways, such as "forensic justification," Luther insisted that God bestows the gift from outside the person, apart from the individual's inherent qualities, worthiness, or works. What may be called the "event" of justification is external to the person who receives the new relationship to God in Christ. It is this "event" which is proclaimed and celebrated through Word and sacrament. Indeed, in the proclamation of God's saving event, sinful people are grasped by God's act on their behalf so that they are made "just" before the tribunal of God.

The Latin version of the *Augsburg Confession,* Article 4, reflects Luther's scriptural insight that no one gains saving righteousness on the basis of human merit:

> Our churches also teach that [humans] cannot be justified before God by their own strengths, merits, or works but are freely justified for Christ's sake through faith when they believe that they are received into favor and that their sins are forgiven on account of Christ, who by his death made satisfaction for our sins. This faith God imputes for righteousness in his sight (Rom. 3, 4).[7]

Five years after the presentation of the *Augsburg Confession,* professor Luther told students who were studying Galatians with him,

> By faith alone, not by faith formed by love, are we justified. We must not attribute the power of justifying to a "form" that makes a (person) pleasing to God; we must attribute it to faith, which takes hold of Christ the Savior

Himself and possesses Him in the heart. This faith justifies without love and before love.[8]

What is the result of this justification? Luther's answer was: good works. Good works are acts of loving service to the neighbor and come from persons who are justified through faith. People do good works because they have faith.[9]

The social implications of Luther's new understanding are interesting, to say the least. Again, we need to recall the context which gave rise to his view of justification and his responses to the sociopolitical situation. The doctrine grew out of a spiritual need to find a gracious God. The Peasants' War gave Luther a golden opportunity to correlate justification to their situation. The poor, dominated totally by the ruling class, did not participate in the political structures. Technically, they could not even marry without permission from their lords. They experienced a society in which there was no justice for them.

Luther, drawn into the controversies at an early stage, proposed some reforms that could have been made by the church and ruling class. The peasants welcomed such support. They recalled that earlier the reformer had admonished the German people to resist the system of robbery by the pope and temporal rulers: "Such power is not to be obeyed, but rather resisted with life, property, and with all our might and main."[10] Yet instead of maintaining active support of the peasants' cause, Luther denounced the peasants and called for the nobles to slay them.[11] What happened? It seems that Luther did not know what stand to take as the peasants' tactics escalated from peaceful petition and protest to violence and destruction as they sought deliverance from oppression. His position was not dissimilar from that of white Lutherans toward slavery in the United States.

By attitude and behavior before the U.S. Civil War, white American Lutherans avoided involvement and even a show of concern about the issues of slavery, race, or racism. The standard Lutheran response was to regard those as "social issues" which belonged in the realm of state and national governments. In contrast, white Lutherans were quite satisfied and even energetic as they took on questions about "pure doctrine" and church polity. But they were remarkably passive when it came to working for justice and freedom on behalf of God's enslaved African-American sons and daughters.[12] This response, as disturbing as it is, satisfied and may still satisfy some white American Lutherans. After all, the status quo was affirmed. I believe, however, that African-Americans took the doctrine of justification and developed it further in the American context than whites were ready or willing to do. In African-American hearts, minds, and action, justification becomes a wholistic doctrine which concerns being justified as a result of God's involvement in our social situations.

## 2.   Justification: An African-American Perspective

*We have come*
*Over a way that with tears has been watered:*
*We have come,*
*Treading our path through the blood of the*
*    slaughtered. . . .*

One of the significant differences between white and African-American Lutherans in the United States is the way in which justification through grace by faith developed in their respective communities. James Weldon Johnson's words disclose the heart of the African-American story in my country. If the white American Lutheran story tells of coming over the Atlantic as immigrants, ours is the story of a people who "have come over a way that with tears has been watered." African-Americans experienced the most dehumanizing tragedy ever perpetrated on humanity: institutional slavery and racism. If at first there was substantial freedom prior to 1619, discourse in that "racial Garden of Eden" soon turned from an African-American/white dialog to a white monolog.[13]

White settlers began to focus on the trading of human beings for economic gain. The planter class made the decision to move toward some form of slavery. Global demands for sugar, cotton, and tobacco strained the small work force. As attempts to use native Americans and whites as slaves proved unsuccessful, the logical choice was African people. Lerone Bennett lists the reasons given for enslaving Africans: "They were strong . . . inexpensive . . . visible . . . unprotected. And the supply seemed inexhaustible."[14] The result was a highly repressive and legal system. Laws only served to strengthen the greed of the planter class. For those who changed to Christianity, the law held that Baptism did not change slave status.[15] The degradation of this oppression can be seen simply and eloquently in a slave's name:

A Negro has got no name. My father was a Ransom and he had a uncle name Hankin. If you belong to Mr. Jones and he sell you to Mr. Johnson, consequently you go by the name of your owner. Now where you get a name? We are wearing the name of our master. I was first a Hale; then my father was sold and then I was named Reed.[16]

African women endured sexism in addition to racism. Sojourner Truth made it clear that she was as good as any man and was able to outwork, outeat, and outlast them. Taking the podium at a women's rights conference, she challenged the white "religious" men present with her renowned "Ain't I a Woman?" speech.[17] The story of Linda Brent, a slave from South Carolina, testifies to her struggle of overcoming being both a slave and a sex object. She wrote eloquently in her autobiography, "The more my mind had become enlightened, the more difficult it was for me to consider myself an article of property; and to pay money to those who had so grievously oppressed me seemed like taking from my sufferings the glory of triumph."[18]

The African-American story, then, is one of racial, sexual, political, economic, and social oppression. Nevertheless, in the midst of this oppression, Africans-Americans knew that they were somebodys. They knew that because they were created in the image of God, they were children of God now! Anthony Burns said it loudly: "God made me a man—not a slave, and gave me the same right to myself that he gave to the man [who] stole me to himself."[19] African-Americans even had the capacity to celebrate and rejoice in the midst of oppression. Mari Evans expresses the paradoxical essence of the African-American story:

> Who
> can be born black
> and not
> sing
> the wonder of it
> the joy
> the
> challenge
>
> Who
> can be born
> black
> and not exult![20]

The African-American experience is knowing that "the grace of God was and is to the black (person) a means of life and strength—a source of support and balance and self-certainty in a world whose approval of blacks is still in extremely short supply."[21]

The first level of meaning for justification from an African-American perspective, therefore, is *self-affirmation*. Our acceptance of God's unconditional act of forgiveness and new life in and through Christ leads us beyond our dependence on those who want to define and oppress us. Justification means that African-Americans can be as fully human as God intends them to be. Accepting, through faith, God's gift of grace means we are equal to and with all of God's other children. Justification means God empowers us to stand upright before God and humanity, knowing that God in Christ is victorious over sin and evil. That is why African-Americans sing, "I got a robe. You got a robe. All God's children got robes." Justification as self-affirmation also means freedom. By freedom I mean the opportunity to make choices and to be held accountable for those choices. To know that she or he has "been justified"—made free—opens the African-American to work for the freedom of neighbors. James Cone says freedom is

> to participate with those who are victims of oppression. Persons are free when they belong to a free community seeking to emancipate itself from oppression. Freedom, then, is more than just making decisions in the light of one's individual taste during moments of excitement. It always involves making decisions within the context of a community of persons who share similar goals and are seeking the same liberation. Freedom means taking sides in a crisis situation, when a society is divided into oppressed and oppressors.[22]

The second level of meaning for justification deals with *justice*. Justification leads justified women and men to act on behalf of and with others who are oppressed. This is what makes justification wholistic for African-Americans. For us it is "a spiritual and social liberation process initiated by God and occurring in the inner lives of persons as well as in the corporate community." Justification is a process within God's purposeful activity to build a kingdom of justice, equity, and wholeness.[23] Dr. Martin Luther King Jr. wrote:

> So by faith we are saved. [People] filled with God and God operating through [humankind] bring[s] unbelievable changes into our individual and social lives. . . . Social salvations will come only through (humankind's) willing acceptance of God's mighty gift.[24]

For African-Americans, justification opens their beings and actions to the sanctifying presence and power of the Holy Spirit. We have a corporate, a people-wide sense of the freedom God gives in Christ. Justification means we are one in the Spirit of the Creator who gives freedom through the Savior. It was no coincidence that in 1526, while Mani-Congo spoke against slavery in his country, Africans in America first rose up in revolt against slavery.[25]

For African-American Lutherans to speak about "justification" necessitates affirming that our forebears went "through the blood of the slaughtered." Because of their faith in the grace of God, they came to understand that God is just. Our understanding of justification as self-affirmation with freedom and as justice in community moves us to consider the social implications of justification for African-Americans.

## 3.  Justification: African-American Responses

*Sing a song*
*Full of the faith that the dark past has taught us;*
*Sing a song*
*Full of the hope that the present has brought us. . . .*

African-American people know that they have come through a dark past through God's gift of faith. We feel within ourselves the stirrings of hope in spite of the conditions of the present because we still have faith in the God who justifies and gives justice. This knowledge and conviction continue the faithful responses of our forebears. They still move us toward using any and all means to eradicate anything that goes against God's will for justice, freedom, equality, and honor for all people. The voices, structures and witnesses from the past urge African-American Lutherans toward grasping the social implications of justification.

There were differing faith responses to the evil of slavery and white racism. Some persons committed suicide before being loaded onto slaveships, others leaped into the shark-infested sea rather than live as degraded images of God. Many planned, organized, and carried out protests and revolts. A number sabotaged equipment, escaped from their masters, or maimed themselves to thwart the dehumanization of human bondage. At the same time, African-Americans were then and still are creative and innovative, devout and determined in expressing as well as living their faith. I will take three vital areas of the African-American story which recount the social implications of justification among us. The areas are spirituals, the African-American church, and the witnesses to justification.

### A. *The Spirituals*

The voices of our forebears sing to us. They remind us that our faith has led us to survive the dark past. Those voices sing to us that we can trust the Creator. Those voices sing songs of hope. Those voices sing about a justifying faith, a faith full of implications for justice now.

An African-American hermeneutic interprets the doctrine of justification and its potential in the context of the people's situation and cultural expressions of their faith. For African-Americans this means remembering the past with its chains and determination to survive with dignity. We remember our story is filled with resistance to the oppressors and wonder at "how we got over." The spirituals grow from our situation and articulate our faith in our terms. In other words, the spirituals tell us where we have been and where we are now. For "what black people are singing religiously will provide a clue as to what is happening to them sociologically."[26] Spirituals also point us toward where we know God will lead us. They become, then, songs of hope and promise to inspire action here and now. Listen as the voices of faithful forbears sing to us.

"He's Got the Whole World in His Hands" becomes a powerful confession of confidence in God when heard in the context of slavery. The masters behaved as if they had the world in their hands, but slaves knew who really was in control and their hope was in the God who ruled everyone. This spiritual sings of a conquering faith which provided the slave community with the inner strength by which they could endure any circumstances inflicted on them.[27]

Equally expressive of African-American faith in God's grace is "Didn't My Lord Deliver Daniel." This spiritual describes the Lord's power to deliver the determinedly faithful Daniel from his oppressors. The song expresses a faith in Jesus who "is the power beyond all the needs of the slave. The Lord readily cuts through laws, conventions, power structures, and all other sociopolitical forms to make things right for those he favors, for those who return his trust."[28] The same spiritual insists on justice and freedom.

Justice and freedom are key themes in the spirituals. Justice is often presented as political action, liberation from the shackles of slavery. When, for example, slaves sang "I've Got a Shoe," they raised their voices in protest against the master who denied shoes to all people. The refrain's double meaning probably escaped self-righteous owners:

*Heav'n, heav'n, heav'n,*
*Ev'rybody talkin' 'bout heav'n ain't goin' dere;*
*Heav'n, heav'n,*
*I'm goin' to shout all ovah God's heav'n.*

The slaves were announcing melodically "that their masters were booked for hell."[29] The African-American slave knew that there was enough of God's creation to include everyone on an equitable footing. Justice, then, became "a universal justice [which] straightens all, clarifies all, judges all. . . ."[30]

One of the most widely known spirituals, "Go Down, Moses," testifies to God's demand for freedom and justice. Slaves knew that God did not will anyone to be enslaved. They knew that to be a slave was to be a nobody. African-Americans, however, knew that through grace, God declared them to be somebodys, that God gave them an identity as his people. So they could identify naturally and completely with the Hebrew people. The African-American story paralleled that of the ancient Hebrews. As the biblical account dealt not only with spiritual freedom but earthly liberation, so the account was applied to the longings of African-Americans. Since God delivered the Israelites from bondage, so, too, would the Lord deliver the African-Americans from their slavery. The ancient story became our story:

*When Israel was in Egypt's land,*
*Let my people go;*
*Oppressed so hard they could not stand,*
*Let my people go;*
*Go down Moses, 'way down in Egypt's land;*
*Tell ole Pharaoh*
*Let my people go.*

"Oh Freedom!" could scarcely be plainer. Those who struggled to be full-fledged persons sang,

*Oh Freedom! Oh Freedom!*
*Oh Freedom! Oh Freedom!*
*And before I'll be a slave,*
*I'll be buried in my grave*
*And go home to my Lord and be free.*

Even a brief sampling of the spirituals shows they were songs about the soul and spirit of a people who have been justified by a gracious God and strove to have that justification be translated also into liberation of the bodies and persons. Through the spirituals, African-Americans affirmed their somebodiness, and claimed that the Spirit gave them a new reality, a new identity, and a new point of departure for living.[31] The spirituals are still songs of strength and faith to keep African-Americans moving on in faith because "God will always make a way out of no way" and because they knew with a just God "trouble don't last always." These songs of our forebears serve a meaningful purpose yet—in the spiritual and social life of our people as we lift our voices and sing about God's design that all persons live together and treat one another with justice and dignity.

They are "songs in which revolution is implied rather than planned or developed. These songs stress situations that cannot take place unless the old [current] order is abolished and new order is established."[32] African-Americans were and are a singing people; we are also organizing people. This gift led us to create another form of fellowship, the African-American church.

## B. *The African-American Church*

The African-American church is the single most important institution in the African-American community. Its very existence is evidence of the power in being justified by grace through faith. Beginning as an organization invisible to slave owners and exploiters, it emerged through those early days to nurture an oppressed people, providing them with the spiritual and social cohesion necessary to be a people with identity and purpose. The story of the existence of the African-American church is the story of our people's struggle against the cruel system of slavery, their wrenching from slaveholders the recognition that they are human, and their raising up of their own spiritual leaders and cultural forms.

At first, the masters felt that Christianizing slaves was out of the question. It threatened the economic basis of the enterprise. On the one hand, these dealers in human lives felt that baptized slaves would be brothers and sisters in the faith with whites, and demand the freedom and equality that relationship implied. Since the legal system was either in the hands of or favorably disposed toward the white owners, laws were enacted that separated political-legal freedom from a person's spiritual status. At the same time, slave rebellions, insurrections, and escapes made the masters unwilling to offer African-Americans anything that would bring them hope or spiritual consolation. On the other hand, there were African-Americans who were given religious instruction and who were baptized. Missionaries went into all the world—even the world of the slaves—preaching the gospel to humankind. Understandably, many slaves were less than eager to "receive" or "accept" the faith professed by those who brutalized them. There was always the risk that such an acceptance entailed also accepting the masters' view that slavery was divinely sanctioned and that bondspersons were to be docile, diligent, and obedient. Still, there were others who became Christian and made connections with their African heritage because "a basic Christian doctrine which would not have seemed foreign to most Africans was belief in God, the Father, Supreme Creator of the world and all within it. The divine sonship of Jesus and the divinity of the third person of the Trinity, the Holy Spirit, would have also seemed intelligible to many Africans accustomed to a plurality of divinities."[33]

The initial "invisibility" of the African-American church deserves comment. Owners who realized that religion could be a factor in promoting loyalty, increased productivity, and meekness created "visible" church structures and opportunities. These were under the supervision and authority of the white power structure. In some instances, slaves were brought to worship in segregated portions of white churches, and usually were denied communion or were offered the sacrament apart from whites. On many plantations, owners provided time and space for worship. Generally, white ministers preached and often white authority figures were present. Obviously, the messages in the "visible" church stressed, "Obey your master, don't steal from your master, and work hard." But in the evening the "invisible" church met. In forests, brush arbors, "Praise Houses," or slave quarters the slaves heard about King Jesus who died for them and who would free them from bondage. It was an expression both of the courageous determination of African-Americans to express themselves religiously in their own ways and of their conviction that they were justified by God's grace. These meetings were risky, yet the slaves would "steal away" for an authentic experience of Christianity. Through their own forms of worship and fellowship, our people communed with their Creator and with one another. Theologically, we may say that God's process of healing and reclaiming the people was occurring within the process of God justifying and sanctifying the slave.

African-Americans did use some aspects of European-American religion, synthesizing and adapting these to African expressions and their experience of slavery.[34] They appropriated powerful truths from the Bible, reinterpreting these to fit their contexts. By the time the masters were willing to "allow" African-Americans to be Christians, and then to have their own preachers and to manifest their faith in their own ways so as to make some of the "invisible" church visible, African-American expressions of faith were well-rooted and already seeking to meet the needs of individuals and communities.[35]

While there were some interracial or biracial congregations and some African-American churches in the states which had abolished slavery, these were few and far between. White denominations, no matter how solicitous they sounded about the plight of African-Americans, still sought to dominate them spiritually and temporally. Yet they often put themselves in a quandary. On the one hand, they did not accept African-American Christians as equals in their pews and at their altar rails, and certainly were unwilling to adapt African-American forms of worship in their services. Yet on the other hand, the white denominations were ambivalent toward and even resisted the formation of autonomous congregations and church bodies led and controlled by African-Americans. Prior to the end of the Civil War (1865), African-Americans in the American South built their own houses of worship where possible. In the middle of the new situation which faced African-Americans after the war (and to the present), their church became a center for hope, identity, and help. The development of the independent African-American church embodied the social implications of justification.

> It is this knowledge of being justified from above and the assurance that being does not require self-debasement of the beloved that impel the beloved toward self-fulfillment in every day and in every generation. The knowledge of justification and the awareness of worth as a justified being moved the oppressed of this land to assert their being while experiencing the contradictions of injustices in their life settings.[36]

Knowledge that they were justified and could move toward self-fulfillment led to theological action. The social implications of justification entailed the creation of the distinctive community called the African-American church, as exemplified in the actions of Richard Allen and others. They witnessed to a faith expressed in the universality of God the Creator, the oneness of humanity, and service to neighbors.[37] Nowhere else in America has this distinctive mission been manifest. Peter Paris identifies this as the "Black Church Tradition" a nonracial concept institutionalized in the historic, independent African-American churches. Paris noted: "Hence it is no understatement to say that the thought and action of the black churches cannot be understood apart from this principle, which to the black churches is what the Protestant principle is to Protestantism, namely, a prophetic principle of criticism."[38] The African-American church, then, stands in protest (from a faith perspective) against the denigrating and racist practices, perceptions, and understandings of the white churches and their members. Theologically, the independent African-American church movement is a necessary corrective to the total "American" religious experience, and there will always be a need for it as long as racial oppression exists in the church and the nation.[39]

Among the central factors of any religious group are its traditions, values, images, symbols, and worldview. Born in slavery, the African-American church presents a worldview which guides, nurtures, upholds, and legitimizes the religious experiences of its people. It was the place which provided necessary skills such as leadership training and communication skills along with personal identity and dignity. It was an inclusive community for men and women, different generations, and the spectrum of class and educational levels. Often it was the institution which spoke for the African-American community, whether or not people were formal members of a congregation. C. Eric Lincoln put it aptly: "The Black Church, then, is in some sense a 'universal church,' claiming and representing all blacks out of a long tradition that looks back to a time when there was only the black church to bear witness to 'who' or 'what' a [person] was as he [she] stood at the bar of his [her] community. The Church still accepts a broad gauge responsibility for the Black community inside and outside of its formal communion. No one can die 'outside the Black Church' if he [she] is Black."[40] A critical point for our discussions is that there are few homegrown African-American Lutherans. Many of us are the products of the African-American independent church tradition. (For example, my family was Baptist and African Methodist Episcopal [AME] before being Lutheran. I was initiated into the Christian family through baptism in the AME Church.) This gives African-American Lutherans opportunities to bring to the Lutheran church some of the distinctive expressions of the African-American church. One of those expressions is the conversion experience. The testimonies of how our people "got over" gives a clue as to how justification by grace through faith was and is felt. W. E. B. DuBois held that slave religion was characterized by three things: the preacher, the music, and the frenzy or shouting.[41] The conversion experience ought be added to the list.

The Wimberlys describe the conversion experience to mean "the radical shakeup in customary patterns of consciousness . . . result(ing) from experiences coming from sources that (are) extrasensory, transpersonal, transcendent, and supernatural. The person felt encountered by something or someone outside the normal channels of consciousness."[42] They identify seven characteristics of the conversion experience:

> First . . . a mystical vision which has an inner experience occurring. . . . Second, the message of the vision was usually conveyed in a stage drama and was acted out by characters taking specific roles. Third, the experiencer was a character in the drama but also was an observer. . . . Fourth, similar characters, images and themes appeared . . . and had transforming significance and meaning in the convert's life. Fifth . . . the new information was described as Christian and supernatural; yet the communal world view helped shape the supernatural interpretation of the vision. Sixth, this world view helped the convert find his or her place in the world. Seventh, radical turnaround in

thinking and behavior which became nurtured and acted out in Christian community.[43]

Furthermore, the principles of interpretation for unveiling the conversion experience and its accompanying vision are: an announcement of need which is usually personal, an agent is introduced to meet the need, and a scene in which the need has been fulfilled.[44] Theologically, the description of the conversion experience sheds light on the African-American perspective of justification and its social implications. Justification (salvation/liberation) is a mutually interdependent process; that is, personal salvation (justification/liberation) is not exclusive of social salvation (social justification/liberation). While investigating slave conversion materials, the Wimberlys found that "Salvation has been revealed as a spiritual and social liberation process initiated by God and occurring in the inner lives of persons as well as in the corporate community."[45] They continue to describe conversion as a "miniprocess" within a larger "macroprocess" which involves the liberating activity of God within the community. The miniprocess of conversion was described as turning the person completely around in another direction from that pursued before the experience began. The miniprocess of conversion began a process of sanctification in which the person becomes a coworker with God to bring about personal and social holiness. Still, the miniprocess was God at work to bring about God's own purpose. The Wimberlys put the purposes of God as simply to heal those in need. The kingdom of God, according to the slave conversion materials, is liberation and wholeness. In conversion experiences, is salvation/justification/liberation a process or a sudden change? The Wimberlys' study indicates

the activity of God on the macrolevel was ongoing and continuous. This means that the activity of God had general purpose and direction for the slave. . . . When the slave was in synchronicity with God's activity, specific direction and purpose were given to his or her existence. . . . The moment of awareness of regeneration was sudden . . . it is clear that regeneration (the moment of new life) was in the context of a process of conviction, withdrawal, inner change, and reincorporation. Thus, conversion was viewed as a sudden change within a process.[46]

All this may be described theologically in terms of the social implications of justification as God's initiating the action (the kingdom of justice), through which God interacts with individuals and communities, whereby the people learn about a Redeemer who walks with them, justifies them, and calls for their complete trust. The miniprocess is justification which leads the individual to acknowledge God as the Creator and Redeemer. Further, that miniprocess leads the individual to work for the freedom of the neighbors who also are in bondage. The African-American church is the place where people get in touch with that miniprocess and learn about the macroprocess. Accounts of profound turnings in which the grace of God is grasped by faith, where the person is changed and energized to work for the liberation of others, are cherished within the African-American church tradition and lend themselves to tracing social implications.

## C.  Witnesses of Justification

Justification by grace through faith and its social implications can be seen in what African-Americans said, did, and believed. It is a process involving both liberation from personal sin and social oppression, and the historic African-American church is the place that nurtures, guides, uplifts, and legitimizes the religious life of African-American people as they express their faith socially. I turn now to two witnesses to the social implications of justification, Martin Luther King Jr. and Harriet Tubman.

First, Dr. King. On several occasions he described what I would term a conversion experience. In his sermon "Our God Is Able" he recounted an incident which took place in the early days of the 1962 Montgomery bus boycott.[47] Using the model developed by the Wimberlys, consider the following quotations from King's report:

1. NEED: Almost immediately after the protest had been undertaken, we began to receive threatening telephone calls and letters in our home. . . . But as they passed, I realized that many of the threats were in earnest. I felt myself faltering and growing in fear.
2. EXTERNAL EVENT: Listen, nigger, we've taken all we want from you. Before next week you'll be sorry you ever came to Montgomery.
3. CONVICTION OF SIN: I was ready to give up. I tried to think of a way to move out of the picture without appearing to be a coward.

At this point, considering escapes such as calling on his father ("Daddy" King), King was being overwhelmed by frustration and deep despair:

4. SEEKING THE DIVINE: Something said to me, you can't call on Daddy now; he's in Atlanta, a hundred and seventy-five miles away. . . . You've got to call on that something, on that person that your daddy used to tell you about, that power that can make a way out of no way. And I discovered then that religion had to become real to me and I had to know God for myself. And I bowed down over that cup of coffee. I never will forget it.

Oh yes, I prayed a prayer. And I prayed out loud that night. I said, "Lord . . . I'm trying to do what is right. But Lord, I must confess that I'm weak now, I'm faltering, I'm losing my courage, and I can't let the people see me like this because if they see me weak and losing my courage they will begin to get weak.

5. EXPERIENCING THE DIVINE: At that moment I experienced the presence of the Divine as I had never experienced him. It seemed as though I could hear the quiet assurance of an inner voice, saying "Martin Luther, stand up for righteousness. Stand up for justice. Stand up for truth. And lo, I will be with you, even until the end of the world."

6. RESOLUTION OF THE DILEMMA: Almost at once fears began to pass from me. My uncertainty disappeared. I was ready to face anything. The outer situation remained the same, but God had given me an inner calm.

7. CONFIRMED BY THE SOCIAL CONTEXT: Three nights later, our home was bombed. Strangely enough, I accepted the word of the bombing calmly. My experience with God had given me a new strength and trust.[48]

The initial and key point in understanding the experience in the context of justification is King's search to resolve the crisis he faced. He could not rely on his academic training. He had to rely on the faith known and experienced by African-Americans. He did what the African-American church trained him to do, take all burdens to the Lord in prayer. Since he was the son, grandson, and great-grandson of African-American preachers, King was familiar with his religious heritage. The role of prayer, Scripture study, and singing (especially gospel songs and spirituals), as well as the social implications of faith were apprehended through the African-American Baptist tradition.

Second, King was also familiar with the injustices and harsh conditions under which African-Americans lived. Although raised in a solidly middle-class family, his eyes were not veiled nor his ears clogged to the sights and sounds of his people's plight. He knew the dehumanizing treatment to which whites subjected African-Americans. His personal encounter as a youth with racial segregation profoundly affected him. A spirit was imputed to him as he continued to participate in the African-American Baptist community of faith. That community of faith nurtured and sustained what God had initiated in the world and in King's life.

Third, King's faith was evidence of the hope connected with African-American faith. African-American people always understood the power of hope as expressed in Romans 5:3-5: ". . . suffering produces endurance, and endurance produces character, and character produces hope, and hope does not disappoint us because God's love has been poured into our hearts through the Holy Spirit which has been given to us." King, through faith actualized in the social situation, fought for social justice and freedom, being open to God's action in the process. He was frank in admitting his occasional feelings of hopelessness: "Yes, I am personally the victim of deferred dreams, of blasted hopes, but in spite of that I close today by saying that I still have a dream, because you know, you can't give up in life. If you lose hope, somehow you lose sight of that vitality that keeps life moving, you lose that courage to be, that quality that helps you to go on in spite of all. And so today I still have a dream."[49]

King, justified by God to do justice, knew he was a person of worth, dignity, and hope. Therefore, he could stand up on the steps of the Lincoln Memorial on a sweltering day in August 1963 and say:

> So, we have come to cash this check, a check that will give us upon demand the riches of freedom and the security of justice. We have also come to this hallowed spot to remind America of the fierce urgency of now. . . . Now is the time to lift our nation from the quicksands of racial injustice to the solid rock of brotherhood. Now is the time to make justice a reality for all of God's children.[50]

From the time he decided to become a minister to the last day of his life, King was dedicated to serving African-American people. He did not seek to become a leader in the protest movement, but the style, theology, and faith of the African-American church prepared him to lead when God and the people called him forth. This led him to say,

> The gospel at its best deals with the whole [person], not only his [her] soul but also his [her] body, not only with his [her] spiritual well-being but also his [her] material well-being. A religion that professes a concern for the souls of [people] and is not equally concerned about the slums that damn them, the economic conditions that strangle them, and the social conditions that cripple them, is a spiritually moribund religion.[51]

Through faith hammered out in the social situation of racial oppression, King was acutely aware of what God was doing, was open to God's actions, and in his ministry organized the community of faith's life around the work of the God who frees the African-American people. While there was still personal and social bondage among African-American people, he was able to transcend that, lifting others out of that bondage and making sense out of the absurd context of oppression. Out of the perspective of the African-American experience and of justification, King made it possible to "sing a song full of the faith" and "full of the hope that the present has brought us."

Harriet Tubman's story is another which we need to hear in order to understand our own voices and to claim our identities as God's people.

*I'll meet you in the morning*
*Safe in the Promised Land,*
*On the other side of Jordan,*
*Bound for the Promised Land.*[52]

Word had arrived, "Moses is here." Another group of slaves was on its way north—the promised land of fugitives. Nineteen times she made the trip back into the South. And nineteen times she defied and beat the system without losing a person. More than 300 people were conducted to freedom by Harriet Tubman along the Underground Railway. While there are many unwritten and untold stories of African-American women who took direct action for justice and freedom, we know best the story of Tubman, the Moses of her people. In spite of a $40,000 reward for her capture, she showed the courage and power to endure the tragedies and travesties of her time.[53]

Born a slave, she experienced the cruelty and degradation of that institution. As a young child she was worked pitilessly by brutal masters, and her health suffered. Once, when seeking to protect another slave, she sustained a head injury which her master thought rendered her useless to him. Enraged that his property was damaged and would no longer produce as anticipated, he let it be known that she was to be sold as soon as she recovered. During that recovery period, Harriet developed a powerful religious faith. At first she prayed that God would change her master's heart, but when she learned that he planned to sell her, her petition changed, "Lord, if you ain't never going to change dat man's heart, kill him, Lord, and take him out of de way, so he won't do no more mischief." The man died. Rather than feeling vindicated, she was filled with remorse. Out of her injury and the prayer for a man's death, Harriet Tubman sensed a deep need for the grace of God. Now she prayed,

Pears [sic] like I prayed all de time . . . about my work, eberywhere; I was always talking to de Lord. When I went to the horse trough to wash my face, and took up de water in my hands, I said, "Oh, Lord, wash me, make me clean." When I took up de towel to wipe my face and hands, I cried, "Oh Lord, for Jesus' sake, wipe away all my sins!" When I took up de broom and began to sweep, I groaned, "Oh Lord, whatsoebber sin dere be in my heart, sweep it out, Lord, clar and clean;" but I can't pray no more for poor ole master.[54]

For our purposes the central issue is the aftermath of her master's death and its effect on her. She experienced the need for personal justification. Harriet needed to know that upon her confession and repentance God forgave her. The Wimberlys noted, "It was at the moment of her spiritual liberation that she realized that social liberation from slavery was possible."[55] Again, justification is experienced as a process with social implications.

In the summer of 1849, Tubman escaped and made her way to Philadelphia. She resolved to bring her family and others to freedom as well. She turned to the Lord, expecting God to protect her in her return trips into the South. She did not doubt God's help, because she had been delivered before. With this faith in and commitment to God and her people, she was able to go on to become the most outstanding African American conductor on the Underground Railroad.[56] Although she could neither read nor write, she was driven by the experience of justification and served her people and country by working for social justice.

As witnesses to spiritual justification and social justification, Martin Luther King Jr. and Harriet Tubman made it possible for African Americans to sing through the way through which we have come.

Our spirituals, church, and witnesses disclose how the social implications of justification have been powerful and how they will continue to be powerful among African-Americans in our struggle for self-affirmation and justice.

## 4.   African-American Contributions to Understanding Justification

*God of our weary years,*
*God of our silent tears. . . .*
*Shadowed beneath thy hand*
*May we forever stand,*
*True to our God,*
*True to our native land.*

How relevant is it to ask, "What do African-American Lutherans contribute toward understanding Article 4 of the *Augsburg Confession*?" If the Lutheran confessional documents are a norm for our participation in the Lutheran church, then the question must be asked. I think there are several major contributions which African-Americans make.

First, we have the gift of memory. Our religious history is based on the faith journeys of our forebears. As we search our history, we learn who we are, what others like us did, and what we can do to create a future that is filled with freedom and justice. We learn, as James Cone said, ". . . there is no truth outside or beyond the concrete historical events in which people are engaged as agents. Truth is found in the histories, cultures and religions of our peoples."[57] The doctrine of justification developed among Germans in the context of spiritual and social oppression. African-Americans can hold the memory of their and our responses in faith to oppression past before the descendants of white Europeans in our society and church so that we may all act for justice in the present and future by the power of faith through grace.

Second, African-Americans are able to call attention to justification as a process that involves bringing healing, wholeness, and freedom to the individual and the community. Traditionally, Lutherans have talked about justification as an *act* with sanctification as a *process*. This has allowed Lutherans both to shove justification into the background as over and done with, and to divorce justification from sanctification—to the distortion of both. It may be more meaningful for 20th- and 21st-century people not to rely on the forensic definition of justification but to interpret justification as God's action and power working in human history, liberating people for wholeness and health. The culmination of that work or process is God's ushering in the kingdom marked by justice for all people.

Third, African-Americans offer an understanding of the mutual interdependence of faith and action. Cone is right when he says, "In order for the poor to experience a justification in which the Lutheran emphasis on the forensic declaration is transformed into liberating social structures, then faith must connect itself with a social theory of change."[58] Using the capitalist system as the frame of reference for applying justification today is inadequate. That system has continued to support the Lutheran church's relationships with the oppressors. It may well be that the Lutheran church needs to be in further dialog with Africans and African-Americans about their resources and methods for doing social and theological analysis in order to understand how socioeconomic factors have oppressive impacts on people.

Fourth, African-Americans contribute a prophetic voice which can lead to diminished arrogance and heightened humility in our churches. African-Americans are living echoes of the defeat of slaveholders and oppressors from the times of pharaoh to the present. There are Amos- and Hosea-like words of judgment, warning, and hope as well as justice which African-Americans are able to speak clearly and effectively to other Lutherans.

Fifth, and finally for this presentation, African-Americans may be a saving presence within Lutheranism. Lutherans have been emphasizing a narrow interpretation of justification and distancing themselves from the context of oppression. We take the letter of James far more seriously and wholly than white Lutherans. It was written out of the expreience of class discrimination in the church and reflects the protests of the oppressed. We join with James in saying, "So faith, by itself, if it has no works is dead. . . . You see that a [person] is justified by works and not by faith alone. . . . For as the body apart from the spirit is dead, so faith apart from works is dead" (James 2:17, 24, 26). A reappropriation of the unity of faith and works will push Lutherans beyond the false functional separations of faith and works, inner experience and action, and even church and state. Advancing justice means taking risks based on one's faith in God's liberating action through Jesus Christ to do justice. Henry Mitchell and Nicholas Lewter put it eloquently (and where they say "Christianity," let's read "Lutheranism"):

> Christianity, which has been so vociferous about salvation by grace, has in effect tried to make orthodox faith statements into a form of works. The impact of grace is lost when conformity of words is the main concern. . . . If a tenet of faith has no *behavioral* implications, it is not worth the trouble to write it down.[59]

In the folk vernacular of African-American people, "pretty is as pretty does," meaning, your actions speak louder than your words. Being justified can be seen in our actions to create a just world where people can fulfill their God-given potential.

## Conclusion

I have attempted to show an African-American understanding of justification with a focus on its social implications, and I have sought to use an African-American hermeneutic in recounting our experiences. Clearly, ours is an understanding of justification actualized in the midst of crisis. Our responses include the creation of spirituals, the institutionalization of a nonracial, nonoppressive understanding of the gospel in the historic African-American church, and individual, yet communal testimonies to the justifying grace of God to do justice. The doctrine of justification is a process which seeks freedom for the whole human race.

For the Lutheran church in North America to be involved meaningfully with the African-American community and other people of color, it will need to pay close attention to what we are saying, where we have been, what we are doing, and certainly, where we are going under the guidance and power of the God of freedom.

We have come full circle, so we sing with our ancestors,

*Lift ev'ry voice and sing*
*Till earth and heaven ring,*
*Ring with the harmonies of liberty;*
*Let our rejoicing rise, high as the listening skies,*
*Let it resound loud as the rolling sea.*
*Sing a song*
*full of the faith that the dark past has taught us,*
*Sing a song*
*full of the hope that the present has brought us;*
*Facing the rising sun of our new day begun,*
*Let us march on till victory is won.*

Let the church say "Amen!"

# 2

# JUSTIFICATION BY FAITH AND ITS CONTINUING RELEVANCE FOR SOUTH AFRICA

## SIMON S. MAIMELA

**M**artin Luther lived and operated as a theologian in a "religious culture." In such a context, "religious" activities are inseparable from "secular" activities, e.g. political, economic, and sociocultural concerns. Our situation is different, so it is often difficult for us really to appreciate the relevance for our lives of the issues and concerns which preoccupied the reformer. His language is saturated with heavy doses of theological rhetoric, and his contemporaries understood what he was saying. But are his thought-world and expressions impenetrable to us? I do not think so. When one strips the religious cloak from Luther's vocabulary and delves into what the reformer said to his generation, one is startled to find that he wrestled with issues of life and death, issues not really different in kind from those which concern us today. This is true even though, for many in South Africa, the issue of highest priority and the question of primary importance is not Luther's "Is there a merciful God?" South African priorities and questions have to do with social justice, freedom, self-determination, political participation, and survival.

Luther's development of the doctrine of justification by faith alone, it seems to me, was an attempt to answer questions his generation raised as they tried to make sense of life and to discover its meaning. Some of those questions were: In a culture that is saturated with religious activities and symbolism, yet which cannot save, how do I, as an individual, obtain salvation? How can I, a sinner, be justified before the righteous God so as to live now and in the next life? How do I lay my hands, as it were, on those things which make for life?

From these and similar questions, it is clear that at the heart of Luther's response lies the concern and quest for a life that has meaning and is fulfilling for individuals. Where there is forgiveness and justification for sinners, Luther argued, there also is meaning and blessing, all that makes life worth living. The late medieval church shared the same quest and concern. The difference between Luther and the church of his time lay primarily in the answers each gave to the question, "How is a sinner to obtain a blessed and fulfilling life in the face of the apparently overwhelming reality of sin even in the life of a Christian?" To understand the context then and the relevance now of Luther's doctrine, consider first the position of the medieval church.

## The Response of the Medieval Church

The late medieval church held that the means by which an individual could protect oneself from the power of sin and the possible loss of life resided in the church itself. Only the church had the power to unlock the doors of life, because Christ entrusted the Office of the Keys of forgiveness only to the church. In other words, the church alone was the way to God; there can be no salvation outside of the church. To put it differently, the medieval church taught that God was unreachable except through the instrumentality of the church. The church stands between God and humans; it alone mediates God to humanity through the sacraments. Indeed, this was a powerful and persuasive argument, and it sounded both fair and reasonable. But its practical import gave the medieval church enormous powers over the lives of the people. Possession of the keys implies in principle that the church alone has the authority to decide who was qualified or justified to have life. The church had the final say about who should and should not have access to the source of eternal life. The need for standards to make such judgments led the church to develop its own differentiated scale of moral and spiritual achievements. To perform the rather onerous task of applying the standards and making the decisions as to who was holy or justified, it was inevitable for the church to construct the self-help system of monastic life.

Now the church was aware that many people were not morally high achievers and so could not be declared justified by virtue of their own merits. Consequently, the church devised the useful system of indulgences secured by the treasury of merits. Through indulgences the gates of heaven were opened a little wider so that even those who failed to achieve an acceptable moral record on their own would have the chance for meaningful life here and in the hereafter.

Under and even through the merciful system of indulgences, the medieval church wielded enormous power over the lives of ordinary men and women. By declaring that it controlled the treasury of merits earned by the saints, the church claimed that it alone could dispense or withhold the means of forgiveness of sins. For the church to claim that only its leaders could decide whose sins were forgiven and whose retained was to claim too much for any human institution. Anyone could see—and did see—that the humans who headed the institutional church were sinners too. Not surprisingly, it was only a matter of time before the church and the papacy were looked upon as oppressive institutions which had to be opposed. Luther opposed the church when he declared that penitent sinners are justified by faith alone.

## A Revolutionary Doctrine

Luther's doctrine of justification by faith alone was and continues to be revolutionary. It constitutes a real threat to the institutional church, because it pulls the rug from under those who would arrogate to themselves the power to decide the ultimate matters of life and death for others. God alone has that power.

Why is the reformer's teaching on justification revolutionary? Because it declares that life or salvation is God's gift and only God bestows it. It declares that a merciful God gives meaningful life freely when God accepts the sinner unconditionally in Christ. It declares that faith in God's promises alone is sufficient to make the most unworthy and unlovable sinner the child of God. It declares that life does not reside in human hands nor does it depend on our ability to please God nor on our capacity to endure the rigors of the monastic life. Instead, justification declares that access to life does not depend on our natural worthiness or background or wealth or achievements, but on the gracious God who gives life to those who dare to believe. It is for that reason that God allowed Jesus Christ to die for us while we were yet sinners and unacceptable.

Luther's teaching on justification was revolutionary because it meant that now women and men could understand that life, meaningful life, was no longer open on the basis of being successful or having quantities of good works or even being leaders in the church. Rather, life was open to the weak, the poor, the powerless, and the unfortunate classes. Life was open to those who were deprived of dignity and true life because the prevailing sociopolitical and economic arrangements declared them unwanted failures. Luther, therefore, upheld the dignity and human worth of every individual before the God who accepts penitent sinners unconditionally. The reformer insisted that this God accepts people without imposing the medieval standards of worthiness. And the reformer accepted especially the underdogs and the downtrodden who embraced his teaching on justification by faith enthusiastically. In short, simple men and women saw Luther as a friend and liberator. In spite of his protests and even actions, they carried his limited reforms to as yet unforeseen consequences for the church.

## Justification's Relevance to the South African Situation

In recognizing that issues about life and living it meaningfully are at stake in Luther's doctrine of justification, we see clearly that his teaching has direct relevance to our situation in South Africa today. We, too, are asking questions about life such as: How can I find a meaningful life, a life worth living? What conditions must exist or be met so that every person will live in dignity, justice, and equality? The struggle we face is also a struggle with those forces in our society that deny a life of quality to the oppressed and powerless majority while giving everything to the powerful and successful.

Talk about concrete life in our divided land translates in Lutheran theological terms to language about the sphere of and existence under the law. In its particularized sense, existence under the law in South Africa means nothing else than existence in multifaceted layers of group identities. Cultural identity, social status, and the color of a person's skin carry enormous sociopolitical values, values that determine the fate and quality of life that is open to each and every person. Put differently, the political system of apartheid places cruel weight on whether one is born white or black. On the basis of such assigned identities a person is declared by civil law justified or unjustified. Racial identity determines that a person *(a)* belongs to a particular community; *(b)* may enjoy certain economic, cultural, and

political rights and privileges; *(c)* resides in a particular area; and *(d)* may
have a certain life-style. In pursuit of this political dispensation, the state
often steps in to break up communities when those communities, in the
state's judgment, are no longer justified in living together by virtue of their
racial or cultural identities. Similarly, the state assumes the power to break
up families in order to maintain racial segregation. In effect, the government tells individuals with whom they can and cannot associate or love,
and with whom they can or cannot be neighbors or coworkers.

To maintain residential segregation, the government has ordered thousands of people to move. They have been shuffled about and resettled at
enormous financial and emotional cost to dislocated individuals and communities. Since it is the black communities which have borne the brunt of
this deliberate attempt to segregate between the "worthy" and "unworthy"
human neighbors, it is no surprise that black persons do not express na-
tionalistic pride in South Africa or feel that they are secure or that they
expect justice there. On the contrary, South Africa symbolizes the negation
of people of color. It negates their humanity, dignity, security, and justice.
South Africa's apartheid system rejects blacks, labeling them as unworthy
people, as persons from whom whites must distance themselves at all costs.
At the same time it tells the white people that they deserve a particular
life-style and enormous privileges. These are merited by whites, says the
system, by natural right and by virtue of the whites' calling to be guardians
of the black races.

To summarize: In South Africa, justification—a life of meaning and
quality—is not seen as a gracious gift from God. Justification is determined
by the state on the grounds of "natural worthiness," that is, on the basis
of race, culture, and economic status. The state grants such a life to those
whom it judges to be the fittest and racially qualified. In South Africa,
unconditional acceptance of other human beings is not the presupposition
of human existence.

The relevance of Luther's doctrine of justification by faith alone should
be tested against the political system that declares justification to be based
on race. Luther reminds South Africans that all humans are unworthy,
unacceptable sinners before God, so no race or group is any better than
another. The good news of Luther's teaching on justification is that God
in Christ accepts (justifies) sinful people not on account of their merits
(racial worthiness) but solely out of sheer grace and mercy. Put differently,
the relevance of Luther's teaching lies in its insistence that all human beings,
especially Christians, are God's children by grace alone because none can
claim to be acceptable and lovable on their own. This is a most important

insight which all South Africans ought to learn for their own good. Without exception, all of us fall short of the expectations that God and our neighbors have of us. Therefore, the fact that any continue to live and are not destroyed is due solely to the fact that God suffers, tolerates, and accepts humans despite their sins, insufficiency, imperfection, and lack of good manners. The theological name for this unconditional acceptance of the unacceptable (unlovable) sinner by God in Christ is what Luther referred to as "justification by faith alone." God's unconditional acceptance of us is the sole basis for Christian ethics and mutual acceptance. And it is the basis on which all South Africans, especially those who call themselves Christians, can begin to work toward overcoming the division that threatens to destroy us all.

## Justification and Hope for South Africa

The gospel which Luther rediscovered for the church is one which we ought to preach loudly and clearly to our people. It is the good news of acceptance and reconciliation for those who live under the law of separation and hostility. It is the gospel which we ought to embody in word and deed in our relations with others. Then those who hate themselves as well as their neighbors, and those who feel themselves rejected by our society, might come to know and experience the liberating love of God in Christ, the Savior. This is the gospel which all fearful South Africans need to hear so that they may be liberated from their fears. This gospel proclaims to them that there is no need to separate themselves from their racially different neighbors. If they hear and believe this gospel, then they will be freed from the drive to defend their lives, their color, and their culture.

Experiencing God's unconditional acceptance of people in Christ can lead South African Christians to venture toward experiencing acceptance of one another. There is no need why Christians in our land cannot take the lead in showing at least tolerance toward their racially and culturally different neighbors. We can demonstrate that it is possible for Christians to accept others on the basis that God has unconditionally accepted them as God's children. Some Christians among us and in our churches still find it difficult to join with Christians of other races on the basis of our commonly professed justification by faith alone. In that case, we ask them by what right they expect others to be what they hold to be perfect, pure, worthy, and acceptable, when God has accepted them despite their sinfulness and unacceptability. What authority do they have to set another standard of acceptability than that which God has set for accepting the unworthy and ungodly? What power do they claim for rejecting and dis-associating themselves from their fellow Christians, persons whom God loves? If God has accepted unworthy human beings, is it possible for us to reject any Christian? Do we not thereby cut ourselves off from God, God's reconciling action in Christ toward all humans, and fellowship with other people—even those with whom we want to associate?

Granted, Christians have their preferences in relation to other persons. Alienation from and rejection of other persons because we consider some to be unworthy of our acceptance differs from whether or not we like or dislike one individual more than another. Luther's doctrine of justification reminds us that we are justified sinners. We are involved in the daily struggle of putting away the "old Adam" so that the "new Adam" might arise. Still, the justifying grace of God is able to overrule our "old Adam" inclinations so that we might become instruments of divine, unconditional acceptance. And it is in witnessing to that unconditional acceptance of sinners by God through faith alone that Christians will find themselves called upon to accept others. Such acceptance of one another will unite us to work for reconciliation among and peace for our divided peoples. The gospel moves us toward mutual acceptance and creative tolerance, pro-viding us with the ground, framework, and goal which may free us to develop solutions to our thorny racial problems.

Yet to be credible witnesses to God's unconditional acceptance of sinners, we Christians must first believe it, experience the joy of its liberating reality, and then put it into practice among ourselves and with others.

Should we do this out of grateful obedience to God for granting us such grace in Christ, then Luther's doctrine of justification by faith alone may be relevant both to our present situation in South Africa and be the key to problems in human relationships elsewhere. That was God's will when he disclosed its liberating message to Martin Luther.

# 3

# THE THEOLOGY OF THE CROSS: THE PERSPECTIVE OF AN AFRICAN IN AMERICA

## RUDOLPH R. FEATHERSTONE

*A theology of glory calls evil good and good evil. A theology of the cross calls the thing what it actually is.*

Heidelberg Disputation, 1518, Thesis 21

For those African-Americans who have been separated from the land of their genesis, home, family, and relatives, and have lived in exile for nearly four centuries, it is a rare privilege to be able to examine the issues of the Lutheran heritage as they relate to the black experience in Africa, America, and the Caribbean. Confessionally, exile has done some rather strange things to and with many African-Americans. In view of this exile experience, we are forced to ask: Have we been away so long that you no longer recognize us? Have we, in being away so long, so obfuscated the faith stories of our ancestors that both we and the faith stories are no longer intelligible to you or us? What, then, are the stories of our exile and how shall we share them at this family reunion? These and many other similar questions cloud the pages of our minds and the essence of our very being. Perhaps in all of this and in the mystery of God's will, the Lutheran church has been appointed as the instrument to effect this homecoming.

At the same time, however, it is fascinating to observe—when speaking of the African experience and the Lutheran heritage—how Africans in America have incorporated the tensions and differences suggested by these perspectives in their way of being in the world. For one thing, the presence and experience of being African-Americans has engendered no neutral response from European-Americans. Lutheranism's record as it pertains to Africa's children in America has been more than questionable at best and one of duplicity at worst (Lutheran apologists notwithstanding). As a point of fact, that record reflects a willingness to stand with and actively embrace the prevailing negative cultural attitude and behavior toward Africa's descendants. Lutherans in America have tended to be found more on the side of the "status quo," "law and order," and "privilege" (i.e., success) for whites than contesting those issues in behalf of Africa's posterity. One cannot help but wonder what this means!

Perhaps in its drive to defend its confessional truth, Lutherans have so emphasized right-thinking (orthodoxy) that they have done so at the expense of the cross and suffering. Right thinking speaks of justification by grace through faith, one side of the coin. The theology of the cross—suffering and cross—is the other side of that same coin. For, as Matthew Scott, a former student of Trinity Lutheran Seminary, has so ably observed, "The doctrine of justification does not mean exemption from the Christian's responsibility to serve others, rather it is our insurance of such service." Had Lutherans taken more seriously the theology they professed—justification by grace through faith and the theology of the cross—it is quite conceivable that a different social expression of that theology would be evident. The "success" motif of the cross would have been more vigorously challenged.

## A Questionable Tradition:
## The "Success" Motif of the Cross

In a world grown increasingly small by technological advances—especially in the areas of mass communication and transportation, not to mention the explosion of knowledge in the life sciences in the last 30 to 40 years—it is more and more evident that the interrelatedness of all life is a given in the global village. Yet if this interrelatedness is more apparent today, and if technology and the explosion of knowledge have had a salutary effect upon our global village, it is equally apparent that these advances have alerted and exposed humanity to the alarmingly disproportionate burden of suffering that the masses of the world's population must endure for the sake and comfort of so few.

Over against this inordinate disparity of suffering by the masses, for more than four centuries now, Protestant Christians—in one form or another—have held before each other and the world the importance of the cross. Pointing to the birth, life, sufferings, death, and resurrection of Jesus the Christ, many of these Christians would naturally contend that the cross is the ultimate answer to all suffering, human and otherwise. In fact, such Christians would be wont to point out how well the symbol of the cross represents Christianity. And in answer to some of their critics and to counter charges of spiritualizing the cross, the proponents of this view would point out how, historically, the symbol of the cross has been a sign of victory and helped "the faithful" to overcome. Not lost in this discussion would be the "example" of Constantine.

In the first quarter of the fourth century (so the argument would go), Constantine, as the result of an "alleged" vision of the cross and his subsequent conviction that this symbol (the cross) led to his eventual triumph in the decisive battle at the Milvian Bridge near Rome, took the necessary first steps which led to state recognition of Christianity. This recognition eventually gave way to a spirit of toleration. Ultimately, however, state toleration of Christianity gradually faded and was replaced by a more vigorous attitude and behavior of acceptance.[1]

Christianity's struggle for acceptance by the predecessors of Constantine, Constantine himself, and his successors helped to overcome the prevailing conviction that Christianity was godless and a threat to the state. As a matter of fact, Constantine and the Christian apologists who came before and after him valiantly sought to ensure "the authority of the emperor and the unity of the empire and to present the Christian religion as the religion which truly sustained the state."[2] More pointedly and disturbingly, as the reality of Christ's passion and death receded in prominence in Christianity's consciousness, the posterity of Constantine increasingly focused upon the cross as the ongoing symbol of success, i.e., as a symbol of victory, conquering, winning, triumphalism, and the like.

When commenting on this story and others with similar emphases in Christian history, Douglas John Hall offers this stinging commentary: "The common theme that unites them [the stories] all (perhaps, ironically, the greatest ecumenical commonplace!) is the theme of success. We tell our Christian story as a success story."[3]

That is, what we have alluded to up to this point is a classic example of what Luther referred to as the theology of glory, about which we will have more to say later on. The point here is that this attitude and behavior stand diametrically opposed to a proper understanding of the cross. This passage says much about many of Christianity's adherents. More pointedly, this passage is suggestive of a unique experience of the cross by a particular people whose experiences in America reinforced the "success" theme.

Seemingly, the arrival of Europeans in America was a signal to Africa's children in this land that the success motif of the cross would be the dominant way in which relations between these groups would be governed. Yet, for Africa's sons and daughters and for reasons which will become more evident later on, this operative appropriation of the cross would reflect a view of the cross that was disembodied, that is, lacking social expression and professing a false universalism of experience, not to mention an incorrect understanding of that same cross. For even when Africans in this land have thought about "success" as it pertains to the cross, their view of this topic has been informed, shaped, and finally understood in relation to their own experience of inordinate suffering and hope.[4] While suffering is real (so goes the argument), God—via the cross—*identifies with and points us to God's ultimate word* regarding African passion.

If any of the foregoing is true, then seemingly what is being advocated here is that those who historically have stood with their backs against the wall have not only a different perception and appropriation of the cross but, in addition, speak from a unique context from which their views regarding the cross are founded. What, then, is the understanding of the cross by Africa's children in America? Simply put, in contradistinction to the apparent prevailing sentiment and interpretation of the cross as "success," what seems to be Africa's children's belief about God and black suffering?

Some Lutheran scholars and theologians—ever sensitive to these kinds of critical questions—would contend that in contrast to the ostensibly prevailing notion and conception of the cross among European-Americans, there is and has stood, for over 19 centuries, a long, obdurate, viable, vibrant, and meaningful tradition that has understood and embraced the significance of the cross differently. This distinctive way of being—God's being with us and in the world and human beings before God and others—found its greatest clarity of expression and theological insight in the person of Martin Luther, the 16th-century reformer. In addition, these scholars would acknowledge and maintain that Luther relied heavily upon the reality of his own experiences and struggles, his understanding of "the righteousness of God," and, among other things, on the scriptural testimony of Paul in formulating what he called the *theologia crucis*, the "theology of the cross."

This theology of the cross, so Lutheran scholars would equally assert, has much to offer Africa's children in America as they also seek to interpret and express their view of God's involvement in and with black suffering. This brief essay, then, will attempt to examine the theology of the cross with a view toward determining its importance for Africans living in America.

## The Context

To genuinely appreciate the radicality of Luther's *theologia crucis*, a brief word must be offered regarding Luther's context. Initially, Luther lived with and participated in a church that, by all human standards, exhibited a penchant for "success." The hegemony of the church in matters political and spiritual assured a control of people's lives hitherto unknown in church history. "The Middle Ages," writes Alister McGrath, "had seen the political power of the church and particularly that of the papacy, reach previously unknown heights. While the spiritual authority of the pope within the church had long been recognized, the medieval period witnessed the extension of such claims to the secular sphere." [5] This all-encompassing claim on people's lives was acknowledged and adhered to by sufficient numbers as to make its impact real. Since Luther lived during the latter part of the Middle Ages, and since the Christian church exhibited a crying need for transformation at that time, it seems safe to maintain "that the genuinely creative and innovative aspects of Luther's *theologis crucis* can only be properly appreciated if Luther is regarded as having begun to teach theology at Wittenberg on 22 October 1512 *as a typical theologian of the later Middle Ages*, and as having begun to break away from this theological matrix over a number of years." [6] Simply put, what is being suggested here is that, in many ways, Luther was product of, victim of, and transformer of his day.

Yet despite the apparent "success" of the church in controlling the lives of the people, there was a spirit of unrest and questioning that was disturbing. Renewed interest in the writings of St. Paul, among other factors, caused persons before, during, and since the time of Luther to continuously ask, "What must I (we) do to be saved?" "How can a sinner be justified before a righteous God?" [7] "Luther," observes McGrath, "was not the only one to ask such questions, and was not the only one to find himself confused by the variety of answers given."[8] It was, however, out of the struggles and experiences of seeking answers to these and similar questions that the cardinal principles of the Reformation—justification by grace through faith and the theology of the cross—were articulated.

## Dawn

"Sometimes—even in middle age!—," writes Douglas John Hall, "a crisis in self-understanding brings about a new way of thinking about ourselves [and about God] that is better than the old way. People sometimes really do 'improve with age.' Coming through these crises of identity, they achieve a more realistic assessment of themselves [and a more critical apprehension of God in their lives]."[9]

For Luther, whose life experiences caused him to struggle mightily to find a gracious God and who initially hated the phrase "the righteousness of God" (*iustitia Dei*), the moment of liberation and truth arrived for him sometime during his middle age. Between the years of 1513–1519,[10] Luther's theological breakthrough occurred. This development led him "to the realization that the righteousness which God requires of [a person] is faith—but this fails to resolve [one's] dilemma, unless that faith is recognized as originating from God, rather than from [persons]."[11] Luther scholars would additionally argue that the whole of God's good news to humanity is codified in the Christian doctrine of justification: the conviction that, through the death and resurrection of Jesus Christ, sinful humanity is now reconciled to God. As the righteousness of God, Jesus Christ is God's decisive disclosure regarding God's hatred for sin and *the way* to overcome it.

This new accent, Luther scholars contend, forced Luther "to begin the long and painful process of revising his understanding of the manner in which God deals with sinful [persons] in a sinful world."[12]

On the basis of his analysis of Luther's theological breakthrough, McGrath maintains that:

Luther's insight into the true nature of the "righteousness of God" represents far more than mere terminological clarification: latent within it is a new concept of God. Who is this God who deals thus with [humans]? Luther's answer to this question as it developed over the years 1513–19, can be summarized in one of his most daring phrases: the God who deals with sinful [humans] in this astonishing way is none other than the 'crucified and hidden God' (*Deus crucifixus et absconditus*)—the God of the *theologia crucis*."[13]

## Theologia Crucis

"Christian theology," maintains James Cone, "begins and ends with Jesus Christ. He is the point of departure for everything to be said about God, humankind, and the world. . . . To speak of the Christian gospel is to speak of Jesus Christ who is the content of its message and without whom Christianity ceases to be."[14] In responding to the question, "What is the essence of Christianity?" Cone contends that the answer can be given in two words: "Jesus Christ."[15]

On April 26, 1518 in Heidelberg, nearly six months after he had nailed his *95 Theses* to the Castle Church door at Wittenberg, Luther presided over a disputation at the Augustinian monastery. Here, too, he spoke of the quintessence of the gospel—Jesus Christ. In fact, in speaking of Jesus Christ, Luther would employ two phrases that stood in contradistinction to each other: *theologia crucis* and *theologia gloriae*. It was the latter against which Luther spoke and of which he had been a part; the former for which he argued and toward which he was moving.

The theology of glory was expressive of a regnant way of life. It had to do with the "success" motif of Christianity and the metaphysical speculations of scholasticism. It had to do with works as humanity's way to salvation. Luther wrote against this understanding and appropriation of Christian theology. Theses 16 through 21 are as follows:

(16) The person who believes that he [she] can obtain grace by what is in him [her] adds sin to sin so that he [she] becomes doubly guilty.

(17) Nor does speaking in this manner give cause for despair, but for arousing the desire to humble oneself and seek the grace of Christ.

(18) It is certain that man [woman] must utterly despair of his [her] own ability before he [she] is prepared to receive the grace of Christ.

(19) That person does not deserve to be called a theologian who looks upon the invisible things of God as though they were clearly perceptible in those things which have actually happened [Rom. 1:20].

(20) The man [woman] who perceives the visible rearward parts of God as seen in suffering and the cross does, however, deserve to be called a theologian.

(21) A theology of glory calls evil good and good evil. A theology of the cross calls the thing what it actually is.[16]

Clearly for Luther, only theology informed by and dependent upon the cross leads to proper knowledge of God. For in the cross God is revealed, yet hidden. The age-old request of Moses, "Show me thy glory," (Exod. 33:18) is an ever-present one. Humanity seeks a direct revelation of God, yet such is denied. What is given is an indirect knowledge of God (Exod. 33:23). It is this revelation which the cross has revealed to humankind and which is open to the eyes of faith. Moreover, it is precisely in the sufferings and cross—*passiones et crucem*—that God communicates most effectively. Summarily, "The cross alone," as Carl Braaten argues, "is the criterion of the church's identity and its mission to the world. *The application of this criterion will disclose what is true and false in the life of the church and its outreach to the world.*"[17]

The primary elements of the *theologia crucis* have been presented most effectively by Walther von Loewenich in his work, *Luther's Theology of the Cross.*[18] Here, in summary fashion, are the main features of the theology of the cross:

(1) The theology of the cross is a theology of revelation and stands in contradistinction to speculation.
(2) As a theology of revelation, revelation must be understood as hidden and indirect.
(3) God's revelation is apprehended via the sufferings and cross of Christ, rather than in the works of creation and ethical works.
(4) This knowledge of God who is hidden in [God's] revelation is a matter of faith.
(5) God is ostensibly and definitively known in suffering.

Clearly, then, the theology of the cross, properly read and understood, is a radical revelation of God and faith in God. At the same time, this radical revelation of God, via the cross, is a clarion call to the community of faith (and by extension, all of humanity), to be with, for, and in community with God and each other wherever there is suffering, weakness, despair, and abandonment in God's world, as God is with, for, and in community with us and the world. The theology of the cross, as God's most decisive revelation in history, is a reaffirmation of God's care and ongoing commitment to wholeness, *shalom* (Gen. 2:4-9). The theology of the cross is the ever-present pull—in Christ—to be what God intended; namely, a new creation: "Behold, I make all things new" (Rev. 21:5) and, "If anyone is in Christ [that person] is a new creation; the old has passed away, behold, the new has come" (2 Cor. 5:17).

## The Theology of the Cross and Africa's Children in America

It is important to note and be sensitive to several realities before proceeding further. First, theology is a human enterprise conditioned by the particularities of race, gender, class, culture, time, place, and audience. As such, theology is never neutral; but is "interested" language and action.[19] "Theology," observes James Cone, "is always done for particular times and places and addressed to a specific audience. This is true whether theologians acknowledge it or not. Although God is the intended subject of theology, God does not do theology. *Human beings do theology.*"[20] As theologians, Christians are called upon to answer these questions: Who are we? For whom do we speak? What community(ies) do we represent? What limitations do we acknowledge in our perspectives? In what ways do we speak and identify with the masses of sufferers in this world? Second, theological methods based on divine revelation and proceeding to other Christian doctrines stand in danger of ignoring the crucial role of human experience. "There is no 'abstract' revelation," writes Cone, "independent of human experiences, to which theologians can appeal for evidence of what they say about the gospel. God meets us in the human situation, not as an idea or concept that is self-evidently true."[21] From the perspective of Africa's children in America, Cone additionally observes that, "God encounters us in the human condition as the liberator of the poor and weak, empowering them to fight for freedom because they were made for it."[22] Third, before forging ahead, it is important to be alert to the danger facing all writers this side of the Reformation. That danger is expressed in the tendency of some scholars to ask and seek ancient solutions to contemporary problems. It is patently unfair to ask or expect from Luther answers to problems concerning Africa's children in America. Yet it is fair and right to inquire of Luther's concern for, interest in, and decision to be with those who, during his day, stood with their backs against the wall. Moreover, it is required and responsible to challenge those, who in the name of Luther, advocate an orthodoxy that has the "tendency actually to contribute to the sense of the absence or silence of God in our *present* lives, here and now."[23] What is called for is orthopraxis!

The existence of suffering in general and black suffering in particular challenges the Christian notion of God. In the words of James Cone,

> If God is unlimited both in power and in goodness, as the Christian faith claims, why does [God] not destroy the powers of evil through the establishment of divine righteousness? If God is the One who liberated Israel from Egyptian slavery, who appeared in Jesus as the healer of the sick and the helper of the poor, and who is present today as the Holy Spirit of liberation, then why are black people still living in wretched conditions without the economic and political power to determine their historical destiny?[24]

With a long history of exile in this strange land, not to mention, slavery, white racism, segregation, discrimination, and the like, the sons and daughters of Africa in this land raise not the question of suffering in an abstract, individualistic, rational, and theoretical way.[25] On the contrary, suffering from this perspective is viewed as a continuous way of being—historical and present—in the world. Furthermore, Africa's children in America collectively exist not as spectators but as participators and victims of ongoing suffering on a massive scale. Stated differently, for Africa's children in America communal black suffering is a given, given the above-mentioned indices.

Any theology, especially the theology of the cross, that does not address this ever-present communal black suffering reveals the bankruptcy and false claims of the cross for all persons. Ultimately, if the theology of the cross can ignore this situation, then it is not fit to be labeled as such and should be called what it rightly is, the theology of glory. For like Luther's theology of glory, it fails to see God in, with, and through human suffering, especially black suffering.

Over 500 years have elapsed since Africa and Europe first experienced significant interaction on Africa's western shores. From this initial contact, slavery eventuated. Slavery's result was to produce a people that whites felt unobliged to respect. On the other hand, slavery forced African people to search for and affirm meaning in the land of their exile. To counter the negative experiences of slavery, Africa's children in America called upon the religious beliefs of their ancestors and eventually the religious tenets of white slaveholders. However this was appropriated, one thing is clear and has remained so to the present:

> Master and slave are in every respect opposite terms; the persons to whom they are applied, are natural enemies to each other. Slavery, in the manner and degree that it exists in our colonies, could never have been intended for the social state; for it supposes tyranny on one side, treachery and cunning on the other. Nor is it necessary to discuss which gives first occasion to the other.[26]

The point that is being made here is that the differences of experience—codified in the above-cited quote—have endured and have, thereby, affected the way Christian theology has been done by these respective peoples. Without a doubt, as time elapsed and as African traditional religion evidenced less embodiment in the social context and as it interacted with Christianity, Christianity gradually took on greater significance in the life of the slave. Yet it is safe to say that religion and, from the African perspective, life remained inextricably intertwined. And on this point the religious understandings and experiences of the slaves and slaveholders remained far apart.

It seems inevitable that, under the circumstances, the life, understanding, and experiences of slaves would drive them further from slaveholders. This happened in the church as well and gave rise to the "invisible institution," the secret meetings or church of the slaves. When discussing the slaves' secret meetings, James Cone makes a critical comment: "While the great majority of white Christians condoned slavery, saying it was permitted or even ordained by God, black slaves contended that God willed their freedom and not their servitude."[27]

Out of the secret meetings the churches of Africa's children naturally began to emerge. Writing in the spirit of the movement toward independence, Lawrence Jones says, "We would be misstating the case were we to leave the impression that the negative attitudes and discriminatory practices of white churchmen [and churchwomen] are responsible, exclusively, for the separation of the darker brethren [and sisters]. Black churches are also the product of the positive self-affirming attitudes of Blacks toward themselves. They testify of the fact that Blacks had heard and believed the Gospel teaching that God is no respecter of persons."[28] The church of Africa's children in America became many things. Significantly, this institution in prayer, worship, song, preaching, and action became a center wherein the question of slavery and African responsibility thereto was addressed. Given the life situation of Africa's children in America, perhaps no question concerned Africans more than the question of theodicy. While it is true that the question of black suffering did, momentarily, experience some withdrawal symptoms, it is equally true that this topic has never been far from the thought of these children of God.

Historically, when Africans in America have struggled with suffering, they, like their ancestors—in the midst of a struggle to find justice in a strange land, and living daily under the constant threat of death as a way of life—have turned to the Scriptures. This is still true today. Beginning with the Hebrew Scriptures, Africa's children both heard and took note of many stories, words, and ideas. As they remembered home (i.e., Africa) and reflected on their plight in the "new world," the slaves listened closely to and rehearsed with each other stories like that of Joseph (Gen. 37:1—50:26). This story, which spoke from the context of a crisis, conveyed to the slaves the notion that in a very unique way God was at work. As in the Joseph narrative, the slaves came to believe that slavery and even imprisonment in a strange and distant land could not frustrate the ultimate purposes of God in human history. As Walter Brueggemann so ably points out, "It [the Joseph narrative] urges that in the contingencies of history, the purposes of God are at work in hidden and unnoticed ways."[29] Perhaps here in some mysterious way a prefiguring of the cross is operative. Perhaps here slaves were sensitive to the belief that God is not immediately recognizable as God by the way in which God is revealed in the world. Perhaps here the revelation of God is hidden and indirect, a cardinal principle of Luther's yet-to-be-articulated theology of the cross. In any case, the Joseph story alerted Africa's progeny to how God works in the world.

God's way of being with humanity and the world—the great reversal—points from the Joseph narrative to the exodus and ultimately to the cross. From this story  the Joseph story—the slaves could anticipate Israel's deliverance in the exodus event, and, thereby, their ultimate deliverance in the cross.

The exodus event, through which God made God's self known in, with, and through suffering, provided occasion wherein slave suffering could be viewed as experiencing ultimate deliverance. As Israel remembered and was delivered (Deut. 15:15), so also did the slaves expect God to interact with them. They took seriously these words: "I have seen the affliction of my people who are in Egypt, and have heard their cry because of their taskmasters; I know their sufferings, and I have come down to deliver them out of the hand of the Egyptians" (Exod. 3:7-8a). "This," writes Bruce Birch, "points to a caring God who takes note of Israel's oppression and suffering. Remarkably, in this verse God also claims to experience it with them. . . . For God to *know* Israel's suffering is a revelation of unique involvement of the divine with the human condition. This is the beginning point of the Christian conception of a suffering God."[30]

The God of the above passage was also the God of Israel's great deliverance in the exodus. Through this decisive event, it became apparent to Israel that God loved them in order to deliver them. Through this passage and event, the slaves sensed God's concern for Israel and by extension God's concern for them in a similar situation. Africa's children, who are biblically conservative, experienced and continue to encounter God as "one who sees and hears." The God who sees, hears, and experiences suffering with Israel and others, via grace, is the same God who has called humanity from oppression and suffering to community and mutual responsibility. The Hebrew Scriptures are laced with passages that support this perspective.

The New Testament claims that the most decisive self-disclosure of God came in the person of Jesus the Christ. This claim reveals that Christians are decidedly convinced that the Hebrew Scriptures' story of Yahweh's involvement with and love for humanity is contained in the New Testament. In fact, Scripture emphatically points to God's most decisive self-disclosure by stating, "But when the time had fully come, God sent forth [God's] Son, born of woman" (Gal. 4:4).[30]

The incarnation—which points backward to the Hebrew Scriptures, and, among other emphases, embraces the Suffering Servant of Isaiah—looms large behind the cross. The cross gives meaning to the other liturgical days, i.e., Christian emphases, Easter, Pentecost, etc., and demonstrates the length to which God goes for the sake of being with (Emmanuel) the creation. From the outset, the Gospels reveal a Jesus who is one with and for those who suffer and are humiliated. It is in him, Jesus, that the radically new reign is brought into being. It is in him that those who are least are called to join him in a liberation movement against powers and principalities. It is in him that the sufferers are given hope that suffering does not have the final word. In Mark 10:42-45 particularly Jesus indicates that there is a radical discipleship required of his followers. It is this perspective that places the challenge before the church, the challenge to come, follow, suffer, and die with him. Much to the chagrin of "success-oriented" Christians, the confession of Jesus as Lord speaks of a cross, a theology of the cross that calls "success-oriented" Christianity what it is, a theology of glory.

Sensitive to that which has been alluded to up to this point, what can we say? The theology of the cross is a theology which does and should continue to challenge the church. In the spirit of Luther, it speaks of a unique way of engaging the theological enterprise. The cross is the litmus test as to the veracity or lack thereof regarding theology. Faith and cross are integrally related and are, therefore, different sides of the same coin. Yet, for those who stand in the Christian faith tradition but do so with their backs against the wall, the theology of the cross, as so frequently articulated, creates some tension.

Black suffering and the theology of the cross, ever-mindful of this "new" method of doing theology, challenge the Lutheran church—in light of its understanding of *shalom,* the cross, and the interrelatedness of all life—in its adherence to *any interpretation* of the cross that is *exclusively personal.* For black suffering calls upon Lutheranism to live out its communal responsibility of love for the neighbor (Lev. 19:18; Mark 12:29-31; and 1 John 3:11-24).

Black suffering and the theology of the cross challenge the church to take seriously the church's theology of the cross in its witness with all relationships *coram Deo* (before God).

Black suffering and the theology of the cross challenge orthodoxy to move beyond the posture of right doctrine and to become more concerned about orthopraxis.

Black suffering and the theology of the cross challenge the church to take seriously the witness and experience of the church of Africa's children in America, i.e., to acknowledge God's work in America has been and is hidden/revealed "under the form of the opposite" (*abscondita sub contrariis*).

Black suffering and the theology of the cross challenge the church to become one with those who stand with their backs against the wall and struggle against the earthly powers of domination.

Black suffering and the theology of the cross challenge the church to view suffering as a call to faith, ever-mindful that God has the final word even with this world's rulers, to live on the basis of "the cross only is our theology" (*Crux sola est nostra theologia*).

Black suffering and the theology of the cross challenge all theology to realize that theology's word about the cross and suffering must ever be open to critique.

# 4

# AN AFRICAN PERSPECTIVE ON THE PRIESTHOOD OF ALL BELIEVERS

## BY JUDAH KIWOVELE

I t is very difficult, perhaps almost impossible, for me as an African Christian to deal with the question of the priesthood of all believers. The difficulty is increased when one must address the topic in the context of the Lutheran heritage. It is only fair to indicate that I write from my own experience and point of view. I was raised in an African traditional religion, the Bena religion of Tanzania. So, in old-style terms, I was a "pagan" until I was baptized into the Christian faith. I was baptized within the Lutheran church in southern Tanzania at the age of 17. That church is a product of the Berlin Lutheran mission. Perhaps it would have been better for me to have been baptized within the Roman Catholic church, because Lutheranism as practiced today is exclusive of elements from African social, religious, and cultural life and thought, and there are elements in Roman Catholicism which may be helpful in the efforts to build a church that is inclusive of people from different cultural and religious backgrounds.

## African Traditional Religion

Most, if not all, Africans have difficulty in reflecting on any kind of priesthood, especially that of all believers, without reference to the concepts of worship and priesthood in our traditional understandings. We have to put the Christian experience of the priesthood of all believers into the terms of the African cultural tradition and its religious heritage. I will discuss this in three related points.

First, for Africans religion is life in, under, and together with the family. More specifically, we understand ourselves and our religion in, under, and through our ancestors. To be human is to be part of a family, a family which extends into the past as well as to relatives in the present. If we could be provided with language which connects our traditional understandings of humanity, family, and ancestors, then we could express what the priesthood of all believers means to us as evangelical Lutheran Christians.

To be human is to be in a family which consists of both what we call the "living-dead" (ancestors) and the living. We are—that is, we exist—because we participate in a community. To be human is to be part of a family. Being part of a family means to participate in its religious and social dimensions. To cut oneself off from both these aspects of one's family is the same as being symbolically dead. "Symbolic death" is like nonexistence, for it separates the individual from both the living-dead and the living members of the family. For most Africans, death is not the extinction of the self or the soul. On the contrary, death is passing from this mode of existence into another mode of existence. The self or soul continues to live after death, and a dead person joins the living-dead. The living-dead are still members of and participants in the family. Indeed, the leaders of the family who have become living-dead are regarded as the defenders of the moral life of the family and the law of the community. So a person "will be born into one's primary and extended family, grow in and with it, and finally die in and with one's family consisting of even one's forebears, in order to experience the unlimited stability of one's existence."[1]

The living-dead intervene in matters concerning the social and religious standards of morality and communal law. An illustration may help. On February 3, 1986, in a congregation of the Lutheran Church in Tanzania, the following incident took place during one of our healing-prayer meetings. Present was a Christian woman who was possessed by the spirit of her mother's father. Her husband was in jail. Her imprisoned husband's relatives were not fulfilling their responsibilities toward her and her children. The children were disappointed and confused, and she planned to leave them to become one of the roaming women in a town. Clearly, the situation was against our Bena tribal cultural-social morality. So the spirit of her grandfather entered her. At the service, the spirit spoke through her and said, "I came into her to prevent her from going into towns and from leaving the children alone. I cannot go out of her until one of the members of her husband's clan comes to talk with me about her and the children being left without support. Then I will leave her." Fortunately, a clan representative came, the spirit spoke to him, the clan made arrangements for the family to be cared for, and the spirit left her. Incidentally, the spirit also disclosed that the woman's husband was imprisoned unjustly and that the people of God were to pray for him. Upon asking those present, we discovered that they, too, believed that he was innocent.[2]

The living-dead also punish those who live contrary to expected moral life expectations. In the account about the woman, she became ill by means of the spirit because she planned to leave her children and roam the town. The living-dead and the living are joined in a communion-like bond. The point of connection is through the social and religious leaders of the families and kinfolk whether living or living-dead. The latter are given intercessory prayers, offerings, and sacrifices of different types. Actually, the living-dead leaders are more powerful than the living leaders. This has parallels in Christianity where living-dead Christians, e.g., saints, are more powerful than living (non-dead) Christians.

Another illustration may further clarify what I mean by the power of living-dead Christians and living-dead non-Christians. At a prayer meeting the previous night in the same congregation, a spirit-possessed Roman Catholic Christian woman was present. The spirit of her living-dead mother had entered her and opposed her becoming a Christian. Her father, however, was a living-dead Christian who had been baptized in that Lutheran congregation's dispensary in his last days. He was buried in the cemetery next to the church building. During the prayer meeting and the exorcism of the spirit in the name of Jesus, the mother's spirit said, "You should not become a Christian as did your father. He became a Christian because he was afraid of death. You should not follow such a religion. You should remain in the traditions of your family." Her living-dead father then spoke through her in opposition to her living-dead mother, "This is the time of Christianity. In the pagan time it was said that to become a Christian was bad, but now it is to the contrary. Children should be allowed to become Christians. I allow my daughter to be Christian." Her living-dead mother's spirit became confused, went away, and called other spirits to counter the father's spirit. He opposed them: "Even though I am alone, you cannot do anything against me. I allow my daughter to be a Christian." Those spirits called yet others, and he chased them all away. The woman was healed and said, "I have been dead. . . . I thank my father (spirit) and you friends who came to pray for us." Then she wept.[3]

Permit another example. This one shows that the living-dead are more powerful than the living. In another congregation, at a healing prayer meeting on February 23, 1986, several possessed women were present. One was possessed by the spirit of her maternal grandfather. He entered her to defend her against the accusation of practicing witchcraft. The charge was brought by her living paternal grandmother. The granddaughter had refused to obey the older woman's orders to continue to practice pagan ways because she was now a Christian. During the exorcism portion of the service it became clear that the grandmother bewitched her grand-daughter. The living-dead grandfather said through the woman, "Your father's grandmother has come to bewitch you. She is here and at her home she cooperates with the father of her own husband. The medicine for the witchcraft is in the old deserted house on the third floor in the ceiling. I am going to fight against her." The grandmother was soon defeated and ran away to her home, over 20 miles away.[4] This was a struggle between the living-dead grandfather and the living witch grandmother.

Both illustrations show that the living and living-dead leaders are engaged in defending the social, religious, and moral life of their families and kinship circles. Whenever the living members of a family or clan want to communicate with their living-dead forebears, they do so through their living elders. These elders hold a special place through the divine right of birth or family position. Living members may want to offer intercession for needy members or make offerings and sacrifices. The living elders, then, are mediators between the living and the living-dead. By the same token, the living-dead are the mediators between the living and the many spiritual powers, including God.

It is quite African to transmit requests through elders who act as intermediaries. The use of intermediaries shows the respect people have for the elders. Petitions are presented to the elders in a proper manner by someone who knows the ways of making such requests. Among the types of intermediaries are those who hold the position because they function as family fathers or succeed in the posts of the family priesthood. There are priestesses in their fathers' families, clans, local communities, and even tribes. These women and men play very important roles on behalf of their people. Social and religious leaders are pillars who uphold African life. The pillars are representatives to and mediators between both the living and the living-dead. To understand Africans locally and nationally, then, it is vital to understand our perception that humanity is a family which stretches back over generations as well as into the present. Perhaps the international community may learn from us the potential for peace which comes in seeing humanity as such a family in continuity!

Second, a key to African life and culture is the role of the living-dead as mediators in our families and kinship circles. *Ujamaa,* familyhood, promises to be the way for Africans to understand what Lutherans mean by the priesthood of all believers. *Ujamaa* is basic to our life, culture, and religion. We are communal people, and we understand reality in terms of family consciousness. Although I may seem to make the same point repeatedly, those outside of our experience seem not to listen as attentively as they ought. Directly or indirectly, the concept of familyhood still shapes most of the sons and daughters of Africa here and in Western societies. Maybe this is because the spirits of our forebears are still in our people wherever Africa's children go. Wherever Africans are, there also are the spirits of our people. Think, then, that the spirits of our ancestors from Africa and the United States are even at this moment here with us, caring for us, even fighting the evils which seek to harm us! Be assured that these spirits are more powerful in fighting evil than we are!

Understanding humanity as a family is a deeply religious point of view. The relationships of a person and group extend through and in family and kinship circles to tribal, national, and international communities. One of the reasons for the sense of the *ujamaa* of all humanity is the African belief that God is the Creator of our first African forebears and the forebears of all peoples. Living Africans communicate with God the Creator through the living-dead ancestors. As spirits, these living-dead intermediaries are close to God and have the capacity to communicate with God on our behalf. As members of our families still, the living-dead are then able to communicate God's ways to us.

I think that behind our emphasis on the living-dead as communicators with the divine is a profound understanding of life. We know that life here and now is ambiguous and insecure. Life has limited "peace, blessing, continuity, stability, harmony, courage, mercy, righteousness, truth, trust, expectation."[5] When humans realize how limited these factors are, they consult the person who is able to be in contact with the spirits in order to find out what the root causes are for the ambiguities and insecurities. Such communicators are the diviners. Any responsible adult member may consult a diviner on behalf of oneself or relatives. Others, such as a spirit-possessed person, may also have the abilities of a diviner or seer. As the illustrations indicate, it is not unusual to have the spirit-possessed person disclose what the root causes are for her or his problems and sickness.

Diviners and seers may also be healers or medicinemen. In most cases, the divine directs clients to approach their living-dead forebears in order to learn the causes of illness. Often problems arise from misconduct which influences and weakens the unity of the primary and extended families and kinship circles. Again, intermediaries are needed to mediate between the evildoers and the offended. The offended may also include the living-dead of other families and communities. Mediation may be through intercessory prayers on behalf of the offenders or through sacrifices and offerings on the part of the offenders to the mediators. The mediators then present the sacrifices and offerings to the living-dead forebears of those who are offended.

One way of expressing an African dimension of human identity is to note that life is given to the individuals by their living and living-dead families and kinship circles. Heribert Bettscheider is correct when he writes, "Life belongs first and foremost to the family hierarchy and then to the individual person as a son or daughter of that person. Without the family hierarchy there is neither individual person nor life and its stability."[6] The life of the individual depends on the relationship which the person has to her or his corporate family and kinship circle, and *through* as well as *in* the relationship the individual has with the living-dead of the person's family and kin. It may be interesting to think about what this could mean on the national and international level. What are the attitudes of and responsibilities nations have toward their living-dead as their living citizens relate to each other and across international borders? How does one nation's understanding of its living-dead and its extended family communities influence its ways of being friendly or hostile toward other nations? Perhaps there is more to the felt-family and the living-dead than many caught up in the East–West struggles realize. But let us return to the topic.

Instability and ambiguity in life is the result of disobedience by individuals and also is the result of the influence of evil powers. When persons have violated the community's morality and traditions, the persons are to repent and promise not to repeat their actions. But repentance alone is not enough. The disobedient members of the community are to include material sacrifices with their confessions. Those sacrifices may include agricultural products such as fruits and vegetables or animals such as chickens and goats. The sacrifices are signs of the confession of disobedience and the promise to live differently in the future. The offerings may be presented as sin offerings and sacrifices to the living-dead ancestors by the family and kinship representatives of the offenders. Repentant and confessing evildoers are presented symbolically in, with, and together with the offerings, gifts, and sacrifices.

When innocent persons are victimized by evil powers, the ancestral spirits may intervene and defend them against evil. Among such powers are those which come through witches. Innocent people may be afflicted by evil powers because someone else in the family or kinship circle has disobeyed the moral traditions of the community. The role of the intermediary living-dead leaders involves fixing the cause for the trouble and then pointing the way toward restoration of harmony and peaceful living.

So for Africans, life on this side of death is both more and less stable, more and less ambiguous. Stability and blessing may be restored in and through repentance, confession, and sacrifice offerings mediated by the ancestral spirits. The living-dead safeguard the family and kinship circles through their mediating actions and through disclosing the expectations and requirements of moral life.

Third, let us consider how the African thought-forms discussed so far appear to non-Africans. Africa's sons and daughters are attempting to be true to their ancestors and, at the same time, relate to people who are not Africans and who do not understand African ways. The traditional European approach has been to think the African is a child and that the white person is the elder brother, that is, the ruling, more authoritative brother.[7] Non-Africans simply do not understand or appreciate our traditional social and religious cultural thought forms. Our ways, at least in regard to religion, are inclusive. We put the religious-social-economic-political dimensions in the contexts of the family, kinship circles, local communities, and nations. Non-Africans are surprised to discover that we think life is unstable and ambiguous. Africans are well aware of the fragility of existence because of our sensitivity to spiritual powers. We look toward the supernatural forces to give us peace and stability. And isn't this the African experience when we have dealt with non-Africans? Human life is menaced by the evil powers of slavery, colonialism, and exploitation. Racism and neocolonialism in South Africa and Namibia are present demons which increase our anxiety. We look toward religion to gain answers to the issues and problems of our environment because we understand the power of the divine to be present in that environment.[8]

Non-Africans understand that so far Africans have not been in the position to relate themselves creatively to their own environment. Yet non-Africans are also aware that Africans understand themselves to be related to the whole living environment of animals and birds, and that Africans

feel that their destinies are bound up with the future of other living creatures. Totems, for example, are symbols of the unity we feel with the totem
animals, regardless of where and when we might live. The animals, birds,
and humans are one family-kinship circle. For that reason, an African
cannot eat an animal which is one of her or his group's totem animals.
The people related to a particular totem animal share in the totem's mystical
power: "Whenever man has more power, one's family and kinship will be
benefited from it, and it will at the same time be dangerous to outsiders
because being in contact with such mystical family power could be harmful
for outsiders. The man will then be taboo."[9] But the danger is only for
those, whether members or outsiders, who act or are contrary to the moral
expectations of the power.

Non-Africans also seem to understand that we regard the soul as including the body as well as the spirit. The soul is the totality of the person.
In a sense, the soul is the energy-like power of the whole living organism,
that is, the person. It is this power-soul which travels during dreams and
which survives death. It is this energy-spirit which continues as the living-
dead and which has power over the living ones related to it. The soul as
force and spirit makes possible communion between the living and the
dead. It seems that some non-Africans not only understand such positions
among us, but have similar ideas in their own cultures and religious experiences. Perhaps now we can understand why some non-Africans tell us
that Africans are not concerned about categories such as polytheism or
monotheism. Africans are concerned about power. We want to know how
the divine power is working, whether the influence a person or living-dead
spirit has is good or bad.[10]

The emphasis on power often brings in the charge that Africans are given
to magic. Non-Africans seem to think that the use of magic by humans
indicates an attempt by persons to control the divine, that magic becomes
a way to make the divine powers give us what we want because we have
followed certain steps, formulas, and the like. The non-Africans conclude
that magic destroys the right relationship between God and persons and
that magic is hostile to religion.[11] Actually, we do not understand magic
in that sense. We take magic, if that word is even useful in this context,
as part of the wholeness of our participation in the family and kinship
circles. Magic enables us to have access to the divine powers in our environment. All Africans know that there are a variety of ways in which
magic power may be used, e.g., contagious (touch), sympathetic (symbolic, imitative), representative (offering), and verbal/communicative

(prayer and intercession). It seems that we have a very different understanding of what is meant by magic and participation in divine power.

Non-Africans from the so-called "developed" or "advanced" societies also err when they think that the religious origins of Africans and other peoples who share the same level of cultural development results from the fear of what they perceive to be frightening power around them. Just the way those non-Africans approach us and our culture indicates that they consider us their cultural inferiors. Those "developed" critics think that cultural and intellectual advances are made when people regard their environment and themselves in abstract and ideological ways. They regard detachment from the concrete realities of life to be superior to engagement with the specific entities and issues of existence. In the long run, their criticism is useless to them and us. One is tempted to observe that the "advanced" societies have reached great heights in exploitation, weaponry, and oppression. They may learn from us that taking concrete realities seriously may be a corrective to their culture's ideological imbalances.

Some Africans have been deceived by these critics into thinking that our traditional ways are "primitive," inferior, and unworthy in comparison to the "developed" cultures of others. In fairness, however I think that some of us Africans are not self-critical enough about our own culture and traditions. We need to recognize that, in comparison to Western culture, ours is less systematic and not given to abstractions. We have a practical, feeling, concrete-oriented life and culture. Such an orientation contributes to our religious forms and symbolic language. As Buthelezi and Toedt have noted, the characteristic motif for African traditional religion is the totality of life to such an extent that the two are inseparable, so there are no real distinctive, institutionalized symbols which mark the boundaries between daily life and religion.[12]

Some non-Africans say that we have no religious freedom and make no free religious decisions.[13] Again, such talk reveals misunderstandings about our culture and values. When religious freedom is an ideology it becomes a matter for the individual to make what appears to be decisions. Westerners seem to equate freedom with an isolating individualism. Africans do not conceive of freedom either in individualistic or ideological terms. Among Africans, religion is not something a person decides for or against. Religion is not a matter of degree, of being more or less religious. The African knows that religion is life. Religion is not an abstract set of doctrines or ornate rituals. On the contrary, religion is concrete, and it is expressed in, under, and together with the concrete realities and structures of life and culture. Religion is the traditional setting which frames our realities expressed in social, political, aesthetical, and mystical means. Our point of departure is not the individual; it is the family. To paraphrase Heinz Brunotte, religion in its highest degree is a matter of communal relationships, and goes so far as to make many rules and customs obligatory only on those who are blood relatives. Strangers do not understand the protective power of the religion. To be born into a community is also to be part of a religious community.[14] African culture holds that religion is a family affair manifested as life and moral law which extends backward in time to include the living-dead, and around the present to embrace neighboring and distant families.

Those who understand African social, religious, and cultural life know better than the "developed" critics. Our forebears have taught us sufficiently and well about the origins of our traditional religions. A personal example may help. While I was a student at our teachers' college some 450 miles from my home, holiday time came around. Before I set out for my father's house, I visited his elder brother. As I prepared to leave, he took me several yards from his house to bid me farewell. As we shook hands, my uncle made the following request of his late father, that is, my grandfather, "My father, I ask you, wherever you are, to be with this child until he comes home safely."

That example discloses the basis of our traditional religion. The origin of our traditional religion is honoring our parents even after they have died and, with them, all of our living-dead family and kin. For us, honoring parents and ancestors is life and peace, and honoring parents and the living-dead expresses our total life together. Honoring the family is both one of the fountains of life and a fountain for peace. The living-dead are among the many powers around us and they defend their offspring. Behind my uncle's request to his living-dead father is the whole sense of Africanness *ujamaa* and inclusiveness in which we are part of a community extended over time in which the ancestors are present to protect, help, and correct their children now.

Africa's cultural heritage has been retained mostly through the traditional religion, while the modern religions which have come to Africa have destroyed and weakened our culture and life. Sad but true, Protestant faiths have been more destructive than others. Roman Catholicism, on the other hand, attempts to retain the whole or almost the whole of our African culture. Perhaps the exception is the official attitude by the pope to polygamy. It may be that Roman Catholic Christianity has overadapted to African culture and life. This may be seen in the prayers to God through the living-dead saints. Is this really the same as African relationships with their living-dead? There may be elements in our traditions which need to be criticized and from which we need to be freed, just as there are such elements in the culture of Europeans and Americans. Here the prophetic power of the gospel, particularly as understood by Protestants, may be creative.

## Summary and Transition

What does all this have to say about the traditional African understanding of priesthood? African priesthood is a representative priesthood in and through the elders of the families and kinship circles. It is not an office which exists by its own right or is independent of the structures of the family and community. It belongs to the whole family and kinship circle, and it is practiced in and through its representatives. These representatives are the elders and their successors. The African concept of priesthood as representative and successive within the framework of the family-kinship circle preserves the continuities between the living and living-dead, the living and the divine powers, and the living with the living. We are able to retain our history because it is constantly present with us through the forebears and the priestly representatives of those forebears in the present. The role of the priests is connected to the preserving of the saving stories of divine powers among, through, and with us. Through the priesthood we retain our history, worship forms, and understandings of who we are. The saving stories and traditions are built into our myths, rituals, magic, offerings, and prayers, so to engage in any of these is to reaffirm who we are and the communities to which we belong. Through this approach, we are able to speak of African traditional religion and still have diverse rites and accounts.

In anticipation of what is to follow, I observe that the African traditional perspective was weakened, sometimes destroyed, by the introduction of Western Christian missions and political-economic-social colonialism. The Western ways which were brought to and imposed on Africa contained the elements of Western ideology which advocated detachment and abstraction from concrete realities. The ideology treats whole peoples as abstractions, so it is also involved in the development of the color bar and segregation which is practiced openly in South Africa and covertly in other parts of the continent. It certainly seems that the transmission of traditions, values, and perspectives from one culture to another carries with it extremely high costs. When the "receiving" or imposed-upon culture is oriented toward concrete socioreligious realities and the "giving" or imposing culture is geared toward abstractions, then the receiver sees the transmission as the imposition of an ideology which is foreign and even suspect. The application to the traditional Lutheran role in Africa seems clear: the Lutheran heritage is the imposition of a Western, cultural, foreign ideology on the African experience. Could the same be true of the black experience in the United States?

## Priesthood in the Old Testament Community

The language about priesthood in the Bible and African traditional religion is similar. Africans understand priesthood in terms of family and kinship, and so did the Israelites. The whole family of Israel, all 12 tribes, were to be priests (Exod. 19:1-8). Christians adapted this to mean that the church was the Christian family, and the church was the royal priesthood (1 Peter 2:5-10; Rev. 1:5-6; 5:9-10; 20:6). The priesthood belongs to the whole community. The whole community is represented in, under, and together with the individuals assigned to carry it out publicly. The public figures are assigned to the priesthood either by divine right through birth succession or through election by the family-community. Whether in family or the wider kinship community, when the individual priests carry out their functions, they do so for their families and their kin. In Israel and the church, then, the priest functions for the immediate circle to which the priest is related and for the community as a whole.

I think that the African understanding of humanity as a family could be related analogously to Israel, the church, and the worldwide community of peoples. Israelite social and religious life centered on the family, and through the family connected Israelites to other peoples. The father in the Israelite family was like a priest to that family. Family priesthood represented in a concrete manner the priesthood of the extended family and kinship circle. From the start, all Israelites practiced the priesthood through the fathers of the families. An official priesthood developed later: "In the earlier times and until the time of the judges, the celebration of the cult did not require a specially organized, consecrated personnel; the patriarchs who were not certainly priests bless, build altars, offer sacrifice, practice intercession." [15] I think that the family priesthood served as a forerunner for the priesthood of believers in Christianity to this day. I also think that Africans are able to relate to such an understanding of priesthood because we already are centered on the family and traditionally regard the father as the family priest. Whenever priesthood is not centered on the family and the participation of its members as part of a religious community, the priesthood of believers and the officially organized priesthood are somewhat empty. The living priesthood is transcendent, immanent, concrete, and horizontal! The official priesthood develops from the concrete priesthood of all believers, and the priesthood of all believers is represented concretely in families. We can say, therefore, that the official priesthood is in the service of the family priesthood and is exercised in, under, and together with families.

Israel's religion started through God's revelation to the head of a family, Abraham. He was the patriarch, the founding ancestor of Israel's faith and family. He left Haran at God's bidding in order to find the land, the fulfillment, which God promised. We may use Abraham as a model in understanding the priesthood of all believers. He was not a member of the organized priesthood, but he did give blessings, built altars, offered sacrifices, made intercessions, and communicated with God as head and father of his own family. In him we are able to see the priestly functions to be exercised by all believers. Africans understand an Abraham-like priesthood. Permit another personal example.

I am the firstborn son of my father's first wife. By divine right, as designated through the order of birth, I am a priest in my father's family. From the time I was eight years old I could offer sacrifices, give blessings, and impose curses. And I carried out those priestly functions before I was baptized. The priesthood I know from my own experience is concrete in terms of the life, needs, and concerns of my family. In comparison, the official, organized priesthood may seem abstract and detached from the realities of specific families and kinship circles. On the other hand, the organized priesthood could be interpreted as coordinating the various family priesthoods. Together the family and the organized priesthoods form a whole and support each other for the life of the community.

The living priesthood, however, is that which is concrete. The living priesthood is that of the family, not the official organized priesthood. I think the priesthood which we see in Israel's patriarchs and family heads was more real and concrete than the organized priesthood we see at a later date. The organized priesthood was divided into levels, and is almost castelike within itself as well as among the tribes of Israel. The priesthood of the patriarchs seems to be closer and more understandable to Africans, and to the Christian understanding of the priesthood of believers, than is the priesthood of Levites and the sons of Aaron. Patriarchal worship and priesthood, as reported in Genesis, was carried on in the family and among kin, and related to the concrete issues of life. Africans may understand such a priesthood better than Western Christians. In fact, it seems that the early Israelites understood their God as the patron deity of the family and clan (Gen. 28:13; 31:42,53; 49:24). The social and religious language employed in the Bible concerning the relationship of God to his people is structured around terms which express family relationships.

Israel's call and election was to be a priestly nation, a nation in which all members were priests who were to believe in God's power and grace. While the whole nation was called by Yahweh to be in communion with him, the priesthood was to be lived concretely in, under, and together with the family. Objectively and abstractly, the priesthood was exercised in, under, and together with the official, organized priesthood. The official, organized priesthood carried on functions related to the public worship of the national "family" or nation. Clearly, the quality of being related to a person's or family's issues and problems is diminished at the national level. It is not surprising, then, that the prophets criticized the official, organized priesthood as it carried on the official, organized worship. One of the risks of the official, organized priesthood and the worship it leads is that both become detached from the concrete life experiences, needs, and hopes of the people who make up the society.

Real priesthood goes further than family membership and communal citizenship. Real priesthood is represented in the righteous, the persons who have faith in God. Such faith is accompanied by contrition and repentance and with acting in love toward the neighbor. At its heart, priesthood involves gratitude to God for God's power, grace, and mercy shown to humans throughout their generations. Real priesthood is service to God through acting in love toward others. The strange human experience is that wherever there are believers in the one God and Father of all, the Creator and Sustainer of everything, there too are the unfaithful and the wicked.

Helmer Ringgren noted that the Israelite priesthood was concerned with "the cultic element, religion of fellowship, theocentric religion, the righteous and the wicked, the concept of god, lament and confession, thanksgiving and praise, myth and history, the Law and the Messiah."[16] Worshipers knew that the God whom they worshiped was the God of their forebears, Abraham, Isaac, and Jacob, the same God who delivered their ancestors from slavery in Egypt. As with Africans, so we see among the Hebrews that myth and history went together. On the one side, their worship went together with their awareness of their own wickedness and the need for lamenting as a result of sin. On the other side, they knew the need for contrition, repentance, and confession to God. On the basis of the latter, they could continue to hope in the promises of God to forgive them and, thereby, to prepare them for the coming of the good news of the Messiah. Through one dimension they prepared themselves for the fuller revelation of God's will through faith in the one God who would grant forgiveness and fellowship with himself. Intersecting with this dimension is the realization that they are part of a human fellowship created by God and had responsibilities within that fellowship. It was natural to combine Deuteronomy 6:5 with Leviticus 19:18: "Love the Lord your God with all your heart, with all your soul and with all your might . . . . You shall love your neighbor as yourself."

Life's concrete problems were experienced first and foremost in, under, and together with the real life-oriented priesthood expressed in families and kinship circles. The Psalms indicate the continuance of the family priesthood and its connections with the official organized priesthood. Some examples: "I was glad when they said to me, 'Let us go to the house of the Lord!' " (Ps. 122:1) and "One thing have I asked of the Lord, that will I seek after; that I may dwell in the house of the Lord all the days of my life, to behold the beauty of the Lord and to inquire in his temple" (Ps. 27:4). The individual righteous believer represents family and kin in seeking fellowship with God and other righteous believers. The members of the family and kinship circle who remained at home shared in the temple-centered worship through their righteous representative who went to the temple, and they were represented by that person in the temple: "I will tell of thy name to my brethren; in the midst of the congregation I will praise thee; . . . From thee comes my praise in the great congregation; my vows will I pay before those who fear him" (Ps. 22:22, 25).

While Israelite religion was theocentric, it did not ignore human concerns. Human concerns, however, were put in the context of the centrality of the one God: "The main concern in the Psalms is not the welfare of the Psalmist, but the glory of God. God deals with man, and man calls for God's attention, but the ultimate purpose in both cases is the advancement of God's glory." [17] Worship in spirit and truth extends toward interceding for others, and such worshipful intercession is a form of faith acting in love toward one's neighbors.

The basis for the priesthood of all believers is present in the Old Testament and passes on into the New Testament Christian community. We are ready to consider the next step.

## Priesthood in the New Testament Community

The New Testament's concept of the priesthood of all believers is rooted in the covenant between Yahweh and the called people: "Now therefore, if you will obey my voice and keep my covenant, you will be my own possession among all peoples; for all the earth is mine, and you shall be to me a kingdom of priests and a holy nation" (Exod. 19:5-6). Yahweh's call to Israel to be his own people was a call to be a holy people, a kingdom of priests. The official organized priesthood, however, was coordinated through one tribe, the Levites, while the nonofficial priesthood of individual righteous believers existed in families. The New Testament priesthood, like that of the Old, was the priesthood of service to God through faith in the one God, and faith active in love toward the neighbors. What was true for the biblical priesthood is still true for the Christian church today.

Nevertheless, the Old Testament priesthood was limited almost exclusively to the nation of Israel and rarely included other nations. Perhaps the expression of this exclusivity today may be seen in the white domination of blacks, in which we are segregated from each other socially and religiously. The national-ethnic limits on priesthood were transcended by the New Testament in fulfillment of the promise to Abraham: "And by you all the families of the earth will bless themselves (Gen. 12:3). God's promise to Abraham is fulfilled in the life, death, and resurrection of Jesus Christ. In Jesus Israel's official organized priesthood and the representative family priesthood are both fulfilled, for as Jesus said, "I am the way, the truth, and the life; no one comes to the Father, but by me. If you had known me, you would have known my Father also; henceforth you know him and you have seen him" (John 14:6-7). He also said with regard to the priesthood of believers, "Truly, truly, I say to you, if you ask anything of the Father, he will give it to you in my name" (John 16:23).

The New Testament priesthood was anticipated in a twofold sense in the Old Testament. First, the general priesthood of Israel is carried into and fulfilled in the Christian church through Christ's calling and empowering his disciples and the community of believers to carry on God's will in the world. Second, Israel's official, organized priesthood was represented to the nation through the Levites, who offered sacrifices and carried on the public functions of worship for all the families. The life, death, and resurrection of Jesus fulfilled this priesthood with Jesus as the one who offered himself for the sin of humanity, once for all (Hebrews 10:26-27). Christ came to and did indeed fulfill what God promised through the Law and the Prophets (Matt. 5:17-20). The twins of anticipation and fulfillment may be seen in numerous New Testament passages, and these often are based on Exodus 19:5-6. In addition, the New Testament transcends the Israelite ethnic-national limitations of the priesthood. People of every nation are called to be priests through Jesus Christ as they repent, are contrite, and have faith in the promises of the one God through Christ (note especially 1 Peter 2:7-10 and Rev. 5:10).

A similar transcendence occurs with the sacrifice of Jesus as the lamb of God. The Old Testament cultic offerings for sin were intended to make peace between God and the sinner. Jesus' vicarious offering was for all persons who expressed repentance, contrition, and hope through Jesus. The conditions for the priesthood of all believers is one faith in one God through the vicarious sufferings, death, and resurrection of Jesus. As a result of making such a confession of sin and of faith, a person could pray to God for the needs and concerns of others. The repentant and faithful believer becomes, then, a member of the priesthood of all believers in Christ.

In summary, the priesthood of all believers, as expressed in the New Testament, has the following responsibilities: believers are to serve one another and to serve all people without making distinctions (John 14:12; 7:38-39). The service of believers to and with one another and all people is realized in and through the preaching of the gospel, intercessions for all people, familial admonition and strengthening of one another, and works of love (1 Peter 2:9; 1 Tim. 2:1-7; Col. 3:16; Gal. 6:1-2; and Galatians 5:6). Such service and work of love are not intended to obtain redemptive propitiation for sin—Christ has already done that for humanity—but is priestly service to God. Where there is faith in the redemptive promises of God in Christ for sinners, there also are acts of love toward our neighbors as the fruits of faith.

## The Priesthood According to the Roman Catholic Church

In Roman Catholicism, priesthood is an office of the church conferred to persons through ordination at the hands of a bishop. Such a priesthood is sacramental and for the life of the recipient in spite of whatever moral or doctrinal faults the person may have or develop. Once ordained, a man remains a priest, although he may be suspended from the right and privilege of exercising priestly functions. Brunotte observed that for Roman Catholicism the priest is another Christ (*alter Christus*), because he is endowed with inalienable signs which make him a living image or representation of the Redeemer. The priest stands there as did Jesus who said, "As the Father has sent me, even so I send you" (John 20:21) and "He who hears you hears me" (Luke 10:16).[18] The functions of the priest are formidable. He is called by God to present the people before God so as to signal their relationship to God, and thereby to offer their gifts and offerings for sin to God (Heb. 5:1). The people are to turn to the priest to receive Christ's life, power, comfort, and spiritual food. They are to turn to him, as well, to confess their sins, show their repentance, and be forgiven their sins.

The basis of the priest's power is ordination, and is exercised largely through the sacraments—especially the Eucharist. The priest is the likeness of Christ to the faithful and represents the faithful before God. While such a view seems similar to the Levitical priesthood, it actually weakens the concept of the priesthood of all believers by making the people passive recipients of the grace mediated through the priest. Along with the understanding of the priest as the *alter Christus* are the restrictions of the priest's gender (male only) and marital status (celibate). These, too, weaken the position of the priesthood of all believers and relegate it to a second-class status. Average believers do not feel that they can be in contact with God without the official, ordained priests, so they are not encouraged to be priests to one another. In fact, the Roman Catholic view, which has influenced the positions of other church bodies to varying degrees, makes necessary the hierarchical and abstract structure of the Christian community. The church is no longer a family but a government in which some have power which is not accessible to others. The sacraments are not shared by the whole family but are dispensed or withheld by the official clergy.

## The Priesthood in Lutheran Perspective

Lutherans understand that the ordained ministry belongs to the whole church and is delegated to some individuals by the church through the rite of ordination. The ordained have the ministry to preach the gospel and to administer the sacraments of Baptism and Holy Communion. A person may be removed from the ordained ministry by the church. The priesthood of believers, at least in theory, is not in conflict with nor subservient to the ordained ministry. The priesthood of believers is the service of all believers to and with one another in God's church and world.

Luther's concept of the priesthood of believers is based on faith in one God in Christ. I think that the *Small Catechism* concretely expresses Christian teaching in the world's Lutheran churches. Through the *Catechism* we see that the priesthood of all believers is carried on through the preaching of the Word of God, intercession for all people, admonishing and strengthening one another, and doing works of love with and to all persons. The *Small Catechism* was designed for use in the family and in schools. The emphasis on the family reflects Luther's understanding that the family is the basis for all life in and leadership for the community. We could say that the *Large Catechism* is an extension of the *Small Catechism* in that it seeks to relate Christians more closely to the wider society in which they live. The reformer intended for both catechisms to be taught and used. Plainly, neither is used as Luther desired, and that omission may contribute to a weakening of Lutheran understandings of the priesthood of all believers since the catechisms aim at equipping the believers for their priesthood in the church and the world.

In principle, the Lutheran church remains in harmony with the biblical and early Christian understandings of the priesthood of believers. Unfortunately, even Lutherans tend to elevate the ordained ministry above the priesthood of believers and see the ordained ministry as a privilege secured for a few and not as priestly service. Frankly, we still understand the ordained ministry in terms of men, and that relegates women to a segregated class similar to South Africa's racial segregation. We should stop condemning South Africa until all the Lutheran churches in the world ordain women! We need to retain a self-critical watchfulness on ourselves lest we misuse the ministry which God has given us.

For practical purposes, the most important place for both the priesthood/ministry of all believers and the ordained is the Christian home and family life. The priestly life grows and extends from a family base to faith active in love in ever-widening circles into society and the world.

## What the Priesthood Might Be Among African Lutherans

It seems to be more difficult for us to speak about ourselves than about others. Traditional Africans, such as I, find it difficult to speak or write anything worthwhile about Africans. I tend to be defensive about our life and culture, perhaps because we have been misinterpreted and regarded as primitives or children by others. Christians in Africa tend to express and present themselves in non-African ways. At the risk of being redundant, I repeat that the point of departure for our religious and cultural life is the African concept of humanity: humanity is a family on all levels, concretely and analogically. On this basis we are able to speak about the priesthood of believers in the Lutheran church in the African setting. African Lutheran Christians could contribute substantially to Lutherans and other Christians if we would go back to our African forebears to listen and learn from them the language and culture of African life. When we do that, then we will be able to relate to other Christians on other continents directly and analogously.

African understandings of the priesthood of all believers would emphasize family, the role of mediators, and the realization that there are powerful forces in the world, some of which we often contend against and some of which defend us. On the last point, we have clear scriptural grounds on which we may stand as well as strength drawn from our African experiences. There may well be spiritual enslavement of peoples who think that they are free and powerful. The priesthood of believers is part of the armor of God in the struggle against evil.

Permit me to sketch some suggestions about what the priesthood of believers in Africa could look like. No matter what the circumstances, we must keep a self-critical perspective, particularly in connection with the relationships we attribute to the living-dead and the living members of a family and kinship circle. Prayer to the living-dead, even to apostles, for protection and help is a denial of our faith in which we say that it is only through Jesus that we come to the Father. Sacrifices offered to the living-dead likewise are denials of our stated faith that Jesus is the only sacrifice for sin. For us to pray and offer sacrifices to our ancestors is to make them into gods. For us to ask the living-dead to intercede on our behalf before God denies that in Christ we have direct access to the loving God who gives us grace and peace.

A Lutheran African understanding of the priesthood of all believers must be rooted in the First Commandment, that we shall have no other gods except the Lord God Almighty. The challenge to African Lutheran Christians is to put at the forefront of our priesthood of all believers the firm commitment that the church will be united in faith in one God in Jesus Christ without combining that faith with other gods; that our faith is to be combined with the proclamation of the Word of God to all people; that in faith we admonish and strengthen one another, that in faith we make intercession with God for all people, and that in faith we serve others and perform priestly acts of love toward all people. If we do that, then the priesthood of believers will express its faith in word and deed, respecting all people equally, defending all people equally, and acting for justice for all people equally. To be genuine and lasting, these commitments of the priesthood of all believers begins in Christian homes and spreads analogously to neighbors and to all people in the world.

# 5
# A TIME FOR AN AFRICAN LUTHERAN THEOLOGY

# AMBROSE M. MOYO

St. Augustine of Hippo, a very distinguished African ancestor and theologian, made the following statement in one of his writings:

> What is now called Christian religion, has existed among the ancients, and was not absent from the beginning of the human race, until Christ came in the flesh; from that time the true religion which existed already, began to be called Christian.[1]

The statement has very profound theological implications for the Christian presence in the midst of other religions and for dialog with them as well. St. Augustine's influence on Luther and on Lutheran theology is particularly visible in the doctrine of the two kingdoms, which has its roots in Augustine's heavenly city as contrasted with the earthly city. The statement quoted above has unfortunately either simply been ignored or found unacceptable as Christians throughout the ages affirmed the uniqueness of their faith and of the church as the sole instrument of salvation. African religions, as well as other non-Christian faiths, have not been regarded in so positive relationship to the gospel of Christ for a long time.

Christianity in Africa dates back to the evangelist John Mark who, according to early church tradition based on the testimony of Eusebius (*Church History* 2.16), established churches in Alexandria, possibly starting in the Jewish community as was the practice. Within a short time the church became rooted among the Coptics, taking within its Christian ritual and practice many elements from the Coptic culture and religion.[2] Through the work of the Coptic church Christianity was spread south as far as Ethiopia, where the faith became very deeply rooted in the life of the people and has resisted the many challenges it has faced through the ages right to the present.[3] Elsewhere in north Africa, the church has produced several outstanding theologians in addition to Augustine, whom Africa has every right to claim as its sons: Tertullian, Origen, Arius, Athanasius, Cyprian, Cyril of Alexandria, Clement of Alexandria, and others, all of whom have made significant contributions to Christian life and thought.

Reference should also be made to the contribution of early Christian movements of African origin, some of which were recognized in their communities as authentic expressions of Christian spirituality, although they were later declared heretical by the church. Egypt, for example, was the home of many Christian gnostic groups of different persuasions, as has now been demonstrated by the discoveries at Nag Hammadi. Both the Coptic and the Ethiopian Orthodox churches insisted from the beginning on exercising their freedom to develop their own distinct African Christian theologies and expressions of spirituality. This explains why so many "heretics" and "heretical" groups such as gnostics emerged in large numbers in Egypt and north Africa as a whole.

Our African Christian ancestors did not hesitate to offer new interpretations of the Christian faith in the light of their own religious and cultural experiences. For me this is a legacy that Africans must be proud of and pass on to their descendants. This is a challenge to articulate unique theological perspectives that are informed by our religious and cultural experiences, and in that way contribute toward the understanding of Jesus Christ and his relevance for all humankind. In other words, as African Lutherans within a wider Christian context in Africa, we have a very rich Christian heritage stretching back to the first century A.D., which we need to reclaim and reinterpret in the light of our African experiences.

It is regrettable that these first Christian churches in Africa did not make an effort to take the gospel further south. It was not until the 19th century that the gospel was preached south of the Sahara by Christian missionaries from the West. Earlier initiatives such as that of Friar Silveira Gonzalo in 1560, were not successful. Since the 19th century initiative, in which almost all Christian denominations participated, including Lutherans, there has been a very rapid growth of the church in Africa, so much so that it is considered to be the fastest growing church today.[4] New African churches, often referred to as African Independent churches, have emerged by the thousands, and are also attracting members from the mainline churches.

The emergence of the new African denominations points to the seriousness with which African Christians take their commitment to the gospel of Christ and attempt to provide new interpretations or new insights into the gospel, so that it becomes an authentically African way of life.

The church in Africa is as divided as the church in other parts of the world. As African Lutherans we are bound by our inherited tradition which informs our theologizing. As we do our theology we cannot afford to ignore our African traditional culture in which most of us were brought up, our African Christian legacy, and our ecumenical context. Most of us are Lutherans not by choice, but because of the comity agreements between mission societies operating in our countries, the Evangelical Lutheran Church being the only church known to us as we grew up. Each mission society insisted on noninterference by the other missions into its zone. This means, for example, that the people of the Mberengwa District of Zimbabwe where I come from had no option but to relate to the Church of Sweden Mission if they wished to become Christian.

The basic question that this essay seeks to address is: What does it mean to be African and Lutheran at the same time in this day and age? How relevant is our Lutheran heritage for the people of Africa in their daily lives, in their situation of poverty, hunger, disease, exploitation, and oppression? What new insights can we as African theologians bring into the Lutheran family and its interpretation of our Lutheran heritage?

Africa is made up of people of different backgrounds and experiences, but, disregarding all that, we see ourselves as one black family, united by our blackness which gives us a common experience, whether we find ourselves in Africa, in the Americas, in the Caribbeans, or in Europe. As black people scattered throughout the world we have a common identity. We need to identify that which gives us our identity and together examine our relationships and our mission within a multicultural global context and within the larger Lutheran family. Black people everywhere belong together, suffer or rejoice together, and are either oppressed or free together. What has Luther or Lutheranism to say to our condition as black people in Africa? Through these questions we are putting Luther and Lutheranism as a whole on trial.

Before attempting to deal with specifically African concerns and relate them to our Lutheran heritage, it will be helpful to define very briefly the nature of African traditional religions and culture, which is the only meaningful context within which we can do our theology in Africa, including black theology in South Africa. We also need to examine the attitudes of our mission-related (mainline) churches to the African's culture and religion. Our task is to redefine the Lutheran approaches to our African traditional cultures which, upon the initiative of Western missionaries, African Christians have been called upon to reject as contrary to the Christian faith and practice. The question is: What specific contribution can we as Africans make toward the understanding of our African cultures, our struggle for liberation, and of Luther in an African context? How can we as African Lutherans appropriate the Lutheran tradition and make it our way of life over against or within our rapidly changing indigenous cultures?

## Encountering African Religions and Culture

Lutheran mission work in Africa began in the 19th century and involved almost all the Lutheran bodies in Europe and the United States.[5] Today there are more than 6,000,000 Lutherans in Africa, the largest concentrations being in Madagascar, Tanzania, Ethiopia, Namibia, and South Africa. There is a Lutheran presence in almost every country in Africa south of the Sahara. Lutheranism has become a force to reckon with, and its contribution to the development/liberation of the people of Africa is very significant.

From the beginning, Lutheran missions to Africa were confronted with people who had cultures and religions of their own, which were different from those of the Western missionary, as well as from the Hellenistic cultures out of which early Christianity emerged. Since the Christian gospel is communicable only through cultural symbols, Christian proclamation in Africa from the beginning was an encounter between the African cultures and the European-American cultures through which the biblical message was filtered before it reached us. Early Christian missionaries, Lutherans included, rejected all aspects of the African's culture and religion as viable ways of living and expressions of spirituality. Let me illustrate this point with reference to specific examples from early Protestant and Catholic missionary attitudes in Zimbabwe.

In 1560, a group of Portuguese Jesuit missionaries led by Friar Gonzalo da Silveira arrived in Zimbabwe, which was then the capital of the vast Empire of Mwenemotapa.[6] They had been sent there by the bishop of Mozambique. On his way to Zimbabwe, Silveira made a brief stop at the town of one Tonga chief who had earlier sent a request for missionaries from the bishop of Mozambique. There Silveira claimed to have baptized

450 persons in one day. In a report to his superiors in Goa, Silveira advanced the following reasons for baptizing such a large number together:

> I made a point of baptizing a large number together immediately because these people resemble children who like to act together and follow each other's lead. They also resemble children as far as their intellectual impediment in receiving the faith is concerned, for none of them have any kind of idol or form of worship resembling idolatry.[7]

The report shows that Silveira did not understand the people to whom he was preaching. First, he made the error of equating their communal way of life with childlike behavior and therefore concluded they were unable to decide independently on matters of faith. Since, as far as he was concerned, the Tonga were like "children," he must have thought that superficial theological explanations would be adequate. He was therefore not able to engage Christianity in a serious dialog with the Tonga and their culture and religion. Their faith, therefore, only lasted for as long as he was with them. They did not understand what the missionaries were asking for in the first place; the Tonga probably thought they were coming as traders in gold and ivory, as there was a great deal of confusion from the beginning between missionaries and traders.[8] They obviously did not understand the implications of what it meant to be African and Christian.

Another error made by Silveira, as observed by Chirenje, was his apparent failure to recognize that the African peoples had meaningful religious experiences prior to the coming of Christianity.[9] He thought of religion in terms of visible religious symbols such as images of gods and temples, the absence of which could only point to the absence of religion. Many 19th-century missionaries made the same error, a good example being Isaac Shimmin, a Methodist missionary, who, in a report to his home board, made the following statement: "The more I see the natives the more I rejoice at the possibilities before us. They are in most deplorable ignorance of all true religion, but judging from their present attitude, they are most willing to learn and judging from their appearance, they are likely to make sound and intelligent believers."[10] Similar prejudices were found among Lutheran missionaries as exemplified by Danell in his report to the Church of Sweden Mission.[11]

The point being made here is that in the past the Lutheran missions have not taken seriously the African traditional cultures and religions. For the early missionary to Africa there could be no genuine conversion without cultural rejection. This meant adoption of the Western way of living. This was the concept which lay behind the creation of mission reserves, such as the one created by the Norwegians at Umpumulo in Natal, South Africa, into which the new converts to Christianity were moved in order to isolate them from their people and their traditional cultures. This same negative attitude toward African cultures and religions has continued in the post-missionary era and is being perpetuated by the church structures which the missionaries set up before they left. The structures of our church leadership, the order of our worship services and its music, our medical, health, and diaconal institutions, and our constitutions, have hardly changed since the missionaries left us. Any attempt to tamper with those structures is seen as sacrilege. But unless these structures are related to the African cultural context, to our aspirations as Africans, and to the African perception of reality, we cannot hope to build a church that will touch the African people at their deepest levels, and we will continue to be deceived by the growing numbers to think that our preaching is having an impact on the African people. Our primary need, as I see it at the moment, is leadership development.

African traditional cultures and religions are very much alive today, despite the efforts of the mission-related churches to suppress them, with the aid of colonial governments. Many of us were brought up within African traditional religions and cultures which continue to inform our experience of Christianity, and which have a place in the Christian spirituality of many African Christians even within the mainline churches. In other words, African traditional religious beliefs and practices have continued even within church circles, including the Lutheran churches, and demand recognition and reinterpretation by the church. The challenge to African Lutheran theologians is to see how our African traditional spirituality can be integrated into our Christian faith in order to remove the guilt that many people feel when they draw on the spiritual and cultural resources from their African traditional culture and religion.

The African experience is first and foremost a religious experience. Religion is seen as an integral part of daily life and inseparable from culture. It expresses itself in the social, economic, and political life of any given community, and determines the individual's and the community's activities and relationships. One is born in a particular community, which means being born in the community's religious faith and going through the rites of passage of that community. Religion is a communal affair, and being an integral part of culture, there can be no separation of the sacred and the profane; our approach to life is wholistic.

According to African thought, God is and has always been very real. God is believed to be the Creator and Sustainer of the entire universe and is known by many names, each of which expresses an aspect of the relationships which God has with people and the rest of creation. This is because Africans are not given to speculation and therefore tend to speak in concrete terms. Benjamin Ray has rightly observed that "African thought tends to be bound up with daily life and hence there is little interest in questions that do not concern practical life." [12] God is real only insofar as his presence is concretely felt in the daily lives of people. It may be mediated through lesser gods and/or ancestor shades, but there is little doubt in the minds of most Africans that these beings serve as bridges beteween them and the Supreme Being. God's presence is felt concretely through their activities.

Since religion is an integral part of the African's culture, a rejection of one's family religious practices can only lead to a crisis of identity, and to what Judah Kiwovele has called a "symbolic death," since one's identity can only be expressed through relationships in the community of the living and of the living-dead, and through them with the Supreme Being. An African community without the living-dead, the ancestor shades, is deprived of life in the present, in the future, and of a life with God. Religion is the filter through which African people see and understand their world. In order for it to be meaningful, Christianity must enter the African traditional culture and religion, die in it to live in it and in that way be able to determine the nature of the relationships with the living-dead as well as with God. This to me is what Christianity in Africa has so far failed to do, by remaining more of an intellectual movement, a religion of the book, unable to touch the deeper emotional levels of the individual and the community. The result has been the emergence of new African churches, the so-called Independent Churches, which not only symbolize "an escape from the political reality of white rule into the solace of ritualism, and . . . an outlet of frustrated leadership talents," but also a search for "a broader theology which [reaches] beyond the past and [offers] a new cultural synthesis oriented towards the present and the future." [13]

The question of the living-dead needs particular attention and study. Ancestors are not worshiped in African traditional religions. They are guardians and living-dead members of the family. They are like the Christian saints who are clearly perceived as the "living-dead" within several Christian communions. Within most of our Lutheran eucharistic liturgies the believers join "with all the angels and archangels and with all the company of heaven" in praising the name of God. [14] The "company of heaven" is popularly understood to include the saints who have gone ahead of us and, in this context of the communion service, can be described as the "living-dead." This popular understanding is confirmed by the proper preface for All Saints' Day which reads as follows:

> Through Jesus Christ our Lord, who in the blessedness of thy saints hath given us a glorious pledge of the hope of our calling; that following their example and being *strengthened by their fellowship* [with us], we may exalt in thee for thy mercy, *even as they rejoice* (present tense, not future) *with thee in thy glory.* [15]

This can also be supported by several hymns in our Lutheran hymnbooks which show that those who have gone ahead of us, although they may be conceived of as sleeping in Christ awaiting the resurrection, are very much alive. Jesus' statement in response to a question from the Sadducees seems to suggest the same notion:

> And as for the dead being raised, have you not read in the book of Moses, in the passage about the bush, how God said to him, "I am the God of Abraham, the God of Isaac, and the God of Jacob?" He is not God of the dead, but of the living.
>
> (Mark 12:26-27)

The Hebrew ancestors are not dead, but are alive; otherwise God would not be described as their God. In other words, they are among the "living-dead." The Fourth Commandment, "Honor your father and mother so that your days in life may be increased" also suggests the same notion. Seen from an African perspective, this commandment, the first one which has a promise connected to it, does not restrict that honor to parents during their lifetime only. The promise of increased days on earth suggests that our ancestors have authority over our lives, all of which is in line with African traditional thought.

It would therefore appear that there is enough evidence from popular Lutheranism and from the Bible to allow us as African Lutherans to seek ways of developing a Christian spirituality which would allow for a meaningful relationship with our living-dead within the Christian faith and practice. The Western Christians, including their missionaries to Africa, take followers to the graves of their deceased relatives regularly, honor them and give thanks to God for their lives with memorial gifts to charity institutions, and even include them in their liturgies as demonstrated above, but when Africans do the same things differently they are accused of ancestor worship. Until Christ is brought right into our fellowship with the living-dead, most of our African Christians will continue to suffer from the "religious schizophrenia" referred to by Desmond Tutu. [16]

Our discussion of important aspects of African traditional religious beliefs would not be complete without reference to what Twesigye has described as its "great flexibility and tolerance of pluralism in beliefs, practices and rituals, as there is no one dogmatic way of doing things." [17] This openness and acceptance of other people's religious traditions is an asset that African Christians can contribute toward a global acceptance of one another as children of the same God, regardless of our different religious experiences of the same God. This would call for different mission strategies in which mission would be perceived more as the sharing of our experiences of God. During that process of sharing and engaging in dialog, we mutually challenge one another to a new relationship, identity, and mission.

The nature of African traditional religions prohibits proselytization or conversion to another religion, as this will be viewed as abandonment of one's community. There can be no competing with one another in matters of religion. This explains why Africans stand puzzled when Christian denominations, particularly in countries where there is no comity arrangement, compete with one another for converts to what appears to the Africans as basically the same faith. The situation is even more puzzling when Lutherans compete with Lutherans or Methodists with Methodists. This African ecumenical perspective becomes very useful in our attempt to give a fresh interpretation of Luther and the Lutheran heritage as Africans, in our attempt to do theology within an African cultural context, and as we engage in ecumenical dialog.

Finally, within traditional thought God has a special place for the orphans, the widows, the victims of unjust laws, the poor, and the oppressed. A society that is given to racism, one which neglects the above-named categories of people, and enacts unjust and discriminatory laws is, as far as African thought is concerned, a godless society with which the Supreme Being (who for the African is the same for all people although called by different names and worshiped differently), will not want to be identified. The role of the spirit mediums and the Mwari cult at Matonjeni in the struggle of the people of Zimbabwe for liberation in inspiring and leading people in their struggle, clearly shows that God and Africa's living-dead will not stand by as neutral observers in the liberation process. [18]

Contextual theology has been defined simply as "the conscious attempt to do theology from within the context of real life in the world." [19] The question is: What does this mean for African Lutheran theologians doing theology in Africa and from a Lutheran perspective? How relevant is Lutheran theology to the people of Africa and what answers does it give to our concerns?

The I.C.T. publication quoted above rightly points out that in a way all theologies are contextual since they are developed within specific contexts and address themselves to particular situations. The same is true of the theology of Martin Luther, which was thought out within the context of the church during the Middle Ages. The question is: How relevant are these inherited theologies when applied without modification to our African context, which, in many respects, is very different from that of Martin Luther and any of the reformers of the Middle Ages, and raises a different set of questions from those to which the reformers were responding? Our task here is to reflect on some of the issues and concerns of the African Christians from the perspective of our Lutheran heritage, and to reinterpret that heritage in the light of our African experience and the biblical revelation.

## The Use of the Bible and the Sola Scriptura Principle

The idea of a religion which is based upon a revelation which is communicated to us through the witness of certain individuals whose message was recorded in some books is foreign to African religious thought. According to our traditional thought, God's revelation comes to us through the mediation of the "living-dead" and/or the lesser divinities, and that revelation takes place through concrete manifestations of these beings as they relate to the community of the living on a continuous and daily basis. People believe they encounter that revelation in dreams, through symbol and ritual, and through contact with nature. God may communicate with people through spirit mediums, through trees, grass, animals, etc., and may express displeasure through thunder and lightning.[20] The living-dead, who are an integral part of the African family, are the embodiment of the Supreme Being, hence it is quite appropriate for Africans to claim that God lives in their midst, and by the same token they affirm God's transcendence through the concept of the "living-dead" serving as intermediaries. Thus regular communion with the Supreme Being is maintained through the ancestor shades, and at the same time the community distances itself from God. The relationship with the ancestors is expressed in concrete terms as these beings are believed to speak with their descendants and encounter each other in real situations of life and death. In traditional thought God's will is communicated to us through the ancestor shades (i.e., the living-dead) with whom people relate as living beings and whose voices are heard through their mediums.

As African Lutherans we have no problems accepting the authority of Scripture and its full inspiration. The Spirit makes God's written Word alive as we read it and hear it proclaimed from the pulpit. For the African people the ancestor shades are our Scripture and their mediums our preachers. Luther's departure with the Middle Ages lies in the fact that he derived the authority of Scripture from its gospel content. For him all Scripture must be judged in terms of the formula *was Christum treibt* (what conveys Christ). Luther saw only one content of Scripture, namely Jesus Christ, and for him all Scripture pointed to Christ, whom he saw as its sole and entire content. What this means is that even within African traditional context our Scriptures should also be judged in terms of the content of their message. Can you imagine what this would mean if our Christian ancestors were to come back to criticize us for not living in accordance with the Christian faith?

Luther's Christocentric approach to Scripture means that those books of the Bible whose content is judged not to be primarily Jesus Christ are seen as peripheral. Luther therefore condemned the letter of James as "an epistle of straw" because it does not mention the name of Jesus, and secondly because it puts faith and works side by side. For Luther salvation was through faith alone *(sola fide)*. As an African I would like to take issue with Luther's narrow definition, which places emphasis solely on faith, and to affirm the letter of James which, from an African perspective, is one of the most profound, most realistic, and practical documents, which needs to be lifted from the piles of "straw" where it was left by Luther.

The African approach to life is wholistic. One cannot separate body and soul, the intellectual and the emotional aspects of people, or faith and works. Our relationship with God and with the living-dead is expressed in concrete, visible action as we relate to one another in the community. The African idea of family is one of an extended clan, which is made up of the nuclear family and all the blood relatives, including what in the West may be regarded as distant relatives. But the African concept has no room for a distant relative since *everyone* is a close relative, no matter how distant they may be. In the extended family system we are all responsible for each other, and therefore no one can go hungry or naked while others in the same family are eating and are clothed. The widow and the orphans are part of that big family in which all share what they have. To ignore the needy and the destitute in the community can only incure the wrath of God and the living-dead. Faith and works in an African society belong together and cannot be separated.

In my view the letter of James sought to fill a gap which had been created by the misunderstanding caused by Paul's philosophical doctrine of justification by grace through faith. An overemphasis on that doctrine can lead to libertine tendencies and to an understanding of the Christian faith which in the long run becomes sterile and too intellectual, making it possible for people to turn a deaf ear to the misery around them, while taking solace in the security of their salvation as long as they have that thing called faith. James is an essential and necessary complement to Paul and his Lutheran disciples. In our African traditional religious thought, the emphasis is on concrete practical action. Consequently we should see the book of James as concretizing Paul's justification by grace through faith, and visibly linking God's concrete action in Jesus Christ with the concrete human response to that action.

Our Christian Scriptures are made up of the Old and New Testaments. However, one notices a tendency in some of our Lutheran churches to concentrate more on the New Testament and to prescribe sermon texts primarily from the Gospels. This unfortunately seems to relegate the Old Testament to a secondary position, and places the Gospels above the rest of the New Testament documents. Our African people, however, find themselves more at home in the Old Testament. The stories about the patriarchs as well as some of their practices, depict real life situations in traditional rural Africa. The relevance of the book of the Exodus cannot be overemphasized, particularly to those of us struggling against racist and oppressive regimes like that of South Africa. The Lutheran churches in Africa need to take the Old Testament a little more seriously, as this is bound to contribute to our search for an African Lutheran theology.

## Salvation in African Context

The church is an instrument of salvation. The missionaries to Africa understood themselves to be on a mission to proclaim the gospel of salvation through Jesus Christ. The gospel of Christ promises a better life and those who believe in Jesus Christ already enjoy the first fruits of salvation. The approach of most of our early missionaries was very pietistic, focusing more on the salvation of the soul, creating very negative attitudes toward the world, and advocating no involvement in socioeconomic and political issues. This is understandable in view of the 18th-century revivalist movement out of which most of them came. In the long run this was not viewed favorably within nationalist circles, which often accused the church of collaborating with colonialists by emphasizing the salvation of the soul at the expense of serious concern with socioeconomic and political concerns, urging Christians to be most concerned with matters relating to the world to come. The charge is often heard from African nationalists that the white man came with the Bible in one hand and a gun in the other, or that while the Africans had their eyes closed in prayer the white man was busy taking their land. Such accusations can only come where there is rather too much separation of the body and the soul, the material aspects of our existence and the spiritual. Such a separation, as we have already seen, is foreign to the African thought.

Salvation in African traditional religious thought is liberation from forces of destruction, and that liberation involves both the individual and the community. Salvation means restoration of the broken relationship within the community, between the people and God, and between the community of the living and that of the living-dead. It also means protection from the forces that threaten to disrupt life, and preservation of the individual and the community in order that all may participate in the wholeness of life. Rituals and symbols of salvation play a very important role in assuring the individual and the community of the presence of God and the living-dead whose absence can only spell disaster.

As we reflect on our Lutheran understanding of salvation, that is, that salvation comes to us as a gift from God to the sinner through faith in Jesus Christ, it will be instructive for us to inquire as to what this means within an African context. The tradition that we have inherited makes sin the responsibility of the individual; everyone suffers for his or her own sins committed individually. There is, of course, the all-embracing sin of Adam, but ultimately everyone suffers for their own sins and they have to repent and be saved as individuals. In African traditional religious thought the individual is seen as part of a larger community, which means that the entire community may suffer for the sins committed by an individual. Among the Karanga people of Zimbabwe, incest may be punished by drought or some epidemic or some national epidemic. If a member of a family commits murder, the deceased may come back as an angry spirit *(ngozi)* and kill members of the murderer's family one after the other until retribution has been made. The situation can only be reversed when the guilty family confesses its crime and compensation has been made to the family of the wronged person. That occasion calls for sacrifice, because any sin is viewed as sin against God and all the ancestors. It must be pointed out that the ancestors of the family that committed the crime are also angered by the crime, hence they withdraw their protection; in the

Karanga language people will say the living-dead have "turned their backs" *(kufuratira)* on their family, thus expressing solidarity with the wronged family.

What we have in an African setting is collective responsibility to ensure that proper relationships are maintained in the community and everyone has a right to enjoy wholeness of life. Any talk about salvation in such a context cannot ignore the communal dimension. It is not only the individual member of the family who is reconciled and forgiven, but the entire family. When a member of the whole family suffers, all suffer; when a member of the family sins, it is the whole family which is disgraced and which carries the punishment.

Christianity also teaches that when any member of the Christian family suffers all suffer, but in reality this does not seem to be always the case. For the Africans this means real suffering, with the individual members of the family actually feeling the pain. It means really taking upon yourself the sins of a member of your family and even dying for it, as is the case when there is a *ngozi* or an epidemic resulting from the sin of an individual member of the community. When translated into our Southern Africa context this has serious implications. We are called to suffer with our oppressed brothers and sisters in South Africa and Namibia. Those who belong to the same family with the white racists in South Africa are collectively responsible for the sins of their white brothers and sisters in South Africa and have to deal with it if there should be genuine reconciliation between them and the black family. Salvation will come to them only when they have together confessed their guilt and, in concrete terms, compensated the black family for the loss of life and their being denied participation in the wholeness of life over the many decades of oppression. This is how the whole issue is seen from a traditional perspective.

The question I am raising here is whether our Lutheran heritage, by making sin to be the responsibility of the individual, is not in fact promoting the kind of indifference that we see toward the human suffering caused by institutions created by systems such as apartheid. Collective responsibility makes us keepers of one another and in a way minimizes crime. Salvation then becomes a meaningful and joyful experience for all, regardless of class or status in the community.

## The African View of Sickness and Healing as a Challenge to Theology

Adrian Hastings has made this very pertinent observation: "No society can operate without a theory of sickness and a practice of medicine, and African societies have certainly been no exception. Faced with illness of some sort or another, human beings need both something practical to do and a wider philosophy of explanation which renders ill health, bereavement and every form of misfortune tolerable by establishing it within a wider frame of reference."[21] He has further observed that the concepts of sickness and healing among the African peoples are "an absolutely integral part of the single mesh of social structure and religious consciousness inside which people live unhesitatingly."[22]

The African perception of reality, as we have already observed, is wholistic, and this applies equally to their understanding of healing, health, wholeness, or wellness. All these involve not just the physical body of the individual, but the entire person in his or her relationships, including the spiritual, intellectual, and bodily life. When an individual is sick the entire village, including its houses and domestic animals, are threatened, and any genuine treatment must include the entire family and everything associated with it. Sickness according to African thought has a cause and a meaning. It is either caused by witches or by some forces of evil, and is an indication of the displeasure of one's living-dead who have subsequently "turned their backs" (*kufuratira* in Shona) on their descendants. When sickness has struck in the family, the elders will consult a diviner who will diagnose the cause of the sickness. Healing will involve application of medical treatment as well as some rituals to bring about reconciliation with the living-dead. Special rituals will be performed to protect both the members of the family and the homestead, including the domestic animals, from the power of evil forces.

I decided to include this subject in this discussion because this has been and continues to be one of the burning issues in African Christianity which we need to reflect on from our Lutheran perspective. In its encounter with African traditional beliefs and practices regarding healing, the mission-related churches both in the 19th and 20th centuries, acting under the influence of Western culture, relegated healing to secular institutions and became intolerant and unsympathetic to the place of healing in the African traditional life. "Missionaries failed to distinguish the doctor from the disease. . . . He became a 'witchdoctor,' as evil as a witch, when he in fact saw himself as opposed to witches and all they stood for."[23] Even in the mission hospitals emphasis was placed on the scientific and nonspiritual approach to healing. The ritual and the communal dimensions of the healing process just did not have a place, thus leaving a vacuum which many African Christians have continued to fill by secretly going to traditional doctors, despite the threats of church discipline or excommunication.

The negative attitude of the mission-related churches toward African traditional healing practices and their inability to deal with the spiritual and communal dimensions of healing are crucial factors in the emergence of the new indigenous churches. Many studies on these churches have demonstrated that diagnosis of the cause of sickness is an integral part of the healing process and that "the diagnoser is merely carrying out a recognized role of the traditional diviners . . . no instruments such as those used by traditional African diviners . . . are used. The only power they use is the Holy Spirit of Jehovah."[24] In the same article Dillone-Malone has observed that "while the new biblical consciousness has become the legitimating framework within which healing takes place by the biblical Holy Spirit, the source of power for such healings, . . . the manner in which illness is perceived, as well as the therapeutic procedures availed of to overcome them, fall squarely within the more traditional indigenous African medico-religious consciousness."[25] As a result of this approach the new churches continue to attract a large part of their membership from both the African traditionalists and the mainline churches, including Lutheran churches.

The whole question of sickness and healing therefore calls for serious theological study from the perspective of the biblical witness and our Lutheran heritage. Healing was an integral part of the ministry of the early church and is directly traced back to Jesus and the apostles. Healing was seen as a gift of the Holy Spirit (1 Cor. 12:10, 28). The process of healing demanded faith in the name of Jesus (Acts 3:6; Matt. 9:27-31), and involved prayer and the ritual of laying on of hands and anointing with oil (James 5:14-15; Mark 6:13; Acts 9:12, 17; 28:8; Matt. 9:18). In the story of the healing of the paralytic in Mark 2:1-12, it is striking to note that the man is healed on the basis of the faith of his sponsors, namely, those who carried him to Jesus (2:5). No reference is made to the paralytic's own faith, which probably was there but seems not to have been of great concern to Jesus. The community participated in and contributed toward the healing process and was itself healed in that process. Second, the paralytic was healed physically and spiritually. The healing process began with forgiveness of sins, with the reconciliation of the patient with God. The process was completed in the restoration of physical fitness. Thus Jesus' approach to healing was wholistic.

The New Testament is quite clear that healing was an integral part of the mission and message of Jesus and of the early church's consciousness and praxis. The approach was as wholistic as what we have shown with regard to African traditional practices as well as those of the new African churches. The question is: What can our Lutheran heritage offer to the church in Africa in its search for a form of ministry which is wholistic and as it tries to respond to the question of healing as perceived and practiced in its constituency? A purely scientific approach to healing will not suffice for the majority of our people in Africa, which makes it imperative that African theologians reflect through this whole question and seek ways to include the African approach in the church's theology and praxis.

## Sacraments as Means of Communicating God's Grace

Rituals and symbols occupy a prominent place in African traditional religious life and thought. They are a means through which the living and the divine or the spirit world are able to communicate with each other. They serve very practical purposes. When life is being threatened, particularly at the critical moments in one's life, most African societies will require that certain rites be performed. Most important among these are the rites of passage, which mark the transition from one stage in life to another, such as when a child is born, at puberty, marriage, and death. At all these occasions specified rites must be performed in order to ensure a smooth transition. Specified rites are also called for in the event of serious sickness in the family, or some misfortune such as involvement in an accident or loss of property or employment, and even on joyful occasions such as the installation of a chief or when one has purchased an automobile. The pouring of libations is a day-to-day experience. The whole of the African traditionalist's life is full of religious activity and no aspect of that life and its relationships can be relegated to the secular as there is no distinction between the secular and the sacred within traditional thought.

The African religious rites and libations have a sacramental character. They involve the speaking of some words addressed to the living-dead or directly to the Supreme Being in some cases (the Nuer being a good example of the latter[26]), and some visible elements and/or human action. They are an integral part of African spirituality.

As African Lutheran theologians we need to examine our Lutheran sacramental principle to see whether it should not be broadened to enable it to meet our religious expectations as Africans. The Lutheran threefold criteria insists that a sacrament must *(a)* be instituted by Christ, *(b)* carry the central gospel message of forgiveness and new life, and *(c)* have an element. The question that I have is whether this threefold criteria can still be justified in view of the advances in New Testament studies through the historical-critical approach. Can it be conclusively established that our sacraments were instituted by Christ? Is it not also true that these Christian rites were already in existence in one form or another before Jesus appeared on the scene, and that whatever adaptations Jesus made cannot make them unique to Christianity?

In the light of these questions and of the fact that in our African context sacraments as means of grace are essential aspects of life, it is necessary that African Lutheran theology reexamines our traditional Lutheran definition of sacraments to see how it can respond concretely to the needs expressed in our African Christian spirituality. If we accept the fact that a sacrament is a rite in which God's grace is uniquely active, what is the justification for restricting ourselves to three, given the fact that the three-fold formula is not that watertight? The sacrament of absolution which is one of the three Lutheran sacraments, does not meet the third criteria. Christendom itself is not united on the number of sacraments that a church should recognize. It is my view that if the Lutheran church should become genuinely indigenous we must seriously search for those elements in our cultures that could serve as means of communicating God's grace. Within an African context the rites of passage and other rites need to be studied with a view to integrating them into Christian practice.

## What about Our Understanding of Marriage in Africa?

The question of marriage is again one of the most pressing problems facing the church in Africa today. As stated above, in African traditional thought marriage represents one of the critical moments in one's life, as it marks a transition into another stage in life. The survival of one's lineage depends on successful marriages and every normal person is expected to and expects to get married. Marriage is extremely important not just for social purposes but because it guarantees the continuity of one's life after death. Only those who have left descendants can become ancestor shades, since that status depends on one's descendant who will remember you, communicate with you, and will need your care and guardianship. Marriage is therefore bound up with the religion of the people.

Another outstanding value of African marriage is that it is not only a commitment that individuals make to each other but also an alliance with the community. In marriage the wife is fully incorporated into the family of the husband, becoming a full member of that family and lineage, enjoying all the rights and privileges of belonging to that family; she no longer belongs exclusively to her own family. This integration is very important as it gives her a sense of security. If her husband should die she would not cease to be a member of the family but would continue to function as wife through leviratic union with her brother-in-law, who then performs all the duties of a husband and father on behalf of his deceased brother.[27] All her needs and those of her living-dead husband, including the need to leave descendants who will remember them after they are dead, are taken care of through leviratic marriage. That type of marriage ensures that not only the children of the deceased are looked after, but also his widow. In African traditional thought the care of widows is comprehensive, and as such includes meeting their procreative needs as well as those of their deceased husbands.

When missionaries came to Africa they found two forms of marriage, namely monogamy and polygamy. But because of the negative attitude toward African culture, they seem to have seen polygamy as the only African type of marriage. And yet, in actual fact, the majority of marriages in most of the African societies were and continue to be monogamous. As a matter of fact, there is evidence showing that some societies were not pleased with polygamy because of problems inherent in that type of marriage.[28]

There are several reasons why people enter into polygamous marriage contracts. If a first marriage does not produce children because the wife is infertile, one would marry another wife. If it is the husband who turns out to be sterile, some societies will arrange, often with the knowledge and consent of the husband (although he will pretend not to know), for the wife to have a love relationship with her brother-in-law in order to beget children for her husband. We must understand that it is extremely crucial and is in fact a matter of survival that one has children, and in African traditional society this is only possible within marriage, as it would cause serious religious problems outside marriage. Second, polygamy enhanced the status of the polygamist in society since only a few could afford it. Some of these marriages were arranged by the wife's parents, even when she was still an infant, although she did not move in with her husband until she was an adult.

The mission-related churches' response to both leviratic marriage and polygamy has invariably been one of condemnation. Those Christian women who go into leviratic marriages are immediately excommunicated, no matter how active they may have been as Christians. Polygamists are required to divorce all their wives, remaining with only one of them, before they can be accepted into the church. In some churches the polygamist would be required to attend catechetical classes for five years, where others took only three years, before they are baptized. In other churches only the man is penalized, and the wives would be accepted as full members im-mediately upon conversion and baptized after the normal period of cate-chetical instruction.

The way the church has dealt with this issue is obviously full of con-tradictions and brings a great deal of pain and hardship on those who are legally married according to African custom, and on the family as a whole. That Christian organizations should delight at breaking up families by forcing even people who were polygamists before conversion, and doing this in the name of the Christ, is indeed very strange, heartless, and cruel in the eyes of Africans. It is therefore necessary that African Lutheran theology reexamine the church's teaching and practice to see how the African concerns can be accommodated.

The practice in our Lutheran churches in Africa is to seek a Western solution to an African problem as seen and defined from the perspective of Western culture. We need to reexamine the problem in the light of the biblical witness, bearing in mind the cultural contexts within which it emerged. This is another area in which Africa's new churches seem to be far ahead of the mainline churches, resulting in many of our members being attracted to those churches. The Old Testament accepts polygamy, and polygamists such as Abraham and David are listed among some of the greatest of God's friends and set as examples of people of faith in the New Testament (Cf. Romans 4; Hebrews 11).

As far as we can tell Jesus himself never condemned polygamy, choosing to remain quiet on that issue and emphasizing only the fact that husband and wife become one flesh in marriage as affirmed in the Genesis account of creation. Paul did not seem to be concerned with polygamy either, placing only one restriction upon polygamists, namely, that they should not be elected or appointed to leadership positions in the church. This absence of the condemnation of polygamy in the New Testament seems to imply that it simply did not matter for salvation.

## Conclusion

The challenges confronting us as African Lutherans are formidable. Space does not allow me to discuss other issues that are concerns for our African churches. We should, however, take our inspiration from Martin Luther, who set an example by breaking with church tradition when it became clear to him that it no longer served as God's instrument of liberation. Luther was a revolutionary who, by translating the Bible into the German language, made it accessible to the ordinary Christians, thus allowing for meaningful participation.

The preaching of Christ in Africa is certainly producing converts, but many of these live in two worlds, namely, the traditional world whose spirituality continues to be meaningful and attractive, particularly during the critical moments in life, and the Christian world in its alliance with modernization and Westernization, which thus offers opportunities for material prosperity. At the same time, we are losing many Christians because of our failure to respond concretely to issues relating to marriage, ancestor veneration, liberation, sickness, and the like. The dialog with our African American brothers and sisters is bound to be of mutual benefit, since as black people we have basic, common experiences even if our contexts are different.

# 6

# THE TWOFOLD KINGDOM— AN AFRICAN PERSPECTIVE

# SIMON S. MAIMELA

n order to introduce the subject of Luther's teaching on the twofold
kingdom or governance of God and the place of that teaching today,
we need to consider an important passage from his treatise on *Temporal
Authority:*

Here we must divide the children of Adam and all mankind into two classes,
the first belonging to the kingdom of God, the second to the kingdom of the
world. Those who belong to the kingdom of God are all the true believers
who are in Christ and under Christ, for Christ is King and Lord in the kingdom
of God, as Psalm 2 [:6] and all of Scripture says. For this reason he came
into the world, that he might begin God's kingdom and establish it in the
world. . . .

Now observe, these people need no temporal law or sword. If all the world
were composed of real Christians, that is, true believers, there would be no
need for or benefits from the prince, king, lord, sword or law. They would
serve no purpose, since Christians have in their heart the Holy Spirit, who
both teaches and makes them to do injustice to no one, to love everyone, and
to suffer injustice and even death willingly and cheerfully at the hands of
anyone. Where there is nothing but the unadulterated doing of right and bearing
of wrong, there is no need for any suit, litigation, court, judge, penalty, law,
or sword. . . .

All who are not Christians belong to the kingdom of the world and are
under the law. There are few true believers, and still fewer who live a Christian

life, who do not resist evil and indeed themselves do no evil. For this reason God has provided for them a different government beyond the Christian estate and kingdom of God. He has subjected them to the sword so that, even though they would like to, they are unable to practice their wickedness, and if they do practice it they cannot do so without fear or with success or impunity. . . .

If this were not so, men would devour one another, seeing that the whole world is evil and that among thousands there is scarcely a single true Christian. No one could support wife and child, feed himself, and serve God. The world would be reduced to chaos. For this reason God has ordained two governments: the spiritual, by which the Holy Spirit produces Christians and righteous people under Christ; and the temporal, which restrains the un-Christian and wicked so that—no thanks to them—they are obliged to keep still and to maintain an outward peace. Thus does St. Paul interpret the temporal sword in Romans 13 [:3], when he says that it is not a terror to good conduct but to bad. And Peter says that it is for the punishment of the wicked [1 Pet. 2:14].[1]

I propose to center my presentation in the South African context and to pose some questions. Within the Lutheran context, the doctrine of the two kingdoms has been a topic of intense concern and sharp criticism. Since I shall attempt to be guided by Luther's teaching on and the distinctions he drew in discussing the twofold governance of God, I shall deal with his situation briefly.

## Luther's Situation

Luther lived and wrote when a theocratic, powerful church attempted to dominate every sphere of human life politically and spiritually. It was exceeding its divine mandate. Along with Luther's reaction against the established religious authorities, he contended with millenarian enthusiasts who wanted to use the gospel as an instrument to press for social rights and political reforms. Against both, Luther argued for the need to distinguish between, and not separate, God's twofold governance through which God cares for and maintains the creation. On the one hand, there was the secular government which, by means of law and the sword, secured and enforced external order and peace. On the other hand, there was the spiritual government. Through preaching and the Spirit, it worked to produce internal righteousness and inner transformations.

By presenting the rule of God in such a manner, Luther intended to acknowledge the dignity, place, contribution, and usefulness of each aspect of God's governance in serving our neighbors. In addition, he attempted to give a theological account to the origin and legitimacy of secular power. Note that he put limits on secular power. The reformer was aware that without a good understanding of the challenges, possibilities, and bounds of secular authority, people would be tempted to endow that aspect with divine qualities and worship it. So he spelled out the biblical warrants for secular power and pointed out that its jurisdiction is limited to external and worldly affairs, such as securing and maintaining civil order, justice, and peace. Secular power does not extend to the ultimate questions of life, such as a person's justification and salvation. Matters which deal with the soul, personal conscience, and convictions are beyond the reach of secular power. Those concerns are under the jurisdiction of the Word of God in the spiritual realm.

Luther carefully balanced the emphasis which distinguished the functions of the two forms of governance by insisting that there was a mutual and necessary interpenetration of the spheres one with another. The maker and ruler of both realms structured their relationship so that neither is complete without the other. For instance, the spiritual governance needs the civil order and peace which the secular kingdom establishes through law and the sword if the spiritual kingdom is to gain a hearing for the preaching which God uses to transform persons. In turn, the proclamation of God's will by the spiritual form cultivates the virtue, good will, and good deeds among people which are needed by the secular side.

Furthermore, both spiritual and secular forms have God's law of justice in common. Again, there is a reciprocity between the two kingdoms. God gives the secular the power of the law to maintain order and peace and to administer justice to the citizens entrusted to its care. The state also has the power of the sword to compel rogues to do by force what the law of God requires to maintain society. To the spiritual kingdom God entrusts the preaching office. Through that office the civil use of God's law (as well as the gospel) is proclaimed, helping citizens to define and clarify God's will for the benefit of the governing authority and of individual Christians. Both rulers and the ruled are summoned to measure their actions against the standard of God's holy will as revealed in law and gospel. By preaching the law and its civil use, the church reminds the state that its laws are to protect the underdogs against powerful exploiters, and that the law exists to serve justice, divine goodness, and love.[2] On the basis of sharing the law, the state administers and the church preaches it. This gives the church a double responsibility: it clarifies both for the state and for itself the proper roles the kingdoms have in God's twofold governance and how these fit into God's plan for the world.

While my outline of Luther's position and context has been necessarily broad and brief, I trust I have avoided the temptation to discuss his views as abstractions which lose touch with the political and social realities faced by people in his time. He made it clear that the church must exercise its divinely instituted mandate in the concrete situations of life. Now I will turn to South Africa.

## Questions and Comments

To discern how the teaching of the twofold governance might or might not apply in South Africa, I will start by raising some questions and follow them with comments.

1. Does the church have any role to play in the social sphere?
2. What kind of witness must the church give vis-à-vis the secular powers which often claim the right to monopolize the sociopolitical sphere?
3. What justification can the church offer for its seeming interference in the sociopolitical sphere as it attempts to carry out its mandate to clarify God's will for the benefit of the secular government and of individual Christians?

While we may be dealt with other questions and issues, these set the tone for this discussion. To pose those questions concretely and adequately, some comments on the present relationship of the church to the government in South Africa is called for. The situation is not unique to us but may be found in the world at large.

Obviously, the position of the church today differs in fundamental respects from its situation in the 16th century. The church then was so dominant that its powers were not merely assumed to exist but were feared. Its attempt to dominate every sphere of human life was a factor to be reckoned with by both rulers and ruled alike. In fact the church's power was so pervasive and total that Luther's issue was how the role and dignity of the divinely instituted authority of the secular power was to be acknowledged, restored, and justified theologically. The reformer's teaching on the twofold governance over humanity was an attempt to place limits on a too-powerful church, and to acknowledge and delineate the legitimacy and limitations of the secular power.

Today the situation is reversed. It is not the church, but rather the state that is too powerful. The state is so powerful that the issue confronting Christians is whether there is any role and room for the church. Most governments enter deeply into all spheres of life, even to the point of encroaching on the areas formerly reserved for the church, namely the spheres of conscience and personal beliefs. Now it is the government which seeks total control. In places such as South Africa, the situation has become so problematic that it is imperative that the church take stock of itself and rethink what its role, power, and divinely instituted office of preaching are. The stocktaking and rethinking are responses to the dynamic of government to arrogate to itself the role of caring for its citizens in body and soul, and then telling the church what it should preach and do. In the face of such a situation, we need to test Luther's two kingdom doctrine for relevance and applicability. If there still are relevant and applicable contributions, then the church could use Luther's insights to warn modern states against the temptation to claim domination over every sphere of life. Even though our situation is opposite to that of Luther, his insights could meet our needs. Perhaps anticipating situations like ours, he remarked, "In the devil's name the secular leaders always want to be Christ's masters and teach Him how He should run His church and spiritual government."[3] The modern problem is "statism," that is, the tendency toward totalitarianism and presumptuousness which tempts states to arrogate to themselves the authority to determine what is good and evil for their citizens, and to claim complete domination over even the most personal spheres of life and thought. We are ready now to analyze and discuss the South African situation, to which the church must respond as it struggles to define its role and exercise the power and truth entrusted to it by its Lord.

## The Situation in South Africa Today

The South African government, like most Western governments, subscribes to a theory in which the state and the church are separated. Some versions of the theory and its practice, unfortunately, are used to relegate the church to a secondary role in which it exists to support the government. So the church is seen as one of the institutions which attends to the "purely spiritual" and private concerns of individuals. Christian practice and witness is thereby blocked from intervening in sociopolitical matters, for these are regarded as the exclusive monopoly of the state. But the South African government professes itself to be Christian, so it has a problem of consistency in maintaining the theory of the separation of church and state. Not surprisingly, under the so-called Christian government, the South African parliament has remained among the few "institutions in the world where theological debate erupts from time to time in the discussion of national legislation. Unlike most modern countries, theology is at least theoretically not pushed to the edge of life but operates at the very core of South African culture."[4]

In itself the attempt by the state to bring theological concerns into debates in the national legislature could be harmless. It could even be applauded by Christians if intended to enact legislation which is compatible to God's will for order with justice and peace. In the case of the South African state, however, the aim is much more than attempting to obey God's will. The interest in theology and the theologization of politics is nothing but an inevitable manifestation of the self-messianism of white Afrikaners' mission in South Africa. The government sees itself as God's elect or appointed servant, called upon to perform a specific, messianic task. That task is to divide and to separate the main components of the South African population into different groups and races, then to allocate to each an area in which to live and to develop according to its respective nature. Put another way, because the messianic task is seen as one of avoiding the chaotic, if not sinful, state of admixture of various races, the South African government believes it is called upon to help God achieve God's divine goals of separating and preserving different racial groups. Is it any surprise that the same calling to separate the races as God ordains also benefits whites? Is it a coincidence that God's will agrees with the desire of whites not to commit ethnic-racial suicide through any form of racial integration? Indeed, the divine calling and the instincts for white self-preservation have become so identical and inseparable that, as a matter of faith, the white Afrikaner government has chosen to perish on "the way to obedience" rather than let the white race "melt into the nonwhites," thereby "forfeiting their white identity and their sacred calling."[5]

Of course, all these attempts by the South African government to theologize politics may sound to outsiders like a bad joke. But to a government which firmly believes that it has a special messianic relationship to and mission from God to right the wrongs of urban South Africa, nothing could be more compelling than to carry out this divinely assigned vocation with all the determination it can muster.[6] Believing that God is on the side of God's "chosen" government, ready to approve its actions and legislation, the story of the South African regime's attempt to design and consistently apply the policy of total separation of the races is a success, and compares favorably with some of the major feats in human history. For within a relatively short time the government's policy of apartheid has reordered South African society into multifaceted layers of group identities in which the color of one's skin, one's cultural identity and social status carry enormous and life-determining sociopolitical values. This system determines the fate and quality of life of every human being in South Africa today.

If we apply Lutheran theological language to apartheid, we could say that the government is the source of justification. Justification is not based on grace but on race, not on faith but on governmentally assigned group identity. On the grounds of such an externally imposed justification, people are to obey rules which determine where they are to live, with whom they are to associate, and even whom they may love and consider family members. Sanctification is attained by going along with the system and, for us, carrying passbooks. Homes, businesses, and even whole settlements have been uprooted and transported to what are (for them) strange territories mockingly called "homelands." The government says that it engages in this out of benevolent concern for all persons living in South Africa, and goes to huge expense and effort to put that benevolence into action. Blacks who show their ingratitude through criticizing such measures are subject to the damnation of detention, banning, and imprisonment.[7] Those who protest more physically are dealt with quite literally by the sword and its more technologically advanced equivalents. For blacks the political dispensation means "bad housing, being underpaid, pass laws, influx control, migratory labour, group areas, resettlement camps, inequality before the law, fear, intimidation, white bosses and black informers, condescension and paternalism; in a word, black powerlessness."[8]

While the political system denies people of color their humanity, dignity, security, and justice, it favors the one powerful sector of society: the dominant white minority. The system tells them that they deserve their privileges, positions, and power over the black races by natural right and divine election. Apartheid promises white people total security, peace, and justice as well as self determination and self salvation from the "black" and "communist" threats in return for their support of the nation's ruling party. That party is presented as God's anointed servant. *The party claims to know how to think better than anyone else, to provide for all South Africans a "proper" kind of personal belief (conviction), and to lead its citizens to Canaan, the land of milk and honey.*

Because the majority of whites place their faith in a government that promises to save them from every danger and to procure for them a rosy future, the government has amassed enormous power. What has it done with this power? It suppresses dissent, controls the press and publications it considers undesirable, and puts down any black uprising with undisguised brutality. The government's actions are logical and consistent, for they are rooted in the whites' understandings of their calling and mission to effect total and permanent separation of the races, and to safeguard the rights of whites to fulfill that divine task. To implement its racial policies and to provide complete care for the white nation in body and soul, the all-powerful white South African theologizes politics through the use of the theological rhetoric of divine calling and mission, so as to involve God in its project of white self-determination and self-salvation. Therefore, it regards the voice of the church and its mission as superfluous and unnecessary irritants. Again, the government's logic prevails. The state often uses its physical power and resources in attempts to silence the church's voices. It does so by intimidating courageous leaders, harassing prophetic church institutions, declaring certain theological emphases seditious and subversive, and banning church persons and publications.[9] The state also stands ready to use its power to promote some Christians in order to help adapt the gospel to the state's power interests. In effect, the government prescribes what gospel the South African churches are to preach.

It is still more frightening to see the responses of the white electorate in election after election. The majority of white Christians are willing to compromise the gospel's teachings by returning to power the government which proclaims that even after the death and resurrection of Jesus, it will ensure that different races, peoples, and groups will be forever unreconciled. The government is divinizing itself without demanding a crude form of state worship. It is being successful with the white voters in projecting itself as the one thing, the sole institution of salvation which is needed by whites. Beyond the state, there is need for neither the church nor divine providence to save them. The cost of winning the hearts and votes of so many whites is fearsome. The price is exacted from people of color, for they are sentenced to a life of humiliation, insecurity, perpetual removals, and break-ups of families through repressive legislation, intimidation, and physical violence in the name of law and order.

## God's Twofold Governance and the South African Church

Against this background we ask whether the church has any role to play, any power to project, any truth to proclaim. On the basis of Luther's teaching on God's twofold governance, I answer *yes!* The most important role of the church is to protect the state from its own presumptuousness, and, therefore, to protect it both from itself and from unreasonable demands made of it by its citizens. The church does this when it proclaims the fact that ultimate authority over and in life is not given by any state but by God. The church fulfills its role when it preaches the gospel truth that true security is not to be sought or found in the total separation of races, as the state alleges, but in the mutual acceptance of people of different races and traditions. The ground of that mutual acceptance is in the name and power of Christ, the one who died for us all while we were yet sinners. Before this Christ no race *qua* race is any better or worse, less, or more sinful than another.

In proclaiming this message, which contradicts the message preached by the state, the church will reclaim its birthright and sacred duty of preaching to unjust and totalitarian regimes which deify themselves. To be sure, such proclamation would bring on a church-state confrontation. It would, in turn, remind the church that in such a conflict it is powerless with regard to possessing the physical means to defend itself, yet powerful through the word which God has committed to its preaching office. The church ought not shrink from projecting this power of interpreting and proclaiming the untarnished truth set forth in the Word of God. That Word is both law and gospel as it addresses the reality of the power of and limits to the government.

Indeed, the church still has the role of reminding the state in South Africa that God's Word alone is the basis of all authority. It is, therefore, only from that Word that we come to learn about and respect and understand the purpose of secular power.[10] For it is the Word of God which establishes and preserves secular power. The state, therefore, is subject to the Word, and the Word can instruct, judge, and rebuke the state if it abuses the authority by pursuing purposes contrary to God's will.[11] The Word which establishes and teaches the secular authority is committed *not to the state* but to the church. The church, then, exercises an appropriate independence from the state and also wields enormous power vis-à-vis the state. That power is the power of the gospel, and on the basis of the gospel, the church defines and clarifies God's will to individuals and the state, and calls the state to account for and to justify its actions before God. In short, by proclaiming the gospel and projecting the power of the Word committed to it by God, the church has the authority to call the state to obey God. The church in South Africa has the authority, task, and potential to counter the self-destruction of the South African state and to avert the potential mutual destruction of the various racial and cultural groups.

In seeking to fulfill its preaching office, the church in South Africa will often be called upon to confess law and justice. The church will be required to summon the state back to basics, that government does not exist for its own sake and is not to seek its own willful interests. Rather, the state exercises a power entrusted to it and rules on behalf of God to establish law and justice, and maintain peace and security for all persons given to its care. In confessing the rule of law and justice, the church would, in effect, be declaring the present government policy, more particularly the legalized political and socioeconomic exploitation and oppression of people on the grounds of color, as contrary to the declared purpose for which God has instituted secular authority. In this case, the government distorts the law as it negates blacks as persons, denies them justice and their human rights, places all sorts of personal and communal restrictions on them, and distributes educational and medical resources, housing, and other social facilities unequally between blacks and whites.

As the church confesses law and justice, rebukes the state, calls on it to give up its racist ideological purposes and urges it to help men and women obey God's commandment to serve their neighbors, the church will be opting for the poor and weaker members of society. This, too, will remind the state that political institutions and secular authority exist to protect the underdogs against powerful exploiters. If the church carried on these functions of its preaching office, it would be doing what Luther attempted in his time, namely, to remind rulers that there is more to government than its ability to punish, harass, and repress its citizens. Next to the preaching office, the highest service of God is that of government. The state is intended to be characterized by divine goodness, blessing, and mercy toward the people entrusted to its care. It is to implement these forms of care by constructing and administering good and just laws to help the poor and defenseless and to further their interests.[12] So the church's preaching of the law and confession of justice is aimed at reminding the state that it does not exist to do violence to the rule of law but to make just laws and to keep the people within those just laws, and, as Luther wrote, to "direct the people horizontally toward one another, seeing to it that body, property, honor, wife, child, house, home, and all manner of goods remain in peace and security and are blessed on earth. God wants the government of the world to be a symbol of true salvation and of His kingdom on earth, like a pantomime or a mask."[13]

Put differently, the preaching office gives the church the duty to warn the government against the abuse of power. The church does so by telling the state that since its authority is derived from the office of parenthood, it ought to support and care for all its subjects as a parent supports children.[14] In acting in the service of love by seeking the welfare of all its subjects, the government would then acknowledge that its lordship over God's people is one of "helping power," and that the proper exercise of parental authority consists mainly in doing what is good and helpful.

Because political power in South Africa has the habit of misunderstanding its proper purpose by oppressing people of color, the church can expect the state to resist the church's confession of justice and even to reject the church's proclamation as an intolerable mingling of religion and politics. The government has the tendency to correct the Word of God and to dictate what the churches should preach and teach. We should expect, then, that the state will investigate the activities, teachings, and publications of certain Christians so as to condemn and silence what it regards as subversive. The church's response should be to declare that it proclaims not its own but God's will, that it has an interest in and responsibility for political issues and how society is governed. If the state promotes that which is contrary to God's Word, then the church cannot compromise its basic obedience to God. It must confess justice for all and publicly rebuke the powers-that-be for their wickedness and oppression before God and humanity.[15] The preaching office puts the church under the obligation to attempt to teach both rulers and the ruled about God's will for them so that social and political abuses will be exposed and corrected.[16]

In addition to the task of preaching the law and confessing justice to the state, the church has another equally important task in relativizing all the absolutes and idols that shackle God's people in South Africa. The ruling party has thrived long and successfully because its policy of apartheid functions as a "golden calf" which promises to care for whites in body and soul, and to give them complete self-determination and self-salvation, both now and in the future. The "golden calf" guarantees their future as a racial entity against real and imagined onslaughts from both blacks and communists. The golden calf will do this as long as the whites support this government and allow it to run everyone's life, even to the most minute detail. The government will determine what to believe, what to read, whom to love, and with whom to live. According to the government, there is no other salvation for them, and certainly no need for a church or providence. In short, we have a state which is busy deifying itself, teaching a political theology-ideology in place of the Word of God. We have a government which calls upon white people to defend the savior-state to the last person in the name of God.

Luther's teaching on the power and limitations of the secular authority should be helpful to the church as it faces the state. On the basis of Luther's insights and as a captive to God's Word, the church must preach the truth about the nature of secular power and the goals of political activity. Both secular authority and political activity are concerned with this physical and temporal life. They are, therefore, limited in time and by finite conditions.

Hence, while they are useful in the world to provide civil justice to all, they are completely useless when it comes to salvation. Any attempt to use political instruments to save souls or people is a serious misunderstanding of the nature, purpose, and limits of those instruments. To think that political ideologies and institutions extend beyond their temporal usefulness and competence is to divinize them, and that encroaches on God's role for the governance of the spiritual kingdom.[17]

The South African government's attempt to shepherd the souls of the whites to some ultimate self-salvation should be exposed as dangerous and misleading self-deification. The government tries to endow the ruling party and its political program with divine and eternal qualities. The fact is that the apartheid policy, however attractive, persuasive, and seductive it may be to its adherents, is one finite and transitional option among many options in South Africa. Because it is not the only way and certainly is not God's way, the apartheid system should be relativized so as not to be regarded and defended as inevitable and divine. The government's allegation that apartheid has the power to save white people is simply not true. Only God has the power to save and guarantee ultimate security, and in Jesus Christ God pledges that God is for us and is prepared to save and defend those who trust in God.

What would happen if the church used Luther's insights on the twofold governance of the world? One result would be to relativize and de-divinize the apartheid system. This would help the South African churches perform the crucial task of liberating people in South Africa from the slavery and worship of the state and its present arrangements. For the church will be making clear, especially to whites, that apartheid is not an inviolable creation of God nor something to which all South Africans are to succumb. As the temporal invention of men and women, apartheid can be changed and replaced by better political structures and arrangements which will enable South Africans to be truly human and open to one another. Not only should the church preach the truth and relativize apartheid, but it should also make clear to all South Africans that the unjust, oppressive system is doomed to destruction with or without their cooperation. Like all imperfect and temporal human products, especially those which are cruel and unjust, apartheid cannot be allowed to stand in the way of the transformation of the world into God's coming kingdom.

## Conclusion

In the conflict with the state, the church has and must project its power, the power of truth set forth in the Word of God. It is that truth and Christ's promise to be with his church which gives the church the courage and authority to confront the state, rebuke it for political abuses, and relativize its attempts to deify itself. In carrying out its God-given task, the church is forced to expose the state's tendency toward presumptuousness. The church plays a critical role in delineating and distinguishing between temporal and ultimate authority, political truth and eternal truth, secular expediency and everlasting justice. The teaching of the twofold governance and its statement by the church will make clear that God is active in both realms, so that we may avoid confusing God's work in political activity and God's activity in salvation.

Armed with God's Word and truth, the church has, I believe, all the power it needs to teach, guide, and help humanity shape God's world into one in which justice is at last the possession of all human beings.

# 7

# THE TWO KINGDOMS: A BLACK AMERICAN LUTHERAN PERSPECTIVE

# JAMES KENNETH ECHOLS

Statements by two well-known American theologians are suggestive of my reflections on the Lutheran doctrine of the two kingdoms and the black experience in America. In 1969, during a time of social, political, and racial upheaval in the United States, Carl Braaten, a white Lutheran, asserted,

> The problem with the two-kingdom doctrine is that the revolutionary dynamic discharged by the kingdom on the right hand did not set off any explosions in the kingdom on the left hand. . . . The two-kingdom doctrine has invariably engendered a conservative political ethic because the eschatological dynamic of the gospel is not released into the power situations which decide for or against the inner historical transformation of society. Its theology of power, essential also in a revolutionary ethic, is made to serve the interests of the status quo.[1]

The black United Methodist theologian, James Cone, who was reared in the African Methodist Episcopal Church, commented in 1984 specifically on the American situation:

> Almost without exception, white American churches have interpreted religion as something exclusively spiritual with no political content useful in the struggles of the poor for freedom. By identifying the gospel of Jesus with a spirituality estranged from the struggle for justice, the church becomes an agent of injustice. We can observe this in the history of Lutheran churches with their emphasis on the two kingdoms, and also in their apparent failure to extend

Luther's theology of the cross to society. Unfortunately all white institutional churches in America have sided with the capitalist, rich, white male elites, and against socialists, the poor, blacks, and women.[2]

From the perspective of the black experience in America, Cone and Braaten identify the key deficiency (perhaps even heresy) in this Lutheran doctrine. The traditional way of articulating and applying the two kingdoms position has denied and invalidated the divine calling of Christians and of the church to become involved in the societally transforming struggle for freedom and justice. And yet, black American Christians need not reject the teaching. If we examine both the doctrine and the life experience of black Americans of faith, we will see that not only can we affirm it, but that we already have affirmed it. The ways in which black American Christians have done so, however, are not exactly what the reformers or white Lutherans today have had in mind.

I want to address this claim by beginning with an examination of the two kingdoms doctrine. Perhaps the results will prove useful as we wrestle with the identities of African and American persons of color and faith who are seeking to be faithful and responsible in the struggle for peace and justice. As I begin this examination, it is crucial to make and maintain a clear distinction between the *conceptualization* of the doctrine and its *appropriation*. The basis for my conclusions is the distinction between *theology as the conceptualization of God's truth* and *ethics as the faithful appropriation of God's truth*. In order to state my position as clearly as possible, here are my conclusions:

1. The black American religious tradition and the Lutheran heritage converge, perhaps even agree totally, in a conceptual affirmation of the two kingdoms doctrine.

2. The black American religious tradition and Lutheran heritage differ radically as regards the doctrine's appropriation in the world. To be more precise, Lutherans have appropriated the two kingdoms understanding in ways which have accorded theological justification to an uncritical acceptance of a given social order. The Lutheran theological heritage, then, has supported societal conservation through an ethical stance that we may term *quietism*. In contrast, black American Christians have appropriated a two kingdoms approach which has led them to demonstrate their commitment to societal transformation. This has been expressed through an ethical stance that we may term *activism*.

3. The Lutheran heritage's appropriation of the doctrine has had the practical political consequence, in situations of oppression, of further oppressing the oppressed (the powerless). It has done so by legitimizing and empowering

the oppressors (the powerful). The black American religious tradition's appropriation has had the practical political consequence of empowering people of faith to stand with and to work for the liberation of the oppressed. Black Americans of faith, then, have stood for and worked against the oppressors, even when the oppressors have been Christians.

I now intend to provide the evidence for these conclusions by analyzing the doctrine and its interaction with the black experience in America. I will look first at how the Lutheran and black American religious traditions have conceptualized the teaching, second, at how they have appropriated it, and finally add a concluding word.

## Lutherans and the Conceptualization of the Two Kingdoms Doctrine

The Lutheran church's affirmation of a two kingdoms perspective is rooted in both the writings of Luther and the Lutheran Confessions. Because Lutherans have pointed consistently to these two sources, they warrant investigation.

First, the reformer. He never wrote a treatise which dealt solely with the two kingdoms.[3] But he was obliged to articulate his understanding of it when he addressed related subjects. For example, both *Temporal Authority: To What Extent It Should Be Obeyed* (1523) and *Whether Soldiers, Too, Can Be Saved* (1526) dealt with the two kingdoms in the course of discussions about other matters.[4] In the former, Luther responded to a political climate in which rulers considered it their prerogative to command what they pleased and subjects were expected to obey.[5] In the latter, the reformer answered the inquiry of a Christian professional soldier, and considered a matter that led directly to the issue of obedience to one's lord.[6]

Two further preliminary but helpful matters call for attention. First, Luther's version of the two kingdoms both reflected and extended a major tradition current in his time.[7] The tradition included Augustine's "two cities" and Pope Gelasius' "two swords" understandings of God's rule related to temporal and spiritual authorities. Two kingdom language and constructions were neither original to Luther nor foreign to his contemporaries. Second, the degree to which the reformer modified the tradition was a consequence of his commitment to the principle of *sola scriptura*. He attempted to develop his views solely on the basis of the Scriptures.[8] Since he was convinced that the core of the tradition was scriptural, he could affirm it, but without being tied to the tradition when he understood that the Bible demanded or allowed the tradition to be changed or expanded. The commitment to the *sola scriptura* principle eventually led the Augustinian monk to abandon Augustine's functional, dualistic view that the city of earth was an evil realm. Luther emphasized that both realms were governed by God.[9]

As he searched the Scriptures, Luther discerned two types of statements which became the foundation for his understanding of God's twofold governance. One set related to civil law and the sword, e.g.:

> Let every person be subject to the governing authorities. For there is no authority except from God, and those that exist have been instituted by God. Therefore he who resists the authorities resists what God has appointed, and those who resist will incur judgment (Rom. 13:1-2).

> Be subject for the Lord's sake to every human institution, whether it be to the emperor as supreme, or to governors, as sent by him to punish those who do wrong and to praise those who do right (2 Peter 2:13-14).

> Whoever sheds the blood of man, by man shall his blood be shed (Gen. 9:6).

> But if a man willfully attacks another to kill him treacherously, you shall take him from my altar, that he may die (Exod. 21:14).

On the other hand, he knew that there were passages which indicated that Christians were not to possess temporal authority or wield the sword. He cited texts such as the following:

> You have heard that it was said, "An eye for an eye, a tooth for a tooth." But I say to you, do not resist one who is evil. But if anyone strikes you on the right cheek, turn to him the other also; and if anyone would sue you and take your coat, let him have your cloak as well; and if anyone forces you to go one mile, go with him two miles (Matt. 5:38-39).

> Beloved, never avenge yourselves, but leave it to the wrath of God; for it is written, "Vengeance is mine, I will repay, says the Lord" (Rom. 12:19).

> Love your enemies, pray for those who persecute you (Matt. 5:44).

> Do not return evil for evil or reviling for reviling (1 Peter 3:9).[10]

Luther resolved the apparent contradiction by recognizing that God had established two forms of government through which to rule the world, one spiritual and the other secular. Secular government (or the kingdom on the left) was established to preserve external or civil righteousness. It was concerned with the earthly, temporal, and physical, and had God's sanction to use the sword of coercive power. Spiritual government (or the kingdom on the right) had the singular task of achieving true Christian righteousness through the proclamation of Christ and the administration of the sacraments so that humanity would inherit eternal life. The kingdom on the right, then, was concerned with the imputed or saving righteousness of God in Christ. Both forms of governance had the same divine author, were complementary, and supported each other. With regard to their permanence, Luther wrote, "Both must be permitted to remain; the one to produce [saving] righteousness, the other to bring about external peace and prevent evil deeds. Neither one is sufficient without the other." [11] In this regard Luther stressed the importance of neither separating nor confusing the two kingdoms.

Luther's doctrine of the two kingdoms rejected the cosmic dualistic aspects of Augustine in which it seemed that Satan was the immediate ruler of this world while God only ruled a spiritual realm. God ruled both realms according to Luther. He emphasized, therefore, that Christians were members of and subject to both kingdoms. Since God ruled both kingdoms, Christians were God's subjects in society and God's children in Christ. [12] The fundamental obligation of a person as citizen-child was obedience to God in both realms. In his treatise *Temporal Authority,* Luther expressed his resolution of the paradox of the Christian's wielding the sword with the injunction not to take the sword:

> You ask whether a Christian too may bear the temporal sword and punish the wicked, since Christ's words, "Do not resist evil," are so clear and definite that the sophists have had to make of them a "counsel." Answer: You have now heard two propositions. One is that the sword can have no place among Christians; therefore, you cannot bear it among Christians or hold it over them, for they do not need it. The question, therefore, must be referred to the other group, the non-Christians, whether you may bear it there in a Christian manner. Here the other proposition applies, that you are under obligation to serve and assist the sword by whatever means you can, with body, goods, honor, and soul. For it is something which you do not need, but which is very beneficial and essential for the whole world and your neighbor. Therefore, if you see that there is a lack of hangmen, constables, judges, lords, or princes, and you find that you are qualified, you should offer your services and seek the position, that the essential governmental authority may not be despised and become enfeebled or perish. The world cannot and dare not dispense with it. [13]

In addition the sword should never be wielded on behalf of self. "A Christian," wrote Luther, "should be so disposed that he will suffer every evil and injustice without avenging himself; neither will he seek legal redress in the courts but have utterly no need of temporal authority and law for his own sake." [14] Actually, the reformer was repeating a position expressed in the earlier *Treatise on Good Works* (1520). In the section which dealt with the commandment to honor parents in the sense of obeying them, Luther argued that it was far more important for Christians to obey the spiritual powers than the temporal powers. He maintained, ". . . the temporal power is but a very small matter in the sight of God, and too slightly regarded by him for us to resist, disobey, or become quarrelsome on its account, no matter whether the state does right or wrong."[15] Disobedience to either form of governance by Christians was justified only when they believed that to obey the human injunctions in one of the kingdoms was to disobey God. A Christian, held Luther, was not to wield the sword on behalf of a ruler if the Christian was convinced that to do so would be wrong and unjust.[16] Invoking Peter's precedent in Acts 5:29 about obeying God rather than humans, Luther declared,

> If your prince or temporal ruler commands you to side with the pope, to believe thus and so, or to get rid of certain books, you should say, "It is not fitting that Lucifer should sit at the side of God. Gracious sir, I owe you obedience in body and property; command me within the limits of your authority on earth, and I will obey. But if you command me to believe or to get rid of certain books, I will not obey; for then you are a tyrant and overreach yourself, commanding where you have neither the right nor the authority," etc. Should he seize your property on account of this and punish such disobedience, then blessed are you; thank God that you are worthy to suffer for the sake of the divine word. Let him rage, fool that he is; he will meet his judge. For I tell you, if you fail to withstand him, if you give in to him and let him take away your faith and your books, you have truly denied God.[17]

In summary, Luther affirmed conceptually that there were two kingdoms or realms through which God ruled. Each had its appropriate functions. The secular or lefthand kingdom manifested itself through structures such as government, marriage, family, business, and property. Its task was to promote the temporal welfare of people, to restrain evil, and to apply the sword where necessary. The spiritual or righthand kingdom had as its proper function the proclamation of the gospel and the administration of the sacraments. The regular institution which provided those functions was the church. Because the manner of God's governance differed, one should be careful neither to separate them dualistically nor to combine them synthetically. Non-Christians were members only of the kingdom on the left, while Christians held dual citizenship and were obliged to abide by the authorities of each kingdom, as long as their obedience to human authority did not require disobedience to God.

The Lutheran Confessions are normative for Lutherans in ways which the reformer's writings are not. Nevertheless, they concur with his understanding of the two realms.[18] Articles 16 and 28 of the *Augsburg Confession* are particularly relevant. The latter, concerned with ecclesiastical power, warned against confusing civil and ecclesiastical power, and went on to deal with the extent and limitation of episcopal authority. Article 16, regarding civil affairs, affirmed the involvement of Christians in governmental tasks, and concluded, "Christians are necessarily bound to obey their magistrates and laws except when commanded to sin, for then they ought to obey God rather than men" (Acts 5:29).[19]

## Black American Christians and the Conceptualization of the Two Kingdoms Doctrine

Black American Christians have not employed the same theological language and categories as did Luther and his colleagues in 16th-century Europe. There is, however, a close convergence if not full agreement between the black American religious tradition and the Lutheran heritage. While the Lutheran tradition has used terms such as two kingdoms, governments, and realms, the black American tradition has spoken of two worlds. The worlds—this world and the "other" or next world—both belong to God.[20] The two worlds understanding essentially incorporates within itself the essence of the two kingdoms doctrine. This is what Henry Mitchell and Nicholas Cooper-Lewter have called the "providence or care of God," for the "two worlds" understanding recognizes that God's care for humanity has both temporal and eternal dimensions.[21]

The otherwordly emphasis of the black American religious tradition was initially the result of white oppression mediated through Christianity.[22] To perpetuate and support slavery while claiming to be concerned about the souls of blacks, 17th-century white colonists enacted civil laws which stated "that the conferring of baptisme doth not alter the condition of the person as to his bondage or freedom."[23] The net effect of such laws for church practice was the proclamation by whites to blacks of a gospel of docility. One cleric of the time wrote about white Christianity's influence on blacks:

> In particular religious instruction would not produce mutiny because true religion enjoins obedience to rulers and superiors. Furthermore it instills an abhorrence of evil and particularly forbids taking vengeance for any injury. The Christian's only sure recompense for injustice is future heavenly bliss. Surely therefore Christian instruction could only make the plantation more secure.[24]

Enslaved blacks had no interest in making plantations more secure by accepting the Christianity forced upon them by white oppressors. In time, however, black American Christians embraced an otherworldly emphasis as one authentic dimension of God's providential care for humanity. No less an individual than Richard Allen, an ex-slave who founded the African Methodist Episcopal Church and worked for the freedom of all slaves in this world, wrote to those still in bondage,

> As life is short and uncertain, and the chief end of our having a being in this world is to be prepared for a better, I wish you to think on this more than anything else; then you will have a view of that freedom which the sons of God enjoy; and if the troubles of your condition end with your lives, you will be admitted to the freedom which God hath prepared for those of all colors that love him. Here the power of the most cruel master ends, and all sorrow and tears are wiped away.[25]

In this respect, Allen's theological perspective conformed to that of the slaves to whom he wrote. The spirituals bore witness to the slaves' confidence in the "transcendent future" God promised them, a future which acknowledged that slavery was not ultimate, and that the wrongs suffered in this world would be rectified in the next world.[26] The black American religious tradition has always held that the grace of God is significant for the hereafter, the world to come.[27] The tradition's otherworldly theme has stressed Christ as the Savior. In the role of Savior, Jesus has obtained humanity's admission into that world beyond the conditions of this life. The otherworldly emphasis is akin to and compatible with the activity of God which Lutherans associate with the kingdom on the right. For both the "next world" and the "kingdom on the right" have as their concern humanity's justification and eternal salvation.

The black American religious tradition's analog to the kingdom on the left, as might be anticipated, is "this world." If the black American's otherworldly emphasis came initially as a result of white oppression mediated through Christianity, the this-worldly emphasis is the black American response to that oppression. Black American Christians have always affirmed "the goodness of God and creation," finding great significance in Genesis 1:31, "And God saw everything that he had made, and, behold, it was very good."[28] That affirmation has implied for black Americans of faith that all life is to be valued and that nothing is inherently evil or demonic. The tradition has never denied that the secular and spiritual structures of reality are good gifts from God. Indeed, the black American tradition and the Lutheran heritage have agreed in esteeming those structures highly.

But the tradition's high esteem for God's creation and its inherent goodness has had to come to terms with a social context in which the white secular (government) and spiritual (church) structures of reality have conspired to deny the essential goodness of black humanity. As black American Christians have suffered white oppression and degradation in the forms of slavery, segregation, and discrimination, they have sought to discern God's will for their lives in this world. Searching the Scriptures, they have encountered the message of a God whose will is liberation, and whose power is directed against oppression.[29] Black slaves, pondering their own circumstances in light of the exodus, concluded that even as God had acted to free the Israelites from their captivity to the Egyptians, so God would free them from their captivity to the whites. In action and song they expressed their confidence that the God who had already accomplished liberation for others in this world would also free them from oppression in this world. This firm conviction gave the slaves the hope and fervor to sing,

> *Go down, Moses, way down in Egypt's land,*
> *Tell ol' Pharaoh to let my people go.*

In addition to recognizing Jesus as Savior, the tradition has also comprehended Jesus as liberator.[30] A key passage has been Luke 4:18-19, in which Jesus announced, "The Spirit of the Lord is upon me, because he has anointed me to preach good news to the poor. He has sent me to proclaim release to the captives and recovery of sight to the blind, to set at liberty those who are oppressed, to proclaim the acceptable year of the Lord." James Cone, citing this passage, stated clearly the tradition's belief in Jesus as liberator:

> Jesus' work is essentially one of liberation. Becoming a slave himself, he opens realities of human existence formerly closed to man. Through an encounter with Jesus, man now knows the full meaning of God's action in history and man's place within it. . . . In Christ, God enters human affairs and takes sides with the oppressed. Their suffering becomes his; their despair, divine despair. Through Christ the poor man is offered freedom now to rebel against that which makes him other than human.[31]

The black American religious tradition certainly has stressed God's action in history *and* (as in the rallying cry of the 1960s, "freedom now!") a staunch commitment to this world. While the tradition has maintained that God and God's creation are good, it has not ignored the disparities between what God intended for this world as a reflection of divine good-ness, and what this world's realities have been. The tradition, as is evident in the spirituals, has called black Americans to live in the light of the "transcendent present." [32] Living in such a way had profound implications for slaves because "if the Kingdom was truly present in their midst, and if it was really ultimate, then they had to disobey all the values that hindered their obedience to the coming Kingdom." [33] Life lived in the transcendent present has extended as well to all black American Christians. For even after the legal abolition of slavery, the persistence of white oppression has encountered the black American Christians' faith in the providence of the God who in Christ has declared God's commitment to liberation. Con-formity to oppression, then, has constituted not only complicity in op-pression but also disobedience to God. It is from this perspective that Acts 5:29 has substantially informed and influenced the black American religious tradition's stance toward the structures of this world.

The black American religious tradition and the Lutheran heritage at least converge, even if they do not agree totally, on a conceptual affirmation of the essence of the two kingdoms. Each refers to two dimensions of the reality of God's rule: one employs the language of kingdom, the other the language of worlds. Both invoke Acts 5:29 in order to establish for Chris-tians the limits of obedience to human authority. Although there may be convergence and agreement on the concept, however, the appropriation of that verse in light of Romans 13:1-2 has been radically different.

## Lutherans and the Appropriation of the Two Kingdoms Doctrine

Lutherans have appropriated the two kingdoms doctrine in a fashion which has been characterized by quietism and which has manifested itself in societal conservation. The source of this quietism and societal conservation can be traced to the reformer himself.

Luther clearly exhibited this quietism in the 1524–1525 conflict between the governing authorities and the peasants. Peasants' reactions against feu-dal oppressors were longstanding and not unique to the German states. In February 1525, German peasants codified their demands in the *Twelve Articles,* declaring to the secular authorities the specific nature of the op-pressions inflicted on them. The preface to the *Articles* appealed to Israel's exodus experience as a biblical justification for their resistance to their rulers. The biblical reference also implied that the peasants understood themselves to be instruments of God's liberating action: "Did [God] not hear the children of Israel when they cried to him and released them out of the hand of Pharaoh [Exod. 3:7-8]; and can he not today deliver his own? Yes, he will deliver them, and will do so quickly (Ps. 46:5)!"[34]

The peasants outlined a program of deliverance which combined elements of what Luther would call the kingdoms on the right with those on the left. The peasants petitioned for the right of the whole community to choose and appoint pastors, and then went on to catalog a host of changes ranging from the abolition of serfdom to changing the tithing system, restoring traditional rights in the use of forest and pond, establishing a fair system for labor and wages, etc. The peasants stated their willingness to withdraw any article shown to be contrary to Scripture, and asked Luther to comment on the *Articles*.

Luther's response, *Admonition to Peace: A Reply to the Twelve Articles of the Peasants in Swabia* (1525), addressed both the governing authorities and the peasants.[35] Luther began by blaming the secular authorities for causing the rebellion because they had cheated and robbed the people so that they, the nobles, could live in luxury. He saw the hand of God in the peasants' revolt: "It is not the peasants, dear lords, who are resisting you; it is God himself, to visit your raging upon you."[36] He urged the princes to consider the justice of each of the articles. Peasants who read the opening of the treatise had reason to expect the reformer's complete support and intervention. He had, after all, chastised their oppressors, invoked God's involvement in their cause, and summoned the authorities to enact changes. But Luther did not stop there.

The second section of the treatise was addressed to the peasants. After chastising the secular rulers and supporting the peasants' grievances, he then castigated the peasants for resisting their wicked, secular rulers. Luther told them that by their resistance against the duly constituted authorities, they were attempting to overthrow the government instituted by God. According to Luther, the peasants were usurping that which did not belong to them:

> The fact that the rulers are wicked and unjust does not excuse disorder and rebellion, for the punishing of wickedness is not the responsibility of everyone, but of the worldly rulers who bear the sword. Thus Paul says in Romans 13[:4] and Peter, in 1 Peter 3[2:14], that the rulers are instituted by God for the punishment of the wicked. . . . It is true that the rulers do wrong when they suppress the gospel and oppress you in temporal matters. But you do far greater wrong when you not only suppress God's Word, but tread it underfoot, invade his authority and law, and put yourselves above God. Besides, you take from

the rulers their authority and right, indeed, everything they have. What do they have left when they have lost their authority? . . . Therefore you are far greater robbers than they, and you intend to do worse things than they have done.[37]

Objecting to the peasants' uprising on the basis of his understanding of the kingdom on the left, he grounded his outrage in the law of Christ. He accused them of claiming to be Christians while discarding that norm by which Christians were to live. After reminding them of numerous biblical passages that embodied the law of Christ, Luther declared,

On the basis of these passages even a child can understand that the Christian law tells us not to strive against injustice, nor to grasp the sword, not to protect ourselves, not to avenge ourselves, but to give up life and property, and let whoever takes it have it. We have all we need in our Lord, who will not leave us, as he promised [Hebrews 13:5]. Suffering! suffering! Cross! cross! This and nothing else is the Christian law.[38]

Instead of resisting the injustice of the secular rulers, Luther challenged the peasants to endure their injustice and to pray for its elimination. Luther did urge both sides to negotiate a settlement rather than resort to combat. If, however, injustice and oppression continued, Luther left no doubt that his overriding concern in matters dealing with the secular kingdom was the preservation of law and order, not the legitimate grievances of the poor and exploited. His bottom line assertion in the midst of turmoil was not the liberation of the oppressed but "Let everyone be subject to the authorities."[39] This bottom line paved the way for Luther's diatribe against the peasants later in 1525. When he learned that there was another rebellion under way and that God's name was again invoked on the side of the peasants, Luther likened them to mad dogs and sanctioned their being killed by the secular authorities. Subsequently, in defense of such action, the reformer wrote graphically and fearsomely,

Let no one have mercy on the obstinate, hardened, blinded peasants who refuse to listen to reason; but let everyone, as he is able, strike, hew, stab, and slay, as though among mad dogs, so that by so doing he may show mercy to those who are ruined, put to flight, and led astray by these peasants, so that peace and safety may be maintained.[40]

Hubert Kirchner has argued that Luther's authoritarian world was so vastly different from ours that it is unfair to judge him for his condemnation of the peasants.[41] Even if this defense is advanced, it does not eliminate a critical consideration about Luther's involvement in the conflict between the rulers and the peasants. In spite of his strong language directed toward the secular authorities, Luther was quietistic. While he acknowledged the reality and injustice of the oppression inflicted on the peasants and urged the rulers to change, his highest priority was the maintenance of law and order. Accordingly, he implored the peasants to "obey and pray and endure," rather than to identify themselves as agents of God's liberating activity. The peasants' rejection of that counsel led to Luther's support and encouragement of their extermination. Thus the reformer advocated societal conservation, and gave priority to his understanding of Romans 13 rather than Acts 5. In the final analysis, Martin Luther legitimatized and empowered the oppressors (rulers) and further oppressed the oppressed (the peasants).

Succeeding generations of Lutherans have imbibed the spirit of Luther's quietism and societal conservation. One of the differences between Luther and those who followed in his stead was their reemployment of the dualistic principle which the reformer rejected. During the 19th century the dualistic interpretation and appropriation of the two kingdoms teaching was reflected increasingly among German theologians.[42] For example, Christian Ernst Luthard (1867) wrote about the doctrine,

> To begin with, the Gospel has absolutely nothing to do with outward existence but only with eternal life, not with external orders and institutions which come into conflict with the secular orders but only with the heart and its relationship to God, with the grace of God, the forgiveness of sins, etc. . . . in short with heavenly life. . . . This means that it is not the vocation of Jesus Christ or of the Gospel to change the orders of secular life and establish them anew. On the contrary, Christ has nothing to do with this sphere but allows it to go its own way. . . . Thus Christ's servants, the preachers, likewise have no reasons to espouse these secular matters but are only to preach grace and the forgiveness of sins in the name of Christ. . . . Christianity wants to change man's heart, not his external situation, as the monastic ethic teaches.[43]

In 1895 the influential scholar, Rudolph Sohm, claimed that, "The Gospel frees us from this world, frees us from all questions of this world, frees us inwardly, also from the questions of public life, also from the social question."[44] To the degree that Christians were in the world, their response to worldly authority, according to Ernst Troeltsch and Wilhelm Hermann, was to be that of obedient submission.[45] Luther's bottom line remained intact among Lutherans.

Lamentably, Lutherans have been all too faithful to Luther with regard to (an appropriation of) the two kingdoms teaching. They have done pre-cisely what he did when confronted with the reality of oppression: they have become the agents of societal conservation, embodying and encour-aging a quietism that has served to empower oppressive governments while further oppressing the oppressed. Thus Lutheran missionaries in Southwest Africa (Namibia) chastised the indigenous African population for rebelling against their repressive, colonial rulers. Pointing to the prodigal son, these missionaries told the Africans that they were on the same path and needed to repent. To ensure clarity the white pastors warned resisters, "You have raised the sword against the government which God placed over you with-out considering that it is written: 'Whoever takes the sword, shall also perish by the sword.' "[46] Several decades later, German Lutherans were among those who stimulated their fellow citizens to an uncritical allegiance to Hitler's regime. They joined in the genocide of millions of Jews.[47] And the ongoing struggle for freedom from oppression in South Africa has been hindered to a significant degree by Lutherans who, until recently, invoked the two kingdoms doctrine in a manner which allowed the church to ignore its responsibility to relate the gospel to this world and, hence, to the apartheid system.[48]

To be sure, not all Lutherans have fallen prey to the tradition of quietism and societal conservation. Dietrich Bonhoeffer is the most well-known exception. Today, there are few Lutheran theologians who would embrace a dualistic and/or quietistic version of the two kingdoms doctrine, and most would affirm the necessity of relating the gospel to the world here and now. Yet the quietist-conservation tradition persists as telling testimony to the practice of giving greater emphasis to Romans 13 than to Acts 5. From this perspective it is ironic that Lutherans consider Bonhoeffer a venerated martyr on the basis of his appropriation of the two kingdoms teaching, for he placed greater emphasis on Acts 5 (obedience to God) than on Romans 13 (submission to humans).

## Black American Christians and the Appropriation of the Two Kingdoms Doctrine

The black American religious tradition contrasts starkly with the Lutheran heritage in appropriating an understanding of the twofold governance of God. On the whole, in situations of oppression, Lutherans have supported the status quo uncritically, invoking Romans 13. In so doing, they have functioned as agents of oppression. While Lutherans have taken a stance of quietism-conservation, black Americans of faith have taken a stance of activism-societal transformation. Black American Christians have challenged the status quo in circumstances of oppression by critically invoking Acts 5. Consequently, black Americans have been agents of liberation, establishing what Gayraud Wilmore has termed a "radical tradition."[49] This radical tradition has been committed to activism and societal transformation in pursuit of freedom, justice, and equality. It has developed in a nation in which white racism has oppressed and brutalized blacks. As a principle of societal exclusion, white racism has manifested itself in the forms of slavery, segregation-apartheid, and discrimination-second class citizenship.[50] As a principle of religious dehumanization and pacification, white racism has expressed itself through theories such as the "Curse of Ham," designed to convince blacks that they were innately inferior, and through gospels of docility and quietism. The goal of such gospels has been to institutionalize in the hearts and minds of blacks a complacency regarding their status in this world.

In fact, the black American religious tradition has affirmed precisely what the white American racism has rejected. The black American tradition has been committed to a "nonracist appropriation of the Christian message" and, therefore, has rejected "Curse of Ham"-like speculations.[51] The tradition has also proclaimed its commitment to activism in pursuit of societal transformation. Consequently it has rejected appeals for quietism, complacency, and societal conservation.[52] The black American religious tradition has proclaimed on the basis of Israel's exodus experience and Jesus' sermon in Luke 4, that God wills the liberation of the oppressed. In this context, black Americans have cited Acts 5 as they have resisted their oppressors, for such resistance has been an indispensable dimension of God's liberating activity and human obedience. As this radical position has unfolded, American society has been made aware of the fact that black Americans have answered the tradition's call to activism.

The historical content of black American Christian activism is important to note here, for such a survey expresses, both ecclesiastically and politically, that the unifying themes of that activism have been freedom and equality. These twin themes were at the center of the events in the late 18th and early 19th centuries which led to the institutional emergence of black American Christianity.

The institutional emergence of black American Christianity in the northern part of the country may be noted in the activism of Richard Allen and his colleagues.[53] A free, black, Methodist circuit rider, Allen was called in 1786, by St. George's Methodist Episcopal Church in Philadelphia, to preach to the free population of African descent. Allen conducted worship at 5:00 A.M. and often in the evening as well. He remarked that his labor had been "much blessed." Allen's and his associates' activism was triggered at one Sunday worship service when they sought to worship with the white congregation. They were blatantly and publicly denied equal treatment.

In more than one sense it represented an 18th-century exodus event. Late morning worship had begun when Allen's group was directed to the balcony where, an usher claimed, seating was available. Upon arriving at the seats, they kneeled to pray as the rest of the congregation had been exhorted. During prayer a trustee interrupted them and demanded that they vacate the seats immediately; clearly those seats were intended for whites only. The trustee would not even permit the Africans to finish praying, and secured the assistance of other church officials to force Allen's party to move. Allen recorded for posterity, ". . . prayer was over, and we all went out of the church in a body, and they were no more plagued with us in the church."[54] Their walkout was an exodus. It was a clear rejection of white racist Christianity with its insistence on black inferiority. It was also an affirmation of a nonracist appropriation of the Christian message which implied that equality in the church extended to seating accommodations.

The activism of Allen and his associates precipitated a series of occurrences which ultimately resulted in the formation of the African Methodist Episcopal Church (1816). Black American Christianity gained institutionalized visibility through actions which transformed the societal context for whites as well as blacks. No longer did whites have a monopoly on interpreting to blacks what God willed for them in this world. Further, contrary to the quietistic-conservationist gradualism of mainstream white Christianity prior to the Civil War, black American Christians in the North denounced slavery as sinful. They made it increasingly clear that they were committed to black freedom and insisted that all humans were equal.[55]

In the South, the overwhelming majority of blacks were slaves. The institutional emergence of authentic black American Christianity was invisible to the eyes of the slavocracy.[56] Masters closely monitored and regulated the religious lives of their slaves. At night, however, the slaves stole away and held secret meetings. There the concern of preaching, singing, and praying was freedom in this world.[57] As a result, the institution which was invisible to the oppressors was clearly visible to the black American community. While we know of the specific activism of few of those black saints, we do know that virtually all black Americans of faith repudiated the message of inferiority and docility proclaimed to them by white American Christianity. Charles Colcock Jones, a white Presbyterian plantation missioner, testified to that activism in his report about the reaction of a slave congregation to a sermon he delivered in 1833:

> I was preaching to a large congregation on the Epistle of Philemon: and when I insisted on fidelity and obedience as Christian virtues in servants and upon the authority of Paul, condemned the practice of running away, one half of my audience deliberately rose up and walked off with themselves, and those that remained looked anything but satisfied, either with the preacher or his doctrine. After dismission, there was no small stir among them: some solemnly declared "that there was no such Epistle in the Bible"; and others, "that they did not care if they ever heard me preach again!". . . . There were some too, who had strong objections against me as a Preacher, because I was a master, and said, "his people have to work as well as we!" [58]

As Jones' account shows, not all were so bold as to leave worship in protest against slavocracy's gospel of docility. Yet even those who remained were empowered by the invisible institution's gospel of freedom to resist what was proclaimed to them as the good news. Such resistance constituted the energizing power of those who walked out. Long before the Emancipation Proclamation and the subsequent legal abolition of slavery, the slaves knew and experienced freedom through the invisible institution. They had been freed in a profound way through the invisible institution's affirmation of the inherent goodness of their humanity and of God's struggle for their liberation in this world.

Political activism by black American Christians in opposition to the oppression of racism has included both violent and nonviolent proposals and strategies. For the most part the tradition has been committed to nonviolence.[59] Whether through violence or nonviolence, black Americans have been united with regard to the goal of their activism: the political realization of freedom and equality for all human beings. Of necessity, that has required the transformation of a society in which bondage and second-class citizenship have been the norms. So black Americans have demanded the demise and dismantling of slavery, segregation, and discrimination. That strand of political activism by black American Christians which has advocated and used violence to achieve freedom and equality extends from religiously influenced slave insurrections, to Henry Highland Garnet, to black theology.

Three slave insurrections, in particular, reveal the close connection between Christianity and violence, a strategy that was intended to achieve liberation.[60] In 1800 in Richmond, Virginia, the slave Gabriel Prosser led what turned out to be an unsuccessful insurrection. Prosser, a student of the Bible whose favorite hero was Samson, planned to seize the federal arsenal in Richmond in order to secure guns and ammunition, and to kill all whites encountered in the effort. In addition, he planned to seize the state treasury and ultimately force Virginia slaveholders to liberate their slaves. Prosser recruited thousands of slaves in his plan, but two informed their masters. Prosser was eventually arrested and executed.

A second insurrection was led by Denmark Vesey, a freed slave. He conspired to raise a rebellion in the area of Charleston, South Carolina, in 1822. As with Prosser, Vesey was betrayed by a slave and later executed. Vesey, too, was a student of the Bible and believed that the slaves were to be the instruments of God's wrath, through whom God would punish whites for supporting human bondage. God would in turn liberate the slaves from that bondage. He may well have been encouraged in his views by the African Methodist Episcopal preacher, the Reverend Morris Brown. Brown was in Charleston at the time and served as secret counselor to Vesey and his associates. Although the planned insurrection was discovered and Vesey's goals were not achieved, this did not deter others from pursuing the same strategy in order to gain freedom.

Nine years later, in Southampton County, Virginia, Nat Turner led a third slave insurrection. Turner, a slave and a Baptist preacher, instigated the bloodiest slave revolt in American history. Fifty-seven whites were killed, beginning with Turner's master. Turner's plan was to capture the county seat, the symbol of local political power. Six weeks after the revolt started it was crushed, and its leaders were apprehended and hanged. Having wielded the sword, Turner perished by the sword. But he was committed to taking the way of violence to achieve freedom because he "discovered that the God of the Bible demanded justice, and to know him and his Son Jesus Christ was to be set free from every power that dehumanizes and oppresses."[61]

Northern black American Christians encouraged these southern insurrections. Among the major proponents was Henry Highland Garnet, the first pastor of the Liberty Street Negro Presbyterian Church in Troy, New York. In his 1843 address on slavery delivered to the Negro National Convention, he declared that it was "sinful in the extreme" for a person to "make voluntary submission" to slavery.[62] He invoked the principle of resistance on the basis of Acts 5:29 and boldly summoned the slave community to an activism which included violence:

God will not receive slavery, nor ignorance, nor any other state of mind, for love and obedience to him. Your condition does not absolve you from your moral obligation. The diabolical injustice by which your liberties are cloven down, *neither God, nor angels, or just men, command you to suffer for a single moment. Therefore it is your solemn and imperative duty to use every means, both moral, intellectual, and physical that promises success.*[63]

His speech issued a rousing call to freedom: "Let your motto be resistance! resistance! resistance! . . . What kind of resistance you had better make, you must decide by the circumstances that surround you, and according to the suggestion of expediency."[64] Garnet was concerned chiefly with the liberation of slaves because slavery. violated the will of God. If violence were the only means to achieve the elimination of slavery, then, thought Garnet, violence was justifiable.

Like Garnet in the 19th century, black theology in the 20th century has refused, on theological and theoretical grounds, to reject violence as a potential tool of black American activism. Practical considerations, however, have precluded black theology from either encouraging or instigating its use. In essence, black theology was the theological response of the black American religious tradition to the black power movement of the late 1960s, a movement which reacted against broken political promises and a lack of social progress, as well as both successful and unsuccessful assassinations. These realities reflected the persistence of white racism in American society and the continuation of black oppression.

Black theology attempted to articulate a distinctive black religious perspective that would address the continued oppression of black Americans. Legally, slavery and segregation had been abolished, but institutional racism and its effects persisted. Reiterating the conviction of the black American religious tradition that God was a God of freedom and equality, a God who struggled on behalf of the oppressed, black theology was forced to reflect upon the use of violence. James Cone, recognizing the necessity of societal transformation and the activism required to embody it, observed concerning violence:

It is this fact that most whites seem to overlook—the fact that violence already exists. The Christian does not decide between violence and nonviolence, between evil and good. He decides between the less and the greater evil. He must ponder whether revolutionary violence is less or more deplorable than the violence perpetuated by the system. There are no absolute rules which can decide the answer with certainty. But he must make a choice. If he decides to take the "nonviolent" way, then he is saying that revolutionary violence is more detrimental to man in the long run than systemic violence. But if the system is evil, then revolutionary volence is both justified and necessary.[65]

Cone deferred making a judgment on whether racist America was beyond redemption without the use of violence, a judgment that would have compelled him to call for its use. Presumably, for Cone in 1969, a black American activism which employed other means to challenge white racism must have been sufficiently adequate to forestall such an appeal. But black theology has refused to abandon totally the option because of its commitment to the liberation of the oppressed. In this regard, it has mirrored both the slave insurrections and Henry Highland Garnet.

Nonviolent political activism has been the predominant strategy through which black Americans of faith have attempted to effect societal transformation. This nonviolent tradition extends from escapes from slavery to freedom (as may be seen in the Underground Railroad), to participation in the Abolitionist crusade, to the militancy of Martin Luther King Jr.

No disagreement existed among black American Christians about the institution of slavery. They believed it violated the will of God and the dignity and worth of black humanity. The issue with which they dealt prior to the Civil War was not whether slavery should be destroyed but how it was to be destroyed. Some pursued the strategy of violence, which led to insurrections, while others chose a nonviolent strategy that entailed escape. This led to the organization of the Underground Railroad. "Steal Away," a spiritual of the Invisible Institution, signaled that a departure to the North and freedom was imminent.[66] Black American Christians like Harriet Tubman conducted those slaves who had "stolen away" from their masters along a route of safe-houses and stations in slaveholding and fugitive-seeking states. Black congregations were among the stops on the route to the North, where freedom existed in either hospitable Northern areas or Canada.[67] The effort of establishing and maintaining the network was formidible indeed, and demonstrated the involvement and commitment of black American Christians to plans of action designed to effect their nonviolent liberation.

In the North, free black Americans who sought to gain the freedom of their enslaved sisters and brothers by nonviolent efforts often associated with abolitionists. With few exceptions, those black American activists were linked with the type of abolitionism dedicated to the immediate emancipation of the slaves and their incorporation into American society. Abolitionism in this sense was compatible with black American Christian goals of freedom and equality for all persons. Black abolitionists, at a meeting in Mother Bethel Church in Philadelphia (Allen's congregation and the "mother" of the African Methodist Episcopal Church) in 1817 declared their complete opposition to the plans of the American Colonization Society, plans by which the white-dominated Society would have transported free blacks back to Africa. They objected not only to the Society's operating assumption that blacks were inherently inferior and could never be the equal of whites in the United States, but also to the fact that the removal of free blacks would hinder efforts to free slaves in this nation.[68]

By 1830 the determination of black abolitionists was institutionalized in the Negro National Convention movement. Assembling in Mother Bethel with Bishop Allen as the chair, the Convention declared its purpose as seeking the abolition of slavery in the South and the advancement of free blacks in the North.[69] The commitment of black American Christians to freedom and equality also caused them to support the antislavery activities of white abolitionists such as William Lloyd Garrison and Isaac Knapp. In fact, blacks constituted the majority of subscribers to *The Liberator,* the newspaper published by Garrison and Knapp. Beginning in 1831, *The Liberator* advocated vociferously what was then a radical abolition policy (immediate emancipation, accomplished immediately with little regard for compensating slavemasters for the loss of their human property).[70] Abolitionists quickly became targets of the violence of their opponents. Yet their agitation for the destruction of slavery remained nonviolent. Dedicated to both liberation and nonviolence, black American Christian political activism was closely associated with the nonviolent tradition of resistance in pursuit of freedom and societal transformation.

One hundred twenty-five years after the organization of the Negro National Convention movement, a national movement for civil rights to end racial segregation was initiated by the courageous and nonviolent political act of Rosa Parks. A devout black American Christian, she became the catalyst for the emergence of significant leaders such as Martin Luther King Jr. A Baptist minister born and reared in the Jim Crow South, King articulated a dream which envisioned the transformation of American society, a dream rooted in the black American religious tradition's enduring commitment to freedom and equality for all. In his "I Have a Dream" speech (1963) delivered on the steps of the Lincoln Memorial and in view of both the nation's capitol building and presidential residence, he said:

> I have a dream that one day on the red hills of Georgia, sons of former slaves and sons of former slave-owners will be able to sit down together at the table of brotherhood. . . . I have a dream my four little children will one day live in a nation where they will not be judged by the color of their skin but by the content of their character. . . . I have a dream that one day, down in Alabama, with its vicious racists, with its governor having his lips dripping with the

words of interposition and nullification, that one day, right there in Alabama, little black boys and black girls will be able to join hands with little white boys and white girls as sisters and brothers. I have a dream today![71]

For King and other black American Christians, the hope was to realize the dream through the nonviolent means of active resistance. Earlier in the same speech, he urged the assembled crowd to continue to work and act nonviolently, a strategy which had characterized the movement since its advent. He warned against allowing their creative protest to "degenerate into physical violence."[72] Demonstrations, boycotts, marches, and ballot boxes were deemed the appropriate instruments of change that would contribute to the transformation of a segregated society into an integrated society. So black American Christians in substantial numbers joined with King in the Civil Rights Movement, extending that strand of their religious tradition which sought freedom and equality for all through nonviolent activism.

This brief historical survey has attempted to delineate how black American Christians have appropriated the two kingdoms doctrine. There is a clear similarity between the experiences of black American Christians and the German peasants of the early 16th century. As did the peasants, black Americans have employed activism in order to overcome their oppressors and transform society. However, since Luther accused the peasants of confusing and mixing the kingdoms in ways which compromised the integrity of the gospel, it should not be surprising to discover that white American Lutherans have responded to black American Christian activists in the same way. In my view there are two reasons to discount this typical Lutheran accusation or response.

First, the black American religious tradition has neither confused nor separated the two kingdoms or worlds. Rather, it has dynamically related the two dimensions of God's reality so as to take seriously both the theological affirmation that this world is God's world and the petition in the Lord's Prayer, "Thy will be done on earth as it is in heaven." Secondly, the white American Lutheran response must be discounted because it has been welcomed by the forces of oppression, the principalities and powers which oppose God's liberating will and activity. The black American religious tradition has acknowledged the gift of authority in this world, the kingdom on the left. But on those occasions when the governing authorities have clearly and blatantly violated the will of God, the tradition has been compelled to declare, in both words and deeds, that Christians must obey God rather than humans.

## A Concluding Word

Given this analysis, the germane question is, "What does all this mean for black Lutherans in America?" After all, they are the heirs of these two significant theological traditions, traditions which have diverged radically in the past and which continue to approach oppressive situations quite differently. Must black Lutherans choose between the two traditions? Or is there some way of remaining both a black American Christian and a Lutheran with integrity?

As black Lutherans in America consider the meaning of the two kingdoms doctrine and its appropriation for life in this world, two thoughts come to mind. The first is that black Lutherans in the United States need not totally reject the Lutheran understanding of the two kingdoms. There certainly are theological approaches other than those of the Lutherans which have been and are sympathetic to societal transformation. Yet if the distinction between conceptualization and appropriation is valid, then it is possible to lament the doctrine's misappropriation by Lutherans without discarding it as an inherently oppressive teaching. Indeed, an important task for black Lutherans might well involve its faithful appropriation.

A second thought is that black Lutherans in America need to acknowledge and discharge their prophetic calling in the midst of white Lutherans. Having been influenced by the black American tradition's legacy of radicalism, black Lutherans should be prepared to summon their white sisters and brothers away from quietism toward an activism committed to the transformation of society. In so doing, black Lutherans can facilitate white Lutheran abandonment of a devotion to societal conservation, even in contexts of injustice and oppression. In so doing, black Lutherans can contribute to the transformation of a tradition identified with oppression. Instead of being identified with oppression, the Lutheran heritage can become dedicated to the liberation of the oppressed in accordance with the will of God.

# 8
# RELATIONSHIPS TO IDEOLOGIES AND NON-CHRISTIAN RELIGIONS

# JOHN S. POBEE

t is common knowledge that the center of Christianity has shifted from the north to the south, particularly Africa.[1] This phenomenon needs to be taken together with other facts. First, it must be understood that *homo africanus religiousus radicaliter,* i.e., "an African is deeply religious." Second, other religions such as Islam and African traditional religions are either also increasing or there has been a resurgence of them, particularly the latter. Third, Christianity is a relative latecomer to Africa south of the Sahara (except perhaps Ethiopia). In the Middle Ages there was already trade between the Maghreb and West Africa across the gold, slave, and ivory routes. Alongside the trade came Islam, so that in medieval times the name of Timbuktu was known far and wide as the center of a great Islamic civilization. The great Islamic empires of Ghana, Mali, and Songhai hardly need mention.[2]

Christians love to think Christianity is the primary and major religion of Africa. This attitude is make-believe, issuing in part from the Eurocentric missionary theory (and practice) of the *tabula rasa,* by which African culture was treated as inferior, if not devilish and of no value for humankind. For example, in the 1970s a Roman Catholic bishop in Ghana by the name of Joseph A. Essuah, now of blessed memory, wrote:

If we think we should keep our traditional ideas as a very important part of

our culture, then is it not yet time to become Catholics and we should openly
go out of the Church.[3]

Several evangelical groups, often of American origin, have adopted similar
attitudes. Ironically, some African Christian Independent Churches, which
are spawned in part by African nationalism, are also very strong in their
denunciation of African traditional religions.[4]

This attitude is futile for a number of reasons. First, as a matter of
communication it is efficient to start with the known and work back to the
unknown and the new. That was a methodology that was found in the early
church itself—as seen in Paul's style at Antioch in Pisidia (Acts 14) and
the Areopagus (Acts 17). Second, this attitude is not practicable. African
traditional culture, which is shot through and through with religion, is
taken in, so to speak, with the mother's milk. Birth, puberty, marriage,
death, widowhood, and installations to traditional offices all partake of a
religious nature.[5] Thus African traditional religion remains one of the important institutional structures making up the total system. As John Mbiti
has put it, "For Africans it (i.e., religion) is an ontological phenomenon;
it pertains to the question of existence and being."[6] For Africans life is
most meaningfully explained in a religious framework of existence, though
the society is not thereby sacralist. In religion *homo africanus* seeks answers
to questions concerning human destiny, the demands of morality, discipline,
and the evils of injustice, suffering, and death. In all of these, religions
serve to give *homo africanus* both emotional adjustment and cognitive
assurance. So it was just not practicable for the *tabula rasa* approach in
mission to be a lasting success. And time has shown that African traditional
religions are still vibrant and strong. The most notorious evidence is that
the same Christian who practices the rites of the church also practices
aspects of African traditional religions, particularly around funerals and
festivals. There is also the evidence of the mushrooming of African Christian Independent Churches which represent a protest against the North
Atlantic captivity of the African churches.

Third, the *tabula rasa* is faulty theologically. At the heart of the gospel
stands the tremendous declaration, "The Word became flesh" (John 1:14).[7]
What this means is that the eternal God, in order to communicate, did not
hesitate to use the contingent, imperfect, and impure form, the flesh which
is the point where sin finds its ingress into humanity. What this says is
that truth is never so sacred that it cannot be negotiated.

The long and short of this story is that there is no way African traditional
religions can be wished away or ignored. *Homo africanus* is an African

first (with all the cultural involvements that implies), and a Christian second. It is to live in cloud-cuckoo-land to think that African culture is substantially dead. The only viable, fruitful approach is to hold a dialog with the taken-for-granted African world. To put it another way, in the words of another Roman Catholic bishop of Ghana, *"Christianity should be Africanised, not Africans Christianised."* [8] No communication of the gospel stands a ghost of a chance of success unless it is pitched at the wavelength of the addressees.

This line of approach is not new. In the history of the church in Africa south of the Sahara, those who had the ears to hear would have heard such ideas. That is the meaning and significance of Ethiopianism represented by such personalities as Holy Johnson in Nigeria, and of the religious dimension of the Aborigines Rights Protection Society (ARPS) of the Gold Coast. The latter, born in 1897, was concerned not only to defend the Gold Coast land but also to counteract the cultural imperialism that characterized the evangelistic philosophy of the line, a policy they called the "denationalization" of the Africans. In place of that they proposed a "Doctrine of the Return to Things Native" or "Gone Fantee" which J. Casey Hayford, known as the Great Moses of West Africa, defined as follows:

> A fusion of what is good in the traditions and customs inherited from our ancestors with the adoption of what is good—and only what is good—of what we learn by contact with Europeans. [9]

And they were at pains to point out that such cultural revival was no revolt against either Christianity or the colonial government. Thus John Mensah Sarbah, known as the *spiritus rector* of the ARPS, wrote as follows:

> To be wholly African in outlook is incompatible with being a good Christian. . . . Pride of place in the African is not a sign of disloyalty. [10]

This is Africa's answer to the assumption by some that Christianity is European and that African culture was a fragment of Boetian darkness.

In our references to Ethiopianism and ARPS we have already come to another important factor on the African and indeed, the world scene, namely, *ideology*, a word that strikes terror into the hearts of many, particularly people in the West. For such people, ideology is synonymous with an oppressive system such as Marxist socialism, which in its history has been associated with the abuse of power. Against that background ideology is defined as "a set of dogmas to be imposed by the government with force if necessary." [11] Nkrumah of Ghana, after leading the people of the Gold

Coast to political freedom from British colonial rule, led the people into an excruciating new captivity under the ideological label "scientific socialism" or "African socialism."

One will make no apology for Nkrumah. But I would say the trouble is not so much with ideology as with human sin and the corruptive effect of power.[12] At this point one recalls a more authentic use of the word *ideology.* Ideology originally meant "Blue-prints of the future made by certain ideologists or groups of elite within the community to move the masses."[13]

Ideology is about a set of ideas, about strategies, about methods with regard to the form the good society should take. This being the authentic use of the word, I do not share the widespread, pathological fear of ideology.

I would also argue that not every ideology may be relevant to each and every place. The experience of Africa is that several ideologies have been foreign to it and have, therefore, been expensive irrelevancies. That means the task for churches is to help people to see what is relevant ideology and what is relevant to our context. This is part of their prophetic ministry. As one looks around Africa and the world one can identify a number of ideologies: colonialism, nationalism, socialism, capitalism, welfare state, apartheid, Christendom, Islam (particularly when it emphasizes the *sharia* as the natural policy), and tribalism. Obviously there is no way one will address each of these ideologies in such a short presentation. One can only make some observations.

First, the Christian dictum that all are sinners forces me also to say no ideology is and can be perfect. There is often a gap between theory and practice. In any case, when it traverses time and space, its relevance may be muted. The experience of Africa is that capitalism and socialism transplanted or implemented in Africa have been disastrous and irrelevant. That is why the very African politicians who mouth Marxist rhetoric are known to keep up with religion, despite Marxism's negative attitude toward religion. I would submit that the usual way the discussion is carried on, namely, whether capitalism or socialism is the greater ideology, is arid. There is a valley somewhere between the deep blue sea of capitalism and the lion of socialism.

Second, we in Africa know from experience that East and West have both been exploiting us in diverse ways. Aid has turned out to be a cover for exploitation and self-interest. In view of the foregoing two reasons, we cannot afford to give a *carte blanche* to any ideology. It is amazing that Christianity is thriving in Africa despite its historical link with colonialism, slave trade, paternalism, etc., all of which are aspects of the interface between Europe and Africa as well as of the interface of gospel and culture. Biblical Christianity has no particular ideology or economic theory. But there are two tenets of the Christian faith which are guiding principles for relating to ideologies. I refer to the kingdom of God and the image and likeness of God (Gen. 1:27). I will return to these two in a little while. For the moment we need to recall that the question of the proper attitude toward ideologies is not a new one but has been with our church almost from its very inception. Historically examined, there have been three answers to this question. First is the Theodosian model, which created a theocratic state in which Christianity was abolished. This model has some roots in the Old Testament idea of the theocratic state composed of the people of God. In one form it appears in the Republic of South Africa, where the Dutch Reformed Church is established and the ideology of apartheid has its roots in that church.

The second answer is Tolstoy's dictum *regnum Caesaris regnum*, meaning that the kingdom of Caesar, the political ruler, is the kingdom of the devil. Before him the Donatists of North Africa had adopted this attitude in their question, *Quid imperatori cum ecclesia?*, i.e., what has the emperor to do with the church? Thus church and state are seen as two different entities which are opposed to each other. The curious thing about the Donatist position is that earlier they had invited the intervention of the emperor. Be that as it may, they drew on some biblical passages such as Philippians 3:20-21, "Our commonwealth is in heaven, and from it we await a Savior." The Jehovah's Witnesses, a Christian sect, still adopts this attitude. This also tallies with a mentality that politics is dirty. However, such a view cannot be the whole gospel truth. In view of what we shall later say about the kingdom of God, the affirmation of Psalm 24:1 that "the earth is the Lord's and the fullness thereof" can only be true when God is seen to be concerned with any and every situation. In any case, there is no way a Christian can realistically and legitimately opt out of politics, for politics is the life that we live.

The third answer is the Augustinian position that while the church as an institution may not be partisan, yet it remains the guardian of all established order and of all proper relationships in society.[14] The problem is the state also claims to be the guardian of society. So the unresolved bone of contention is: Where does the conscience of society reside, in the church or in the state? One thing is clear to me, that insofar as Christians pay taxes, they are entitled to call the tune as well. Therefore, churches as institutions should educate their members so that in their involvement in national life they may infuse the insights which they gain from the ideas of the kingdom of God and humanity with the image and likeness of God.

As guardian of society the church will have to be prophetic, discerning between the will of God and idolatry in economic, political, cultural, and ecclesial life. In this regard, because ideologies offer salvation, the church's task will include helping the people to see that "salvation is found neither in a system nor as a system but only wherever real life, freedom, and happiness shatter the salvation systems and the planned and the predictable can expect to be disturbed. Resurrection? judgment? grace?"[15] And in my view the track record of all these ideologies in Africa is that they have often not been able to give to all people in society the salvation which they promised.

Of course, if the church is to carry conviction as the guardian of society, it must be credible. It must be a church that lives its word; it must be a church that puts itself out for people, especially those who find themselves in a hopeless situation; it must be a church that is not corrupt or compromised; it must be a church that corporately and in its individual members lives out righteousness, justice, truth, and freedom; it must be a church that wields spiritual weapons, a church that is ready to stand up and be counted. It must be a people of God who are reconciled one to another and therefore can courageously offer reconciliation to the political arena which is based on division.

It is time to return to the two guiding tenets for addressing ideologies, namely, the kingdom of God and the idea of the image and likeness of God. Jesus' message was about the nearness or coming of the kingdom of God. The prayer which he taught included the following parallelism: "Thy kingdom come, thy will be done on earth as in heaven." That message is about the sovereignty of God over all life. This puts Christians under the obligation to ensure that the totality of life, individual and communal, is brought under God's rule. Psalm 144:12-15, which may be read as an offering, is an exposition of the kingly rule of God as it defines the blessedness of the kingdom in very wholistic terms: it is material, political, economic, and social wholeness, as well as religious and spiritual wholeness. So as we address ideologies, the issue is not so much the label as whether it makes for material, political, economic, social, religious, and spiritual wholeness. The indicators of this wholeness include righteousness, justice, freedom, love, and truth. These then are the tests of any ideology presented before churches as they go about their business of being the guardian of established order and of all proper relationships in society. I would suggest that this is the prophetic role of the church. But it should not be only negative, always denouncing; it should also be positive and evenhanded, affirming its tenets that cultivate the characteristics of the kingdom of God.

The other principle as we face ideologies is the idea of the image and likeness of God. This is the biblical understanding of what it is to be human. According to Genesis 1:29, "God created man in his own image; in the image of God he created him, male and female he created them." Of course, here already we meet the first battle. According to some ideologies that image is not found in non-Caucasians, as the racist anthropologists and upholders of the apartheid ideology have sometimes argued. Or as some have alleged, women do not bear that *imago dei*. Not only is the text clear that "male and female he created them," but also in the light of Galatians 3:28 which states that "there is neither Jew nor Greek, there is neither slave nor free, there is neither male nor female, for you are all one in Christ Jesus," the sexist and racist theologies based on Genesis 1:27 can only be regarded as godless and infamous heresies that the church universal should in its prophetic ministry demolish. Such heresies are the lie and deception that mark the sinful and demonic world, doomed to destruction (cf. 2 Thess. 2:7-12).

But what does that shorthand *imago dei* mean? First, it means a human being is a total living personality, physical as well as spiritual. Rooted in the *humus,* the soil, he/she has a calling to transcend the material. It is here the rationality in one's being and actions becomes a characteristic of a human being. And in being natural they express their responsibility for the world. In South Africa, when more is spent on security than on human beings, rationality has been lost. Second, *imago dei* speaks about human beings who are created for community, and a sense of community is an indispensable factor of the created order. Any ideology that polarizes society or marginalizes some cannot escape the prophetic ministry of the church. Any ideology that does not express genuine solidarity with and compassion for the needy and the less fortunate of society cannot be left alone by churches. In this regard the church's antennae should detect the many seemingly respectable doctrines of our day and demolish them, e.g., the cult of individualism or the trickle-down theory of the growth ethic.[16]

Be that as it may, an element of the community emphasis is the love ethic. Human beings have the capacity to love and need to be loved. But that love is not a condescending act of charity; it is rather selfless and self-sacrificing devotion to fellow human beings.

Thus, to bear the *imago dei* is to be cocreator with God and thus have dominion over creation. But dominion is to be seen not in terms of power, but of impressing God's image of order and dignity on all creation, humans included, and thus reverence God. This is the issue at stake when ideologies create ugly specters such as refugees, with their sense of social uselessness, which violates the integrity of creation. Here the churches need to engage the ideologists in the question: What are the true indicators of authentic modernity and authentic progress? And what should be the true ethical content of authentic development which should inform our work as co-creators with God? As I see it, these are the keys to the goodness of the created order for which men and women are responsible.

Let us pull together the threads vis-à-vis relationships to ideologies and non-Christian religions. As these ideologies and religions live willy-nilly in one world which God created, Christians have no choice but to be in this one world with them. Such a coexistence is impossible if the church adopts a superior attitude—humility on the part of the church is a must. Second, dialog becomes the style of the church: openness to others and openness about the outcome of such dialog and tolerance, which demands full measure of realism about the particularity of existing religions and critical thinking. This means serious and candid interfaith dialog which takes seriously the people as adherents of their religion and ideology and is willing to be vulnerable. That is the only way forward.

# 9

# A SOCIAL AND POLITICAL ANALYSIS OF APARTHEID/RACISM FROM A BLACK LUTHERAN PERSPECTIVE

# SIBUSISO M. BENGU

This essay shall present a sociopolitical analysis of apartheid/racism from a black Lutheran perspective. More specifically, my focus is on the black South African experience.

The most negative contributions which Europe gave to Africa are racism in general and apartheid in particular. I will attempt to trace the links between the apartheid and racism experienced by black Africans with the exploitative economic system imposed by Europeans on Africa. Racism will be shown to be a tool of that system. I will also deal in some detail with the exploitative economic system and the racism of the white messengers of the gospel of Christ—and we have to recognize that some of those messengers were Lutheran.

## Apartheid and Nazism

Some scholars have called apartheid the South African brand of nazism. We must recognize it as such and realize what that means in the present situation. The only form of racist tyranny which the world has known since the days of nazism is apartheid. Progressive forces the world over have condemned apartheid by using terms such as "inhuman," "repugnant," "abhorrent," "fundamentally immoral," "a catalyst of violence," and "a crime against humanity." Although its proponents define apartheid as a policy of racial segregation or, more benevolently, "politically separate development," it is plainly a policy of racial supremacy. The Nazis first proposed a policy of "separate development" toward Jews in Germany. Behind Hitler's ideology was the conviction that Jews, among others, were subhuman. As we know, that policy led eventually to the total persecution and systematic genocide of Jews in territories dominated by the Nazis. It is just as plain that the white government in South Africa deals with blacks as though they are subhuman. Blacks are economically exploited and systematically denied their human rights.

Some people may believe that oppressors can convert themselves into being liberators. Under that mistaken belief, they buy Pieter Botha's propaganda that his government, on its own, is moving away from racist policies and that apartheid is dead or dying. We know better. Before the same government lowered the curtain of censorship, the world saw how bloodthirsty South African police and soldiers gunned down their own people, even unarmed children. Today we are witnessing a ritual slaughter of the African people. For the government's representatives to shoot at the slightest pretext reveals a palpably low regard for black lives and black humanity. Obviously, these are steps in the vicious, genocidal policy toward black people being pursued by P. W. Botha's racist regime. Genocide is an international crime. But it seems to be condoned when the victims are black.

When the Nazis perpetrated genocidal exterminations of Jews and others, the whole world joined hands to put an end to the iniquity of nazism. Why isn't the world horrified into action by the latter-day nazism of the ruling Afrikaner clique in South Africa? Because the victims are Africans. Remember that the Nationalist Party in South Africa was founded by Nazis before the Second World War. During the war a number of its members were interned. Among the internees were John Vorster and Hendrik Verwoerd, men who were developers of apartheid and leaders of the nation. P. W. Botha and most of his cabinet are proving themselves to be no better than Vorster and Verwoerd.

As I speak of apartheid as a form of nazism, remember that Lutheranism came to Africa with some Nazi influence. Even if Lutheran missionaries may not have been formally identified with the Nazi party, many were influenced by Nazi racial attitudes and thinking. So numerous German missionaries to South Africa also supported apartheid. It has now been

proved that among the architects of apartheid were some German missionaries and the children of those missionaries. The Bantu education system, for example, was conceived by Dr. Eiselen, a Lutheran of German
extraction and the son of a Lutheran pastor.

Let us be honest. We who are black Lutherans have to face the fact that
some founders of the evil system of apartheid are members of our confessional group! What does it mean for us to share the same faith with our
oppressors? Is it the same faith? Is there a common identity between white
and black Lutherans within the apartheid system? Or let us ask an even
wider question: Is there a common rejection of the sin of racism and
apartheid among those who have blood ties with the oppressors?

And let us also be clear. Apartheid has not changed; it has become more
vicious. Originally the system's inventors said that it was devised in the
name of Christianity, Western civilization, and economic efficiency. As
other evils do, apartheid subtly covers itself under those Western values
which assure the West that apartheid is its honest ally in the struggle against
communism. Nowadays, P. W. Botha declares arrogantly and self-righ-
teously, "I am going to keep law and order in South Africa and nobody
in the world is going to stop me." What he really means is that he is going
to murder Africans. And no one, Botha and his supporters think, is going
to stop him. The only sin of those Africans is their demand to be treated
like human beings in the country of their birth.

But we must be even more clear. Botha and his clique will never destroy
the determined spirit of the African people to liberate themselves from
oppression and persecution. No government is stronger than the wrath of
its aroused people.

## Culture and Race

In order to deceive the world, the proponents of apartheid deliberately
confuse the concept of race with that of culture. They claim, therefore,
that apartheid is based on culture, not race. Look closely at these two
concepts.

A race is a group of people connected by common descent. The variables
of the concept of race are fixed by history and cannot be changed. On the
other hand, culture is the generic term for the values people uphold at the
present time. Culture can be defined as the totality of the values, institutions, and forms of behavior transmitted within society through the process of socialization. Culture may be learned or unlearned. Race, however,

is not a matter of habit. Some black people who are discriminated against have adapted to and internalized European culture. In fact, if discrimination were based on culture, they would pass as Europeans. But apartheid is not based on culture: it is based on *race*.

At one time the South African propaganda slogan was "separate but equal!" The truth is the same in South Africa as it is in the United States: racial groups are kept separate in order to maintain *in*equality. "Separate development" would have no purpose if the races were to be separate in order for them to be equal. The separation of races is the old British imperial policy of divide and rule.

What, then, is racism? I share with you a definition offered by the Reverend Cedric Mayson. Owing to his commitment both to Christ and the struggle for liberation in South Africa, he was tried for high treason but skipped the country. He lives now in London. Mayson says, "Racism is a white way of thought. Blacks suffer it but seldom instigate it. Racism is prevalent and racism is wrong but it is also a symptom and not a disease. Racism is more than skin deep—the heart of exploitation is greed, exploitation and oppression. . . . Racism is in itself evil but getting rid of racism is not enough. Racists believe that others are inherently inferior to themselves and use this as a justification for manipulating them." [1]

The whole world condemns apartheid as inhuman, cruel, unjust, immoral, etc. But what are the people like who govern South Africa, who direct the armies of soldiers and police, who try to strangle the lives of millions? These people are the rich elite.

## Racism and Economic Exploitation

The first black president of the Methodist church in South Africa is quoted as saying, "Never forget, our problems are really the same as in the rest of the world, the conflict of rich and poor. Because our poor are mostly black and our rich mostly white it seems to be a problem of race, but the heart of the problem is the question of wealth and poverty." [2]

It is crucial to understand the powerful link between racism and economic exploitation. If the problem of racism in South Africa or the United States were separable from capitalistic exploitation, the world would long ago have found a solution for racism. When P. W. Botha and Ronald Reagan speak in favor of "reform," what they mean is that they are prepared to change their structures on race if there is a profit in it for the ruling elite. Changes that are proposed in the racist system are cosmetic. The changes are of appearances only and are determined by what is good for business. Do we want to reform an evil or do we want to end it?

For a convincing example of the South African government's behavior which proves that racism is a tool of economic exploitation, turn again to Cedric Mayson:

> This is the clue to understanding the apparent ambiguity by which the South African authorities will permit some people to criticize them and not others. Andrew Young or the Rev. Leon Sullivan are allowed to visit South Africa even though they are black Americans who are strongly critical of apartheid, because they are promoting a version of black capitalism which is acceptable to the South African government which knows that it can control and administer it. Chief Gatsha Buthelezi of KwaZulu and Chief Mangope of Bophutatswana are given much license in their criticisms of apartheid because they accept the capitalist structure and are seeking a place in it; but boys are sent to jail for five or ten years for possessing T-shirts or literature which suggests a link with the ANC [African National Congress] because the ANC advocates economic and political change.[3]

We might also note that the South African government moved swiftly to ban the Christian Institute shortly after it began a research project called "Christianity, Capitalism, and Socialism in South Africa." The government neither wants to hear nor to have others hear about the realities of or alternatives to capitalist exploitation.

And what of the churches? Most of the church bodies continue to limit their vision largely to racial attitudes. They refuse to accept the fact that the churches, too, are part of the oppressive structures. Many of the Lutheran churches from which we come have not openly condemned capitalist exploitation either. They condemn racial discrimination and apartheid, but they do not address capitalist exploitation. Let us mark it plainly: capitalist exploitation is the root cause of injustice in South Africa, the United States, and the rest of the world.

When we focus on the linkage between racism and economic exploitation, we see that South Africa is a microcosm of an unjust world. For eight years now I have spent all my time in the service of the Lutheran World Federation's member churches and their related agencies. I have carried on research and stimulated studies on national and global root causes of social and economic injustice. At various levels I have seen that the question of race is strongly tied to poverty and affluence. As you know, our world is broken into North and South. The rich North is inhabited by white people who consider themselves "developed." The materially poor countries of the South are inhabited by black and other people of color, and are euphemistically considered to be "developing." The whole economic system which is based on the North/South division of the world perpetuates economic exploitation based on race. Who are the so-called "developed" and the alleged "undeveloped"? What causes material "underdevelopment"?

In order to maintain their consumption of food, energy, and luxuries, the Scandinavian nations, for example, are dependent on the use of 5,000,000 hectares (about 11,000,000 acres) of agricultural land in those southern world countries where people are starving. The economy of the Western nations is still based on the poor countries' production of raw materials at starvation wages, while the West demands more for the finished goods they deliver to the South.

The resources of God's world are being shared inequitably. Consider that 30% of the world's population lives in the industrialized countries of Europe (including the USSR), North America, Japan, and Australia. These nations consume seven-eighths of the earth's riches and products. Two-thirds of the world's population lives in "underdeveloped" Asia, Africa, and Latin America—and they use only one-eighth of the earth's bounty.

Now put those statistics in terms of race to see the bond between racism and economic exploitation. We have found that the poorest people in Brazil and the United States are black. Even in a country like Tanzania there is a link between current food production policies and Western agribusiness interests. Foreign control of the economy goes beyond the control of international markets and trade, and reaches into controlling the actual production of food and other goods in the Third World. How is such control exercised? Various mechanisms are used. These include the use of aid. Loans and grants are very often tied to and geared toward particular forms of production.[4]

The connection between the racist apartheid policies of South Africa and the capitalist economies of the West is exposed as we seek ways to dismantle apartheid. Western nations such as the United States, West Germany, and Britain are the strongest opponents to the imposition of economic sanctions as a peaceful way to force the Afrikaners to abandon apartheid. For years the representatives of foreign businesses in South Africa have argued that they were there for purely business purposes. They were there, according to them, to develop the country and not to support apartheid. We now have evidence that foreign investments and loans have been used to support the prevailing patterns of power and privilege in South Africa. For example, over and above the usual business gains resulting from cheap labor, foreign companies pay a special defense tax which supports the

South African army. This is the same army which terrorizes freedom seekers in South Africa and Namibia. This is the same army which raids frontline states like Angola, Mozambique, Zimbabwe, Zambia, Lesotho, and Botsawana—all under the pretext of defending South Africa.

If racism and economics are tied together, what might be done through economic measures to end apartheid? One step involves disinvestment and economic sanctions. The people of South Africa believe that they will liberate themselves. They also feel that disinvestment and the application of economic sanctions will help weaken and isolate the South African government. Do black South Africans want an economy which is tottering even more than at present? Do they want to pay the price in jobs and stability? Opinion polls have consistently shown that black South Africans are overwhelmingly supportive of international sanctions against the government. Against the tense atmosphere and unrest in which nearly 1000 have been killed, 77 percent of oppressed blacks voted for economic boycott and sanctions against the Pretoria regime.

Another step involves the realization that apartheid is economically disastrous. Just consider the staggering costs in funds, energy, and structure. There are separate facilities for different ethnic groups with budgets for nine homelands, instead of one government with one budget; segregated schools and universities; and separate housing and social facilities. Add to that the expenses, both human and fiscal, of recruiting, training, equipping, and maintaining a large army along with the costly raids on the frontline states. Apartheid cannot continue with a weakened economy.

And the economy is weakening. The deepening financial crisis is evidence that economic sanctions have political impact. The drastic fall in the value of the rand is an indicator that continued economic pressure will be successful in South Africa. Even before mandatory, comprehensive economic sanctions are imposed, the threat of those sanctions has induced some movement toward change.

Foreign businesses cannot be neutral in a situation in which so many people are being killed each day. Those corporations either are on the side of the racist government or on the side of those who struggle for freedom. To stand with and for the oppressed, foreign businesses need to defy all the racial discrimination laws. They need to defy the influx control laws, provide jobs, and offer accommodations to workers without regard to race. Above all, the corporations must object to paying the defense tax. Foreign businesses need to protest the use of their funds to kill people who struggle against the denial of citizenship and political rights in the country of their birth.

In seeking to hide their own vested interests, some persons, institutions (including churches), and governments argue that black people will be the losers if foreign companies were to disinvest in South Africa, and so they decline to support disinvestment and economic sanctions. Of course, there is no logic in this argument. The argument is advanced by that segment of society which gains the most through investments and cheap labor. They certainly do not want a pullout by the international corporations! No scientific studies have supported this false argument. For all we know, the business sector—both foreign and South African—has not shown any serious interest in addressing the problem of systemic unemployment in black communities.

Exposing the link of racism/apartheid to economic exploitation must not be misconstrued as suggesting that racism is not an abominable evil in itself. We know it is precisely that. This Lutheran audience might find it helpful to recall the resolutions of the Seventh Assembly of the Lutheran World Federation (Budapest 1984) on *Racism in the LWF and the Member Churches:*

> Because of the extreme violence of apartheid, which we as a working group have condemned as a heresy and for which the Assembly has suspended the "White" member churches in Namibia and South Africa, all other member churches must be called on to cease all support of apartheid. To support institutions that support or condone apartheid is to participate in the sin of apartheid itself.

> The Seventh Assembly resolved:

> —to urge all LWF member churches to take visible and concrete steps, including boycott of goods and withdrawal of investments, to end all economic and cultural support of apartheid, even as they continue to urge their own governments, business organizations, and trade unions to observe strict enforcement of military and oil embargoes and boycotts concerning culture, sports, the transfer of nuclear technology, and the importation of nuclear materials in order to isolate and cut off South Africa until such time as apartheid is totally dismantled.
> —to ask each LWF member church to take action to remove all vestiges of institutional racism from their structures, reporting to the LWF Executive Committee on these efforts by January 1988 in order that these reports can be shared with the other member churches for their edification and prayerful support.[5]

## Black Lutherans as Revolutionaries

The Lutheran community reacted to apartheid and racism in South Africa as did our Reformed brothers and sisters. We disciplined the white South

African churches within our confessional fellowships until such time that those churches denounce the sin of apartheid. Meetings, such as the one in Harare in 1986, provide an opportunity for us to reflect more on what else can be done about racist Lutherans. What have Lutheran churches and the LWF done to eliminate institutional racism from their structures? The Black Lutheran Caucus may very well be a force which will push forward the antiapartheid and antiracist movements.

Many black Lutherans in South Africa, the rest of Africa, and the United States confess that their common experience of *oppression and economic exploitation* makes it difficult for them to identify with their Lutheran oppressors. Shouldn't the Lutheran World Federation take the practice of racism and economic exploitation more seriously than ever before?

Dr. Martin Luther was a fighter and a revolutionary. Why aren't Lutherans as revolutionary as Martin Luther? Like Christ, Luther was a revolutionary. On the other hand, "Christendom" is reformist. But Christianity is revolutionary. Many black Lutherans, myself included, find it easier to identify with Martin Luther than with Lutherans in general.

May God raise up among us Martin Luthers who will have the commitment and the courage to purge the church and society of apartheid/racism and economic exploitation.

Nothing short of a revolution will rid us of these evils.

# 10
# ON BEING BLACK, LUTHERAN, AND AMERICAN IN A RACIST SOCIETY

## ALBERT PERO

O utside of Lutheranism, so much has happened between Africans, African-Americans, and third world people within the Christian church, that some of us will have to do double time, if we have not already, in order to catch up with our brothers and sisters.

In particular, from the Pan-African conference of third world theologians (Dec. 17-23, 1977, Accra, Ghana) to the present day, many theological issues have been examined and discussed. While these colleagues have forged ahead in addressing the gospel to the context of African and African-American Christians, some African and African-American Lutherans have been somewhat silent (for whatever reason) in their participation in a Lutheran theology which has been void of meaning for many of their people.

Our time has now come to serve the Lord on our own terms and to do so within our own Lutheran context, without being turned into European-Americans before we accomplish our goal. Our time has now come to abort the questions and answers of white theologians such as Barth, Brunner, Tillich, and others, and rather, ask what God would have us do in our own present, concrete situation. For too long, we black Lutherans have been preoccupied with what white pastor A or white pastor B told us about our Lord Jesus Christ in regard to the Lutheran church and the world outside.

Our task and struggle, like others before us, is to find a theology that speaks to African and African-American Lutherans where we are; to enable us to answer the critical question of our Lord Jesus Christ: "Who do you [black Lutherans] say that I am?" The essays in this book represent a significant attempt to rescue theology from the hands of white Lutherans; from the shelves of the seminaries and universities; and from the sanctuaries of "dying" black Lutheran churches; to make Lutheran theology a living, dynamic, active, creative reality in our societies; and most of all, to join our other African and African-American theologians and bishops in the liberation struggle to free all of God's people with the gospel of Jesus Christ.

I see our theological task directed from the organizing principle of the poor. The challenging question they have for us is beyond our human capabilities but within God's resources. Millions of poor people are asking Christian Lutherans and therefore Lutheran theology: Where is this "abundant life" (John 10:10)? because they see nothing but pain, suffering, disease, hunger, torture, rejection, oppression, and depersonalization all around.

Since Lutheran theology has a doctrine of justification by grace, a message of faith and hope, then it must be a hope for the hopeless, a voice for the voiceless, and a love for the loveless. Above all, our witness here should be healing and reassuring. Lutherans should free themselves from empty arrogance and dogmatic absolutism, thereby allowing the Holy Spirit to direct their path toward wholeness.

Finally, our task is too urgent to be left any longer in the hands of the white missionaries, bishops, pastors, or theologians; rather, the involvement of all black Lutherans is called for—those nameless, faceless, African and African-American Lutherans—men and women from all walks and stations of life. I am talking about theology: city theology, rural theology, street theology, home theology, global theology.

Let us then launch into our tasks under the guidance of the Holy Spirit and remember while we work the motto of Martin Luther King Jr.:

Power without love is reckless and abusive and love without power is sentimental and anemic. Power at its best is love implementing the demands of justice. Justice at its best is power correcting everything that stands against love (*Where Do We Go from Here: Chaos or Community?* 1967).

## Black Existence in Lutheranism

The idea for this book came out of a long overdue personal, professional, and community need on the part of black Lutherans to express in coherent language the meaning of our struggle to be black and Lutheran; specifically, to lift up to a consensus level the joys, sorrows, pleasures, and pain of being black Lutherans.

Hopefully a variety of purposes will be attended from this work. It will serve to help black Lutherans particularly, and black Christians generally, see how they must relate to other black people around the world; it will give black Lutherans some clarity and coherence concerning their identification as black Lutherans; it will provide some theological substance for study and discussion among the laity for meaning as to being black and Lutheran; it will help white Christians in Lutheranism to better relate to black Lutherans and members of other ethnic groups. In short, this book should help black Lutherans "get it together," i.e., get in touch with their identity, relationships, and their mission as they reflect upon their history and what God would have them do from the stance of Lutheranism.

Most people, especially black people, do not like others speaking for them. One learns this quickly in a black caucus or assembly of black Lutherans. I have not been asked to represent all of black Lutheranism, but hopefully many will be able to find some clarity and direction themselves within the witness and testimony of my experiences as a black Lutheran.

## Living with Two Souls

I have been a black Lutheran all my life. Symbolically speaking, I have been "Black by day and Lutheran by night." Literally this means that I have lived in two worlds paradoxically, one black, the other white. This paradox is not a new one. Around the turn of the century, W. E. B. Dubois wrote about the general paradox of black life in America in *The Souls of Black Folk*. His classic statement is as follows:

> It is a peculiar sensation, this double-consciousness, this sense of always looking at one's self through the eyes of others, of measuring one's soul by the tape of a world that looks on in amused contempt and pity. One ever feels his twoness—an American; a Negro, two souls, two thoughts, two unreconciled strivings; two warring ideals in one dark body; whose dogged strength alone keeps it from being torn asunder.[1]

Black Lutheran thought is not the same as European Lutheran thought. Nor is it identical with traditional African beliefs. It is both African and Lutheran, but interpreted in behalf of the cultural experience of black people's struggle for justice in a context dominated by white racism. It is the African side of black Christian faith which enables us to see beyond the white contradictions of the gospel and discover God's liberation/salvation. It is the Lutheran element that helps us engage our African roots so that they become useful in our affirmation of life and struggle to become more than a mere imitation of Lutheran theology from Europe.

While there are many similarities between black Lutherans and white Lutherans, the dissimilarities are perhaps of greater importance. The similarities are found at the point of a common Christian identity, the dissimilarities are found between black and white cultures. Whites utilize their culture to dominate others, blacks utilize theirs (empowered by the gospel) to affirm their dignity and seek justice and walk humbly with God. As white Lutheran theology ignores the contradictions of oppression, exploitation, and nonrepresentation of black life, black Lutheran theology is the thinking of oppressed, marginalized, exploited black people, whom many white Lutheran theologians regard as unworthy of serious theological reflection.

A theology is needed to establish a constructive interpretation of the biblical, theological, and political dimensions of the black Lutheran churches in America and Africa. More specifically, its focus is on developing an official thought of the Lutheran heritage and the black experience in Africa and America.

There are no appreciable differences between African and African-American Lutherans regarding their respective social teachings but, rather, that both are united by a distinctive principle of coherence which we shall call the "black Christian tradition", i.e., the institutional embodiment of the Christian faith in a nonracist form. Most importantly, this tradition designates the unique contribution of the black churches to Lutheranism and the world. It forms the rock of their existence and, because of its primacy in the black community, it has had enormous effect on the moral and political thought of all African and African-American Lutherans.

Analytically, our task consists of a clarification of the basic values underlying African and African-American religion—those values that caused the emergence of the black independent churches from Africa to America and which have sustained their life up to the present day. Further, rigorous criticism is brought to bear on the way those values have functioned in the internal life of the Lutheran churches and their effect on all the efforts of the churches to enhance racial, sexual, and class justice in the society at large. In accordance with the insight of W. E. B. DuBois, this book demonstrates that the "dual-consciousness" of black Lutherans has led the black American churches to internalize an ambiguous social ethic that has served, on the one hand, as a lure toward an ideal vision of society and, on the other hand, as a serious restraint on the race's sociopolitical development. This moral conflict permeates all aspects of their common life; i.e., their autonomy, moral agency, political orientation, understanding of power. In short, our principal task is to analyze the nature of those theological, moral dilemmas in order to point out their implications for thought and action in the religious, moral, and political spheres of the black community.

Clearly, it is no understatement to say that the African and African-American experience has been characterized by the severest conditions of oppressive injustices. In the U.S., 300 years of slavery followed by another century of racial segregation and discrimination evidence those conditions (to say nothing of the present apartheid system in South Africa). But throughout that history, black Lutheran Christians have had a prominent role in shaping, maintaining, and enhancing social order and communal solidarity by adaptive and expressive functions. In addition, they have inculcated in their peoples fundamental moral responses to such conditions which, while varying in accordance with the intensity of the adversity encountered from one period to another, nevertheless, comprised (then and now) the authoritative basis for moral existence from Africa to the Americas.

These brief observations rest on the assumption that the social cohesion of every society is based on a set of shared values that find significant expression in various communal symbols, ideas, rituals, and pronouncements. Those values constitute the paramount cultural paradigm in which the people find their sense of solidarity in identity, relationship, and mission. But more importantly, that root paradigm constitutes the ultimate authority in Christ for all moral obligation, legal enactment, social organization, and political association. In fact, no social or political black Lutheran advocacy in the society can gain legitimacy apart from an appeal to that paradigm. Further, we contend that the African and African-American Lutheran churches have always understood that paradigm to be grounded in the Judeo-Christian understanding of human society as reinterpreted through their culture.

The purpose of this inquiry is to set forth a constructive interpretation of the relation of the Lutheran church and society in the black experience in order to explicate the elements of a *united black American* and *African religious* social ethic, chief among which being the value of and quest for liberation, freedom, and human dignity for all people. Consequently, our scholarship should differ from other forms of black scholarship that modeled themselves methodologically after those which sought to explain the impact of oppression on the oppressed. The results of such endeavors were predictable, i.e., high levels of pathological disorder psychologically, socially, politically, and even religiously. That type of scholarship prevented the emergence of black Lutherans as agents of constructive social change and development in church and society.

The recent rise of black and African liberation thought occasioned the vision of the Harare conference and hopefully the birth of a united African and African-American Lutheran revisionist genre in scholarship by developing a new hermeneutic, i.e., that of dealing with the experience of oppression from the perspective of the oppressed.[2] This genre assumes a high measure of cognitive, moral, religious, social, and political agency on the part of the oppressed in spite of their crippling environmental conditions. This genre can and should reject all philosophies of history that presuppose a generic understanding of human thought and action. Rather, it should radicalize the notion that all perspectives are grounded in specific sociocultural experiences. The result of this new approach should be liberating for all oppressed Lutherans because it validates their experience by relativizing the perspectives of their oppressors. Moreover, it enables oppressed peoples to be studied as agents rather than mere victims. This study stands in that tradition.

Although the essays in this volume address themselves primarily to the problems of Lutherans within a multicultural context separated by race, nationality, and sex, the insights apply equally well to problems between religious denominations and other cultures separated by national boundaries. Such problems are becoming more visible if not more intense. It is becoming increasingly difficult for persons who identify with different groups (because of cultural background, age, race, color, creed, family, national origin, politics, education, etc.) to ignore one another and coexist under conditions of imposed separation or segregation. The world is too small, and communication and transportation too rapid, to live apart. Too many persons are becoming aware of their rights and deprivations, and too many others are developing humanitarian concerns, to allow segregation and inequity to continue. We no longer have a choice. People must learn to live and work together with tolerance, respect, and understanding, or the human being as a species cannot survive.

Subsequently there is a growing concern and new agenda on a global level over the lack of adequate preparation of persons to live, work, and understand one another. Especially among black Lutherans do we find these stirrings, which in turn generate new perceptions and new articulations of reality.

## Roots, Community, and Theology

Alex Haley's book entitled *Roots* directed attention to a huge missing link in the various stages of development in civil rights in the U.S. In uniquely powerful fashion, *Roots* momentarily directed the attention of the nation away from our preoccupation with power, material things, etc., and drove us to contemplate (if only in passing) questions of who we are and what we are like. This has heightened the awareness that being human—or inhuman—is something that transcends both ideology and color. It drives us to ask theological questions. These theological questions, however, are highly political and social. Often new stirrings are present a long time before the symbols and the articulations of what is being felt and what is happening emerge.

The major white institutions must be deeply concerned about the massive stirrings among the people of color. The new feeling that something is wrong and the new quest for models of perception and for social and political understanding and action are again coming out of the thoughts and struggles of leaders of the historic black churches.

The content of these new stirrings cannot be capsulized in a few words. At the risk of distortion, however, it deals basically with the dead-end nature of systems of violence. It perceives that the "upward" quest of every definable segment of the nation for a "piece of the action" is on a collision course with survival itself. Such systems have delivered for a few, but the masses remain worse off than ever before—not just economically, but more importantly, left with even less of a sense of worth or perception of their humanity.

The problem, however, is that in the past years the doctrine that all segments have a prior right to a piece of the action has been uncritically bought by *everyone*. The more serious question is: What happens to our humanity where the name of the game is not only to grab more power for me/us, but where that power is perceived as salvation?

Such a question will be resisted by majority and minority alike—except that the deep, undefined hunger and distress of human hearts at this moment in history is raising massive new questions which the church has a mission to amplify and for which the church has something to offer. Consequently,

African and African-American Lutherans are faced with a definition of the basic questions of theology, namely:

1. What is the essence of identity?
2. What is the essence of community?
3. What is the essence of mission?

The ultimate answer to these questions will push us toward identifying God as the source of our resources, and furthermore enable us to clarify the correlation of indigenousness and universality. What some have hoped for in the past and many hope for today is the formation of a new community of diverse cultures in one organism.

There are particular questions which this new community must address corporately:

A. What have we learned and do we continue to learn about our identity through our religious experiences as synthesized from our cultural traditions to our denominational heritage within the context of the Americas?

B. How do we know what is real, and what isn't real (authentically tested)?

C. How do we conserve, celebrate, and share that which is behind the learning which becomes the certification of new learnings? What is the praxis?

However, a more important question is, How do we get there? It is the nature of this book to deal with this question as a major foundational concept and action of our search for the key to establishing a culturally inclusive community amidst diversity.

## Lutheran Theology and Identification: A Ventured Summary

The basic issues addressed within this book are critical for coming to an understanding of its rationale, goals, and scope. The issues are simultaneously contextual and universal; contextual in the sense that it grapples with the Lutheran denomination, universal in that it dares to define Lutheranism beyond its cultural roots. The question then is, What does it mean to be black and Lutheran within the community of Christian theology? What is the coherence and function of the foundational article of the Lutheran theological system? How do black Christians relate to it and the subsequent Lutheran doctrines and ecclesiology?

The issues and problems of Lutheran theology and cultural identification are vast and formidable. I shall not attempt to discuss them all here; but I shall venture to summarize Lutheran theology and identity as it could be utilized in this consultation. The Lutheran identity which I shall advance, I trust, will be more useful for a black understanding of the *Augsburg Confession*. It is, I believe, an identity which is more closely akin to the original Lutheran coherence.

It has been suggested by some theologians that Lutheranism as a movement offers to the whole Christian church a proposal of doctrine which posits that we are *justified by faith alone*. This doctrine has a Christian identity to which our *Augsburg Confession* would give witness. Given this proposal, instead of black Lutherans asking what a Lutheran is from a denominational point of view, we could put it as follows: What do we have to say to Lutherans as to the content of the gospel relative to our identity and praxis?

Moreover, Lutheran theology can be summed up most adequately in terms of law and gospel. Law and gospel implies a dialectic process by which a person experiences the demands of the law that finally break through into freedom in the gospel. How the dynamic of law and gospel is experienced is of the utmost importance. The result is a better understanding of the law/gospel *process* that can be applied to different contexts/settings with unique content. The gospel is the story of Jesus, who was delivered for our sins and raised for our justification. This message among black people, along with others, is of ultimate concern because our ultimate concern is that which determines our black being or nonbeing. The task of this book, then, is enabling black people to deal with ultimate concern, and doing so with all the resources of the world in which they live. So what we are attempting to advance is a historical conscience correlated with a gospel perspective.

Furthermore, it has been said that the Lutheran church is a confessing church. If confession is proclamation (preaching) in crisis, then black Lutherans have established many confessions. If confession is proclaiming that "Jesus is Lord" in the face of those who, with might, power, and authority *by their actions* insist that he is not, then black Lutherans hold forth the banner of a Christian Lutheran proclamation in protest of racism in a profound way, both in the U.S. and in South Africa.

In this sense, it is important to understand ourselves as black *confessional* Lutherans. This is our primary identity, for we do not confess the Lutheran *Confessions;* rather we confess what Lutherans confess, namely that "Jesus is Lord." Finally, there is really no such thing as a Lutheran Baptism or a Lutheran Eucharist, nor can we forgive sins in the name of the Lutheran church—we can do so only as servants of the Word.

It is to be expected that some Lutherans and other Christians will ask: Why explicate a theology from the black Lutheran experience? Is it not true that God is color blind? That in God there is neither black nor white, etc.? This book answers these questions by stating that there can never be a theology in general. Theology is always reflected in a particular community. It seems that some would place theology only in the context of white racist community. When such a theology claims God's approval of white racism, classism, and sexism, Luther himself would probably call it a theology of the anti-Christ. Moreover, in a racist society, God is never color blind. To say this is analogous to saying that God is blind to justice and injustice.

The appearance of this theological material coming from the experiences of black people with God within and without Lutheranism is due to the failure of white Lutheran theologians to relate the gospel of Christ to the pain and suffering of being black men and women in a white racist society—of which Lutheranism is a part. It arises from a long historical struggle of black people trying to develop a culturally inclusive church where unity in diversity is celebrated.

Because African people are Lutherans in the U.S. and Africa, black and African Lutheran churches must also become the context of the major content or repository of the black Christian experience. It is from this root that we gain the inspiration primarily to engage the past in order to live in the *promissio* of the one, holy, catholic, and apostolic church. It is from this black Lutheran context that our theological reflection links up with other black Christian theologians. This is why black Lutherans are so important, namely, to help articulate the black religious experience of Lutherans. The black theologian and bishop becomes a "power broker" in articulating the faith of black Lutherans and their peculiar mission, role, and function as a part of God's chosen people in and out of the context of Lutheranism.

## The Black Cultural Experience as Prolegomena

As we have posited, the dissimilarity between white Lutherans and black Lutherans is found in our cultures. It is therefore indispensable to our reflecting and living of theology to have a full grasp on the uniqueness of the black culture in general and the black Lutheran community in particular.

We need to remember that the perennial struggle of black people within a society whose controlling motif is economic and political power results in contradictory modes of interaction with the overall situation. A delineation then of the areas of experience where pressures are most severe will provide a background for dealing with a necessary clarification of our identity, relationships, and missions in the context of the struggle for survival, liberty, cultural transcendence, meaning, expression, and a relevant theology.

Black people are a unique people. There is nothing new about that statement in and of itself. White people have always said that black people are different from white people. They have put a value on that difference, saying not only that black people are different from white people but also that this difference means that black people are inferior to white people.

The message that blacks are different from and inferior to whites has been continually communicated in different ways through the various political, religious, and social media from the period of slavery down to the present. Therefore, when we say that black people are a unique people, we need to be careful to differentiate what we are saying from what the white racist says. We are not saying that blacks are biologically different from whites. The difference we are pointing to is a different experience that blacks have had. Blacks have grown up and developed in a different environment. Cobbs and Grier put it this way:

> The American Black man is unique, but he has no special psychology or exceptional genetic determinants. His mental mechanisms are the same as other men. If he undergoes emotional conflict, he will respond as neurotically as his White brother. In understanding him we return to the same reference point, since all other explanations fail. We must conclude that much of the pathology we see in Black people had its genesis in slavery. The culture that was born in that experience of bondage has been passed from generation to generation. Constricting adaptations developed during some long ago time continue as contemporary character traits. That they are so little altered attests to the fixity of the Black-White relationship, which has seen little change since the birth of this country.[3]

So the uniqueness of blacks comes from what has been called the black condition or the black experience.

Part of the black experience is the fact that blacks and whites have been told in all kinds of ways that blacks are different from and inferior to whites. The religious, political, and social structures have said this down through the years, and it has been reinforced over and over again. As stated previously, there are no basic biological or personality differences between blacks and whites, but there is a different experience or life-style.

Leronne Bennett, in his book *The Challenge of Blackness*, defines black ness as "that universe of values and attitudes and orientations which rise like dew from the depths of our ancestral experience and pulls us toward the distant shores of our destiny."[4] The black experience is a certain dark joy, celebrating the triumph of human beings over a social order which would degrade them. The black experience also includes cultural styles, social patterns, and behavior of blacks that have been developed in order to cope with the racism in America. Leon W. Chestang, in a paper, "Character Development in a Hostile Environment," characterized the black experience as one of social injustice, inconsistency, and personal impotence.[5] By social injustice is meant the denial of legal rights experienced by blacks in the United States since the beginning. Social inconsistency speaks of the disparity between what white Americans have said about America, and what they have done to blacks despite what they have said.

One of the clearest examples of the institutionalization of the inconsistencies can be seen by comparing the Dred Scott decision to the *Declaration of Independence*. The Declaration of Independence said:

> We hold these truths to be self-evident: that all men are created equal; that they are endowed by their creator with certain unalienable rights; that among them is life, liberty and the pursuit of happiness.

But the Dred Scott decision countered,

> . . . too clear for dispute, that the enslaved African race were not intended to be included, and formed no part of the people who framed and adopted this declaration; for if the language, as understood in that day, would embrace them, the conduct of the distinguished men who framed the Declaration of Independence would have been utterly and flagrantly inconsistent with the principles they asserted; and instead of the sympathy of mankind . . . they would have deserved and received universal rebuke and reprobation.

The framers of the Dred Scott decision knew that they were on sound ground with white Americans. They were well aware of the fact that the early drafts of the *Declaration of Independence* contained a clause objecting to the imposition of slavery in the colonies by the English. They also knew that the clause was taken out of the final version because they were afraid of alienating southern support. When it came to blacks, America's practice has always been inconsistent with what it preached. The inconsistencies are summed up in the words, "Blacks have no rights that Whites are bound to respect." [6]

Another characteristic of the black experience is personal impotence. Here we are speaking about the powerlessness felt by blacks as they try to effect change in their lives. One of the clearest examples of this is an incident that Alvin F. Poussaint related that happened to him in Jackson, Mississippi. He was leaving his office with his black secretary when a white policeman yelled, "Hey boy, come here." Somewhat bothered,

> I retorted, "I'm no boy." He rushed at me, inflamed, and stood towering over me, snorting, "What did you say, boy?" Quickly he frisked me and demanded, "What's your name, boy?" Frightened, I replied, "Dr. Poussaint, I am a physician." He angrily chuckled and hissed, "What's your first name, boy?" When I hesitated he assumed a threatening stance and clenched his fist, as my heart palpitated, I muttered in profound humiliation, "Alvin." He continued his psychological brutality, bellowing, "Alvin, the next time I call you, you come right away, you hear?" I hesitated. "You hear me, boy?" My voice trembling with helplessness, but following my instinct for self-preservation, I murmured, "Yes sir." Now fully satisfied that I had performed in acquiescence to my boy status, he dismissed me with, "Now boy, go on and get outta here." [7]

This incident from the life of an eminent psychiatrist illustrates on a personal level the impotency of blacks to deal with the situation in which they find themselves. But not only is there personal impotence as a part of the black experience, there is group impotence.

James H. Cone has also given us some characteristics of the black experience. Cone put it in philosophical and theological terms. He described the black experience as an existential absurdity. [8] In 1969 he stated that when the black man first awakens to the face of America he feels sharply the contradiction between things as the way they are and as they ought to be. He recognizes the inconsistency between his view of himself as a man and America's description of him as a thing. His immediate reaction is a feeling of absurdity. The absurd is basically

> what a man recognizes as disparity between what he hopes for and what he seems in fact to be. He yearns for some measure of an orderly and a rational world. He is oppressed by the disparity between the universe as he wishes it to be and the way he sees it. [9]

Cone talks about the black experience as one of oppression, that blacks are oppressed by a white society. Still others have simply described the black experience as blacks being victimized by whites who are guilty of attitudinal and institutional racism. Racism, according to this definition, is any attitude or activity which subordinates a person because of color, and then rationalizes that subordination by attributing to that person undesirable biological, psychological, social, or cultural characteristics. This has happened with blacks in the United States. They have been victimized by whites who have subordinated them. This, then, is the black experience and it is that experience that makes blacks unique.

When one begins to talk about the uniqueness of black experience, many people will try to point out that this experience is not uniquely black. They point out that other people have had the same experience. They say that what I am describing as the black experience is an experience that has been shared by all who are at the lowest place in our social scale. One has to concede that this is partially true. Native Americans, Spanish-speaking people, and women, both black and white, have had this experience. But there are a number of other things that must also be said.

First, we need to be careful lest we fall into the trap of what has been called attenuation, that is, the endemic tendency on the part of Americans to see less and less difference between one thing and another. While one has to guard against making too much of differences, one also has to guard against minimizing all differences.

Second, while it is true that there are people in the world who have been and are being victimized by the system, one has to point out that blacks have been victimized for a very specific reason: they have been victimized because they are black.

In addition, even though the research has been quite meager in this area, a number of studies provide evidence of qualitative differences between black and white children, even when living conditions are held constant, such as family income and neighborhood. In fact, as the research of Deutsch and Lott, among others, points out, no matter how carefully one may seek to equate groups, qualitative differences will emerge. A white and a black child, though living on contiguous blocks, do not live in the same world.[10]

One of the results of the black experience that has been demonstrated is the impact this experience has had on black character and personality. No serious student studying the black situation will deny the fact that blacks have developed certain character traits and behaviors that are uniquely black in an effort to survive in this racist society. Allport described this impact on one's personality:

What would happen to your own personality if you heard it said over and over again that you were lazy, a simple child of nature, expected to steal, and had inferior blood? Suppose this opinion were forced on you by the majority of your fellow-citizens. And suppose nothing you could do would change this opinion—because you happen to have Black skin.[11]

Now where did these unique behaviors and character traits that are uniquely black come from? There have been basically two schools of thought on this question. One school has attempted to show that some of these character traits result from the survival of Africanism among blacks. Among those scholars are Melville J. Herskovits and W. E. B. DuBois.[12]

But other scholars reject this position and state that the behavior and character traits of blacks are the results of the way in which blacks were socialized into that American scene. They go so far as to suggest that nothing, or at best very little, of Africanism survived in American blacks. In their view Africanism was largely erased through the process of slavery. They hold that because of contact and interaction with whites, blacks adapted and adopted the culture of white America so that what one sees is a manifestation of the mediation and synthesis of two cultures. Among the scholars who hold this view are E. Franklin Frazier and John Hope Franklin. Cobbs and Grier speak rather forcefully on this point:

Traits of character and patterns of behavior that appear more often in Black people than in other groups can all be traced to various aspects of life in America. Cultural anthropologists have searched intensively and interminably and have found no contemporary evidence for the persistence of African patterns of culture. The experience of slavery was unbelievably efficient in effacing the African and producing the American Negro. As a result, the cultural and characterological patterns developed by American Negroes provide a unique picture of a people whose history was destroyed and who were offered in its stead a narrow ledge of soil on which to live and grow and nurture children. All that is uniquely Negro found its origin on these shores and provides a living document of Black history in America.[13]

New tools of research are constantly being developed in this field, and one has every reason to believe that these will be refined even more. Until scholars have used these new tools of research to examine the depth of the psyche of blacks and compare it with the psyche of Africans, the question of the survival of African character traits and behavior in American blacks will have to remain open.

One thing is sure, research has demonstrated that one's environment influences one's social functions, behavior, and character traits in a powerful way. Most of the psychosocial theorists, along with pointing out that one is influenced by what is inherited from one's parents, also concede that environment plays an important role in the development of personality, behavior, and character. The sociocultural theorists point to the same things. In the case of blacks one can study the work of Allison David and John Dolland to substantiate this.[14]

What are some of the character traits and patterns of behavior that appear more often in blacks than in other groups? Cobbs and Grier list the following: "The Black family as an extended family, the ability of Blacks to divorce themselves emotionally from an object, the streak of hedonism and the capacity for joy, drinking more, dancing more, loving more."[15] While they recognize that these characteristics are often used as stereotypes, they hold that there is a grain of truth in them. As we have noted, these character traits and patterns of behavior are prevalent in blacks because of the impact of the American ethos on their culture.

Another factor that has some effect on black character and development and social function is the fact that blacks have been denied full participation in the dominant culture despite the fact they have accepted and internalized the values of the dominant culture. Their behavior is circumscribed and conditioned. As a result black people have developed what has been called a "duality of response." (We shall later look at this duality theologically.) Andrew Billingsley, in his book *Black Families in White America,* states the same idea in somewhat different language.[16] He says that blacks have been forced to live in two environments, the "nurturing environment" and the "sustaining environment."

In the nurturing environment, blacks find their being; in the sustaining environment, they are involved in matters of survival. This survival, more often than not, is in a hostile society. Those factors in a nurturing environment which give blacks their being are their families, community, norms, values, and traditions. They receive their basic training in their nurturing environment as to how to survive in the sustaining environment. They are able, in this environment, to develop and operate in an expressive way. They are free to be who and what they are in relationship with their peers.

In their sustaining environment, on the other hand, they have to be concerned about their survival needs, goods, services, political power, and economic resources. In short, they have to be concerned about those factors which make it possible for them to live a reasonably successful life in both their nurturing environment and their sustaining environment.

Now, to a large extent, what is said here is true of all people. The difference is that those who are part of the white community in America and South Africa are better able (though not completely) to merge the nurturing environment and the sustaining environment. These two are brought closer together and they can respond in either of them in much the same way. Blacks, on the other hand, must give one response in the nurturing environment and a different response in the sustaining environment, in order to survive. To develop expressively, relationships in the sustaining environment are filled with risks for the black person. An attempt to develop expressive relationships here may be rejected by whites, and at worst the black person may be excluded from that particular environment completely. We will discuss this in greater detail below.

So in the sustaining environment black people have to develop what scholars call instrumental relationships. Here they are subject to having to hide their real feelings. They develop feelings of distrust and suspicion, and they manipulate in order to survive in the sustaining environment. In the sustaining environment black people operate out of what has been called their depreciated character. That is, in this environment the goal is survival, to succeed at all costs. This may mean relating to others as things.

Another problem that blacks face as the result of having their nurturing environment separated from their sustaining environment is that oftentimes behavior or social functioning and character traits that are learned in their nurturing environment as to how to survive in the sustaining environment can cause conflict. The nurturing environment may put a high value on the particular social response, but in the sustaining environment a low value is put on it. This becomes especially complicated when survival in the sustaining environment is dependent on a different behavior than the one learned in the nurturing environment. And it becomes even more complicated, for if blacks use the survival tactics that whites value highly in the sustaining environment they will be rejected. The failure to use the behavior that is valued highly in the sustaining environment will also be penalized. Blacks find themselves in a "damned if you do and damned if you don't" situation. I will use two examples to illustrate this point; both of them apply directly to those involved in teaching black children.

The first example is the characteristic of self-assertiveness and aggressiveness. Now among those in the white society, where the nurturing environment and the sustaining environment are merged, self-assertiveness and aggressiveness are well-understood and a high value is placed on them for whites. Whites are expected to have these traits. But blacks get mixed signals. In the past they knew that to make it in the sustaining environment, one had to be passive and nonaggressive. They were taught this in their nurturing environment. For instance, for blacks to be self-assertive and aggressive in the sustaining environment has in the past (and even to the present) meant to be killed, to be destroyed. Black parents knew that and they began very early in the development of their children to instruct them to behave nicely and say "yes sir" and "no sir" when the white man talked to them. Black males, especially, have been told to keep their self-assertiveness and aggressiveness controlled, lest they get in trouble with society. Parents have taught this to their children by word and action. Even religion has been used to develop the characteristics of passivity and non-aggressiveness in blacks. Blacks were not to show too much aggression, or else they would be destroyed.

Benjamin Mays did a study on the Negro's concept of God and discovered that a large number of blacks had a concept of God that was compensatory. [17] He also discovered that there were a growing number of blacks who had a God who was concerned about social reconstruction. The compensatory nature of God and the socially reconstructive nature of God were both widely perceived until the time of the Second World War. The God who was concerned about social reconstruction was not talked about very much, but that God was still there. Religion, however, ceased to have such a God until the civil rights movement in the late '50s and early '60s. That there was a God who rewarded people in the afterlife became the rule of thumb, and what happened was that the black intellectuals began to do something that they had not done before—to develop a skeptical understanding of God. These are just illustrations of the fact that a lack of self-assertiveness and aggressiveness is a value blacks taught their children and lived by in order to survive in the sustaining environment.

This is not as true today as it once was. But we are still confronted with a confused picture. Whites say that blacks ought to be self-assertive and aggressive and consider it a negative character trait that they are not. But one wonders if white attitudes have changed on this point.

There are a number of factors that one must keep in mind when we discover the way blacks respond or behave as a result of the black experience. While on the one hand blacks share common experiences, on the other hand we need to keep in mind that blacks as well as all other people respond differently, often to the same stimuli. For instance, all blacks have been forced in one way or another to submerge their aggressiveness, but they do it in a number of different ways, depending on factors such as socioeconomic level, family life, past relationships with whites, and geographical location.

Some blacks suppress aggressiveness and substitute an opposing emotional attitude—compliance, docility, or a "loving" attitude. Sometimes rage can be denied completely and replaced by a compensatory happy-go-lucky attitude, flippancy, or—an extremely popular mechanism—"being cool." Or the aggression may be channeled into competitive sports, music, or dance. Another socially acceptable means of channeling rage is to identity with the oppressors and put all one's energy into striving to be like them. It is also acceptable and safe for oppressed people to identify with someone like themselves who, for one reason or another, is free to express rage directly at the oppressors. Another technique for dealing with rage is to replace it with a chronic resentment and stubbornness toward white people—a chip on the shoulder.

The different responses on the part of blacks have caused considerable confusion in both the black and white communities. Once again this demonstrates the urgency of obtaining a psychological analysis from an indigenous perspective. For the most part, psychology has, until quite recently, been guilty of an irrelevant analysis of the black experience. This has been partially due to psychology's origins and partially to its inability to separate itself from the racism so prevalent in America.

There is today an increasing appreciation of the richness of the various cultural heritages in America from the perspective of black psychologists and psychiatrists. White Lutheran involvement in ending exclusionary practices in this discipline as well as others will convince the youth of our sincerity, and prepare them to approach blacks in the larger society without prejudice and utilize their studies as foundational sources for education.

As pastors, teachers, and lay people we must try to develop emotionally and psychologically healthy people in a society that is basically racist. A black perspective is indispensable to this process.

Within this black historical perspective, we should remember that the ideas of *hope, liberation,* and *justice* have always been viewed in relation to the important theme of love. We remember this in order to separate our reflections and thinking from white theology. For us, God's love is made known through "justification by grace," liberating the poor for the future of God, as is so evident in the thinking and praxis of Adam Clayton Powell,[18] Howard Thurman,[19] Benjamin Mays,[20] Martin Luther King Jr.,[21] Malcolm X,[22] James H. Cone, Gayraud Wilmore,[23] and others.

The focus of the Harare conference on the black American and African cultures in light of the Lutheran heritage has led many of us to an emphasis on liberating "praxis" as the context out of which Lutheran Christian theology is now being developed. This means that to do black Lutheran liberation theology, one must make a conscious choice and commitment to the poor and against those who produce poverty. It is my prayer that this volume will change not only how we reflect on God, but also strengthen what we do in God's world so that our witness to the victims of society might make a future that is defined by God's freedom and justice and not by slavery and oppression.

# 11
# INTEGRITY IN THE PRIESTHOOD OF ALL BELIEVERS

## CHERYL A. STEWART

**W**ords are important because they bear meanings and power. *Integrity* is one of the critically important words for us. The Latin root, *integer,* has a wide variety of meanings:

(1) complete, whole, entire, intact, restore a thing to its former condition;
(2) unspoilt, pure, fresh, innocent, uncorrupted, balanced, unbiased, impartial, free from prejudice, open, undecided;
(3) renewed, begun afresh.
   Hence adverb *integre* honestly, uprightly, impartially, purely, correctly.

The Latin *integritas* means an unimpaired condition, soundness, health, moral purity, uprightness, and correctness.[1] The Latin renderings are flavored in English with an emphasis along the lines of ethics and wholeness: "1) adherence to moral and ethical principles, soundness of moral character; honesty, and 2) a sound, unimpaired or perfect condition."[2] *Integrity* is a word that runs deep in human hopes and goals as well as ideals. No wonder, then, that words such as *integrate* and *integration* have tremendous emotional and psychological impacts.

One of the problems with words like *integrity,* however, is that a person's frame of reference determines how the word is used, interpreted, and applied. White, Western society's frame of reference is structured by power, specifically, with white Westerners having control (especially white, Western *males* exercising power). In that context, integrity has to do with how a person or institution maintains faithfulness to the "system," the "white male club," the power brokers. The frame of reference is arranged along the linear path of past, present, and future in which "progress" is inevitable as long as the power structure is maintained.

This puts persons of color in a peculiar position. For them to be accepted/integrated into white, Western, male-dominated society would mean their accepting a similar understanding of integrity. The price of such acceptance/integration is being deaf to the moans and groans of other persons of color who understand integrity to be the synchronizing of creed and deed. The "integrated" person of color then turns from espousing and acting out of love, justice, and peace because to be accepted by the white community means to turn away from the community-oriented, cyclical frame of reference which characterizes people of color.

The Christian understanding of integrity is based on the frame of reference modeled and taught by Jesus Christ: to love God with our entire being and to love our neighbors as ourselves.

Yet why discuss integrity in connection with the priesthood of all believers? I contend that Luther's interpretation of the priesthood of all believers depends on one's understanding the incarnation of integrity. To put this before us more clearly, I will briefly explore the historical bases of the priesthood, recall the traditional Lutheran understanding of the priesthood, examine the African-American culture's historical and present involvement with the priesthood, and posit directions in which black Lutherans from Africa to the Americas may want to go. In a sense, I will be telling the story of the priesthood of all believers from its Old Testament roots to today's challenges.

## The Story

*The Old Testament*

> Now therefore, if you will obey my voice (and keep my covenant, then you shall be my own possession among all peoples; for all the earth is mine, and you shall be to me a kingdom of priests and a holy nation.
>
> (Exod. 19:5-6)

Shortly after their unexpected and abrupt departure from Egypt, the Israelites entered the Sinai desert and made camp in front of Mount Sinai.

Moses went up on the mountain to receive God's promise that henceforth the Israelites would be set apart as a kingdom of priests. Each person could approach Yahweh separately on behalf of the community for purposes of dedication, worship, and service. The Israelites accepted Yahweh's demands and promises, and Moses consecrated the nation to be priests to one another. In return for their obedience and faithfulness, Yahweh made this promise: "I will make my abode among you and my soul shall not abhor you. And I will walk among you, and will be your God, and you shall be my people" (Lev. 26:11-12).

The ideas of priests and priesthood were not new to those assembled at Sinai. They knew from previous experience that priests were the mouthpieces of Yahweh, who taught God's ways and discerned God's will for the community. As the Bible presents it, prior to Moses commissioning a priesthood, there was no formal priesthood among the Israelites. While Yahweh spoke through individuals and listened to their petitions, God did without priests. People spoke directly to Yahweh. The family setting and its domestic activities were comparable to Yahweh's sanctuary and its ministry, so that all domestic affairs were carried on in an atmosphere of priestly sanctity. A father was teacher and informal head priest, while a mother was guardian and informal high priestess of the sanctuary. Each family was a witness to other families as the whole community prepared and equipped itself to be a faithful servant-community.

Formal or set-apart priestly functions and persons developed during Israel's sojourn in the wilderness. The tribe of Levi and the house of Aaron were selected and the responsibilities given included: first and foremost, teaching; then guarding the sacred vessels and tabernacle, presiding at worship to insure that Yahweh was properly approached, and bringing the words of Yahweh and the people to one another. Moses had these responsibilities first, then Aaron and his sons were consecrated to this official priesthood. The Aaronic-Levitical priesthood was new and distinct from the universal priesthood of the faithful Israelites. Generally, this arrangement worked well during the wilderness wanderings. The portable tabernacle was the Israelite's proof that they had a special relationship with their God. It was also the symbol of Yahweh's presence and their election.

Israel's perception began to shift with the institutionalization of a set-apart priesthood. Cyril Eastwood comments, "Israel's mistake was to see priesthood as a right instead of a privilege."[3] Over time they came to believe that this right could be protected and performed only by a special class of person. Consequently, conflict arose between those who fulfilled their religious duties and those who did not. "The attention of the people was focused on holy persons, holy things and holy places instead of the Holy One."[4] This shift resulted in "religion" being understood as observing the law instead of as a revelation of Yahweh's grace. The priesthood—rather than Yahweh—was emphasized. In turn, the Levitical priests performed the sacrifices and good works on behalf of the Israelites who sought Yahweh's presence. They forgot that Yahweh's presence was offered freely to all.

Once settled in Canaan, the Israelites radically changed their worship life and the roles of the priests. Instead of a portable tabernacle and temporary shrines, permanent temples were erected which had to be maintained and staffed. There was an increase in the amount of written materials as a transition was made from oral to written traditions. As a result, there was an enlarged place for Levites to be custodians and scribes. The priests developed increasingly more complex rituals for approaching Yahweh through sacrifices, and the supervision of sacrifices became the sole domain of the set-apart priests. This shift from a didactic to a sacerdotal priesthood meant that the primary responsibility of the priest was no longer teaching but offering sacrifices. So "instead of being the interpreter of the Word and the Law and the will of God, [the priest] became the indispensable intermediary between [the people] and God, and Judaism became a theocracy ruled by a hierarchy."[5]

The ideal of Yahweh, a nation which would be a kingdom of priests, was compromised early and throughout subsequent Israelite history. Instead of understanding Yahweh's kingdom of priests as an experience through which they would grow closer to Yahweh, instead of seeing the set-apart priests as dedicated to and consecrated for special service to Yahweh, instead of seeing themselves as elected to be a guide to the nations, instead of realizing that Yahweh was accessible to all humanity as pledged servants of God, instead of turning to their history to reclaim their covenant relationship to Yahweh, the Israelites compromised their integrity as Yahweh's chosen people. Their completeness, wholeness, and freshness were lost because they did not adhere to Yahweh's moral and ethical principles. Yet once more Yahweh came to their rescue by creating a realized priesthood to replace the idealized one which they lost.

*The New Testament*

> Grace to you and peace from him who is and who was and who is to come, and from the seven spirits who are before his throne, and from Jesus Christ the faithful witness, the firstborn of the dead, and the ruler of kings on earth.

> To him who loves us and has freed us from our sins by his blood and made us a kingdom, priests to his God and Father, to him be glory and dominion for ever and ever. Amen (Rev. 1:4-6).

Israel's laws, cult, and covenant became its revelation instead of pointing the way to the revelation. Unable to fulfill the priestly function for which it had been chosen, Israel was unable to change its concept of redemption to include Jesus Christ as the redeemer and to see that the new revelation was Jesus Christ. The Israelites were unable to see that "Christ has fulfilled and done away with the priesthood of the Old Testament."[6] They were unable to see that Jesus Christ was the final fulfillment of the idealized old covenant priesthood. As the New Testament presents it, there is a point-by-point correlation between the responsibilities of the Old Testament high priest and Jesus as the new covenant's high priest: both were called by God, both were consecrated by being washed and anointed with oil, both were teachers of God's law, both entered the Holy of Holies and brought the blood of the sacrifice before Yahweh for the atonement of the people's sins. Because Israel could not see the similarities, neither could it see the differences: Jesus needed no successor, and did not need to repeat the sacrifices. He was the eternal high priest and the once-for-all sacrifice.

The incarnation ended all other priestly functions and responsibilities. A new priesthood was inaugurated because Christ was the sacrifice and became the priest-mediator for the entire creation. Christ's blood was the foundation of the new priesthood, and we all share in the benefits and privileges of Jesus's high priesthood: we become Christ's kingdom and Christ's priests. Hans Küng notes, "The significance of these ideas for the New Testament is that all human priesthood has been fulfilled and finished by the unique, final, unrepeatable and hence unlimited sacrifice of the one continuing and eternal high priest."[7] The motif of Jesus's priesthood is elaborated by the author of the letter to the Hebrews. Addressing Christians who were ready to abandon their faith in the face of Roman persecution, the writer underscored that Jesus was the culmination of God's revelation as well as God's high priest (cf. 4:4-16). Jesus was the only high priest who opened to all the way into the Holy of Holies, heaven. Through Christ, then, there is direct and immediate access to God, ". . . since we have confidence to enter the sanctuary by the blood of Jesus, by the new and living way which he opened for us through the curtain, that is, through his flesh, and since we have a great priest over the house of God, let us draw near with a true heart in full assurance of faith, with our hearts sprinkled clean from an evil conscience and our bodies washed with pure water" (Heb. 10:19-22).

The setting aside of the set-apart priesthood and the inauguration of a new high priest leads to the conclusion that all believers share in Christ's new universal priesthood. If the church is the body of Christ and Christ is its head, then the church shares in the priesthood of Christ.[8] The new and universal priesthood is empowered by the victory feast, the final sacrifice, provided by Christ in which he himself is both the host and the celebrant. Hans Küng lists five signs and marks of the new priesthood:

1. Direct access to God (through faith, baptism, and the Spirit);
2. Spiritual sacrifices (praise and thanksgiving in the world);
3. Preaching of the Word (the Christian story, the message of salvation, personal witness);
4. Administering Baptism, Eucharist, and forgiveness of sins; and
5. Mediating functions (service, prayer, bearing one another's burdens).[9]

The new priesthood in Christ had been gathered, educated, empowered, and sent out. The integrity of God's intention for priesthood had been regained. New life, new moral authorization, new unity had been initiated. There was renewal in all aspects of the life of the community summoned to be a kingdom of priests and a holy people. The new priesthood of all believers, bought by the unconditional love of God and paid for in the blood, sweat, and tears of Jesus Christ, was at the center. The mission of the body of Christ was to the world, not only to churches and synagogues. So the early Christian missionaries took this radical gospel on the road, in obedience to Jesus' commands.

## The Early Church and the Middle Ages

Come to him, to that living stone rejected by men but in God's sight chosen and precious; and like living stones be yourselves built into a spiritual house, to be a holy priesthood, to offer spiritual sacrifices acceptable to God through Jesus Christ. For it stands in scripture:
"Behold I am laying in Zion a stone,
    a cornerstone chosen and precious,
    and he who believes in him
    will not be put to shame."
To you therefore who believe, he is precious, but for those who do not believe,
"The very stone which the builders rejected
    has become the head of the corner,"
    and "A stone that will make men to stumble
    a rock that will make them fall";
for they stumble because they disobey the word, as they were destined to do.
(1 Peter 2:4-8).

These words, written to churches in Asia Minor, must have given the saints tremendous encouragement! As the early church grew and its written tradition became more entrenched, discussion among church leaders led to honing and clarifying basic Christian doctrines. As time passed and Christ's return in glory was not realized, the need to have a tradition became increasingly significant. I can survey only briefly what some of the early church "fathers" contributed to the development of the doctrine of the priesthood of all believers.

In a late first century letter from Rome (named after the supposed bishop of that congregation, *Clement of Rome*), we see that a local congregation was administered by elders and a bishop with the assistance of deacons. Initially, the congregations were autonomous and were led in worship by a presiding officer (bishop) who also preached and represented the congregation to the wider public.

*Polycarp,* the bishop of *Smyrna* who was martyred around A.D. 156, intentionally included women in the idea of priesthood, thereby creating the notion and potential for the ministry of women as a special group in the life of the church.

*Justin Martyr,* a mid-second century philosopher-apologist who was born in *Samaria* and taught in Rome, described services of worship in which he held that the spiritual sacrifices of thanksgiving and service were most evident during the eucharistic feast. He also maintained that all Christians had a high priestly character because of their uniqueness, election by and worship of God, and their mission to all humanity.

*Irenaeus,* an Easterner who became a bishop in *Lyons* in the late second century, considered the church to be priestly because of the priestly character of its members, God's bestowal of spiritual gifts on all humanity, and the spiritual sacrifices offered by Christians in prayer, thanksgiving, and in the Eucharist.

To be sure, there were African contributions. *Clement of Alexandria* (late second and early third century) understood the gospel to have universal presence and appeal. Those who possessed the knowledge of the gospel formed a spiritual priesthood. He described Christians who practiced the spiritual sacrifices of prayer, preaching, Baptism, and Eucharist as persons of apostolic character who participated in the special succession of the priesthood.

His contemporary in *Carthage, Tertullian,* insisted that Christianity was the knowledge of God based on spiritual reason and held that the rule of faith was the true authority for doctrine in the church. His definition of Jesus as divine and human, clarifications about the persons of the Trinity, and uses of terms such as *justification* and *sacrament* became standards in the West. Tertullian took the priesthood to be a community of spiritual people who offer God the spiritual sacrifice of prayer. He insisted on a self-disciplined and ascetically moral priesthood.

*Origen,* also of Alexandria and sometimes thought to be Clement's successor, also believed that Christians revealed their priesthood in the holiness of their characters, spiritual sacrifices, and confession of Christ in the face of martyrdom.

*Cyprian,* an avid reader of Tertullian's works and martyred bishop of *Carthage,* held that bishops had special priestly functions related to maintaining the unifying orthodoxy and morality of the church. He made bishops responsible for being the guardians of orthodoxy because they were the successors to the apostles. Cyprian's expressions about the unity of the church and the authority of the bishops were used to advocate a high priestly caste in the later church. Eastwood wrote of Cyprian's understanding of the authority of the local bishop, "The supreme authority of the bishop in the local church presupposed the possibility of a supreme authority over the universal church. So the passing of the universal priesthood rested ultimately, perhaps inevitably, in the sole priesthood of one man whose powers were immeasurable, whose position was unchallengable, and whose words were infallible." [10]

At the start of the fifth century *Augustine of Hippo* (now Annaba, Algeria) inferred that the universal priesthood is based on the universality of the gospel. The latter teaches the universality of the Christian faith and the need to extend the gospel throughout the world. A bishop himself, he claimed that the gospel offers eternal life to all through God's presence in history and in the sacredness of every human life.

By the beginning of the third century, a distinct separation began to emerge with the use of the words "laity" and "clergy." Separate and hierarchically arranged orders emerged. Bishops, presbyters, and deacons were the major orders, while subdeacons, acolytes, exorcists, lectors, and janitors made up the so-called minor orders. The inauguration of the system of a treasury of merits and indulgences and the experiences of the Inquisition gave the hierarchy of the Western church centered in Rome more authority and subjugated the universal priesthood to the ordained and consecrated ranks of the clergy. From the fifth through the eleventh centuries a set of four serious conflicts wracked the church and made tremendous impacts on the doctrine of the priesthood of all believers.

The first conflict was one of the East vs. the West. The power and authority of the Roman Empire had spread rapidly. When a new territory was conquered by the Roman military arm, the inhabitants became Roman citizens and Rome sent a governor to rule in the annexed area. Hand-in-hand with the military came the church. Monks and missionaries brought the Roman church as the military brought the Roman legal and political systems. On December 25, A.D. 800, the Emperor Charlemagne ushered in the age of the Holy Roman Empire with the groundwork laid earlier by Pope Gregory the Great (A.D. 540–604). It was Gregory's missionary campaign which reestablished the Roman ties with the churches in Spain, France, and England. The universal priesthood had a universal message to bring, according to Gregory's teachings; the duty of daily Christian witness was applicable to both priests and laypersons in the studying of the Scripture, the unity of all believers in Christ, and the promised inheritance for a kingly priesthood of a heavenly kingdom.

The second conflict was that of Islam vs. Christianity. Shortly after Gregory's death a little-known Arabian began to preach a new doctrine of expansionist policy to a united people who were not Christian, yet came through the same Father Abraham as did the Jews. The Catholic church was unprepared for the challenge the rise of Islam posed. "The new Israel, the elect race, the people of the New Covenant, failed to see in Muhammad a divine judgement upon their apathy and a stirring challenge to their waning faith. The new Community was already suffering from the malady of the Old. The Elect race had forgotten the purpose of its election and the Royal Priesthood had neglected its priestly responsibility and consequently had lost sight of its unique mission to the world."[11] The body of Christ was already at odds with itself because of internal division. The ethical values and moral standards reflected those of the world, not the mandates of Christ—the integrity of the church was once again being called into question. The church can only be strong when its values lie in the priesthood and sacrifice of Jesus Christ. A result of the separation of clergy and laity was that the education was centered in the clergy and the laity were ignorant of the Scripture. As a consequence the priesthood was unprepared to defend Christianity and the church's own calling to be priests for one another. Islam was built on a community base and bound together in fellowship by its faith in Allah as their story was recorded in the Koran. God's message to the church might be read in hindsight as what can be accomplished when a community is united in faith and in mission. The community of Islam had indeed become a priesthood of believers. But Christianity was too busy trying to maintain the power and authority of the papacy to stop in midstride and take stock of its lack of integrity.

The third conflict which arose during this period was that between the priesthood and the laity. The conflict centered around three major issues: (1) the veneration of icons, (2) the penitential system, and (3) the doctrine of the Eucharist. The question of icons drove a wedge between the clergy and the laity which was alarming. The veneration of icons turned Christians into passive onlookers deprived of grace instead of being active participants in Christ's gift of life. It increased the power of the priests while making the laity into uneducated, superstitious people. The penitential system took the fear and ignorance of the laity one step further into out-and-out exploitation. Public confession gave way to private confession to a priest and a system of indulgences grew to monstrous proportions. The doctrine of the Eucharist, a sacrament of unity, was the final straw in the separation of the clergy and the laity. The mass was spoken in Latin, a language unfamiliar to the laity, and the wine was withdrawn from the people. The whole attention of the congregation focused on the priest in worship and the laity were virtually, if not actually, excluded from the holy priesthood. The net effect of these practices was to deny the doctrine of the priesthood of all believers.

The fourth and final conflict during the Middle Ages was that between church and state. After Charlemagne's death the power of the Roman Empire began to wane and collapse. As the empire collapsed the independence of the papacy rose. In 1073 Hildebrand (Gregory VII) was enthroned as pope. His goal was to establish, beyond the shadow of a doubt, the authority, independence, and purity of the church. Under his leadership papal infallibility was asserted, the centralized authority of canon law was strengthened, interference by the state in church affairs was greatly reduced, and clergy and laity were separated physically by the altar rail and spiritually by celibacy. The doctrine of the priesthood of all believers was totally overshadowed by this high-powered conception of ecclesiastical rule. And "it was inevitable that voices of protest would be raised."[12]

## The Reformation

> But you are a chosen race, a royal priesthood, a holy nation, God's own people, that you may declare the praises of him who called you out of darkness into his marvelous light.
>
> (1 Peter 2:9).

The groundwork for the Reformation had been in the process of preparation for a long time, as we have seen. During the first 250 years of Christianity the priesthood of all believers was very important and received much attention. The fourth through the seventh centuries saw this universal priesthood being slowly pushed into the background. The eighth through the eleventh centuries saw the church's increasing involvement in the struggle for power and control, with the priesthood of all believers very much ignored as the church struggled to achieve dominance. The twelfth through fifteenth centuries saw glimmers of light as small groups and individuals sought to appeal to the spiritual conscience of the church in order to bring it back into harmony with the ministry of Jesus Christ and the apostles. Marsiglio, the mystics, Wycliffe, the Lollards, the Humanists, and the Franciscans, in their emphasis on the spiritual life and a personal relationship with God, "unintentionally undermined the foundations of a sacerdotal church which expressed itself mainly in sacraments and social ordinances." [13]

The purpose and meaning of the church is obscured if the office of pastor is set above the doctrine of the priesthood instead of within it. The doctrine of the priesthood of all believers posits that all believers are priests to each other because of the priesthood of Jesus Christ. The initiation and consecration of the priesthood is through Baptism, continued renewal is through the Eucharist, the spiritual sacrifice and mission are through ongoing worship and service to others. Out of Luther's understanding of the authority of the Word of God and the doctrine of justification by faith erupted a renewed emphasis on the priesthood of all believers. Let us make no mistake, however, in thinking that Luther stepped into a void of a "dead age." The times themselves were filled with unrest, unsolved problems, and unfulfilled longings. The climate was right for reformation—the *kairos* had arrived.

> The Lord has sworn and will not change his mind,
> "You are a priest forever, after the order of Melchizedek.
>
> (Ps. 110:4)."

In his exposition of this text Luther wrote:

> Every baptized Christian is a priest already, not by appointment or ordination from the pope or any other man but because Christ Himself has begotten him (sic) as a priest and has given birth to him (sic) in Baptism.

And again:

> For although we are all priests, this does not mean that all of us can preach, teach, and rule. Certain ones of the multitude must be selected and separated

for such an office. And he (sic) who has such an office is not a priest because of his (sic) office but a servant of all the others, who are priests. When he (sic) is no longer able to preach and serve, or if he (sic) no longer wants to do so, he (sic) once more becomes a part of the multitude of Christians.[14]

Luther's lectures on the Psalms (1513–1515) are his earliest works. We can see his theology taking shape already. His early perception of the priesthood included not only the universal focus, but also the understanding of God's gifts of inclusiveness and diversity. Perhaps the most eloquent statement of Luther's position in regard to the doctrine of the priesthood of all believers is found in his treatise *To the Christian Nobility of the German Nation* (1520). In this work Luther attacked the Romanists who had "ensconced themselves within the safe stronghold of these three walls. . . ."[15] The three walls were:

(1) the pretended superiority of spiritual power over temporal power;
(2) the exclusive right of the pope to interpret Scripture;
(3) reforming councils could only be called by the pope.

Luther's refutation to all three walls was his assertion of the doctrine of the priesthood of all believers.

In tearing down the first wall Luther said that all Christians have spiritual power and the only difference is office. Our baptism, the gospel, and our faith give us spiritual power and make us Christians. What he said in the exposition of Psalm 110:4 (quoted above), he reiterated in this treatise:

Therefore a priest in Christendom is nothing else but an officeholder. As long as he (sic) holds office he (sic) takes precedence; where he (sic) is deposed, he (sic) is a peasant or a townsman (sic) like anybody else . . . there is no true, basic difference . . . except for the sake of office and work, but not for the sake of status . . . those who are now called "spiritual" . . . are neither different from other Christians nor superior to them. . . .[16]

The second wall was more loosely built than the first wall, Luther said:

Their claim that only the pope may interpret Scripture is an outrageous fancied fable. They cannot produce a single letter [of Scripture] to maintain that the interpretation of Scripture or the confirmation of its interpretation belongs to the pope alone . . . although they allege that this power was given to St. Peter . . . it is clear enough that the keys were not given to Peter alone but to the whole community. Further, the keys were not ordained for doctrine . . . but only for the binding or loosing of sin.[17]

In addition to the lack of scriptural authority for ultimate papal interpretation of Scripture, Luther insisted that all Christians had the responsibility for reading, teaching, espousing, and understanding Scripture. The second wall was a pile of rubble.

The third wall, that reforming councils could only be called by the pope, was built on the first and second walls, according to Luther. Without the first two walls, the third could not stand. He appealed to Matthew 18:15-20, where Jesus told the disciples how to handle a church conflict:

> Here every member is commanded to care for every other. How much more should we do this when the member that does evil is responsible for the government of the church. . . . But if I am to accuse him before the church, I must naturally call the church together.[18]

The rest of the treatise is devoted to a practical program for the reformation of the church from other aspects of papal authority and abuse.

Luther's purpose in these early years was, clearly, not to create a new Christian church, but to clean up the old one. And his writing undergirded that goal. In 1521 he told his Augustinian brothers in Wittenberg that there was no set-apart priesthood except those raised up by the devil and that there was only one priest in Christendom, Jesus Christ himself. Luther further explained to the council of the city of Prague that any and all other priests are born of water and the Spirit through the sacrament of Baptism, not through ordination. In discussing those who administer the sacraments, Luther went on to state that under no circumstances should these persons be called priests because the name

> priest stems either from the custom of the heathen or was drawn from vestiges of the Jewish people and adopted to the great harm of the church. According to the evangelical writings they should more correctly be called ministers, deacons, bishops, and stewards. . . . [Paul] speaks as he does in order not to set up a rank, an order, a right, or a kind of dignity . . . but to commend the office and the work alone, allowing the right and dignity of the priesthood to remain with the people (*in communi*).[19]

Finally, in 1523 Luther explained 1 Peter 2:9, the passage quoted at the beginning of this section:

> But we are all priests before God if we are Christians. . . . Therefore I would very much like to have this word "priests" as commonly applied to us as it is customary to call us Christians; for it is all one thing: priests, baptized, Christians. Just as I dare not allow the anointed and tonsured alone to be called

Christians, so I dare not allow them alone to be considered priests. . . .
Therefore mark this well that you may know how to make a distinction between
the way in which God calls us priests and the way in which men (sic) call
themselves priests.[20]

As Luther's "dear German people" became more and more liberated,
they also became increasingly violent. As suasive and powerful an orator
as Luther was, he was unable to stem the tide of the Peasants' Revolt, and
instead of channeling the peasants' anger into creative reform patterns,
Luther sided with the elite nobility against the peasants. What began as a
single-minded church reform program soon came to be a movement divided
within itself. The legacy left by Luther and the other European reformers
has impacted Christianity ever since the 16th century. The story of Protestantism and the story of the Catholic church after the Second Vatican
Council (at which time it becomes the story of the whole catholic and
apostolic church) is the story of the extent to which all Christians have
understood and applied the doctrine of the priesthood of all believers.

*Colonialism*

> I hate, I despise your feasts,
>     and I take no delight in your solemn assemblies.
> Even though you offer me your
>         burnt offerings and cereal offerings,
>     I will not accept them,
> And the peace offerings of your fatted beasts,
>     I will not look upon
> Take away from me the noise of your songs;
>     to the melody of your harps I will not listen.
> But let justice roll down like waters,
>     and righteousness like an ever-flowing stream.
> But you have turned justice into poison
>     and the fruit of righteousness into wormwood.
>
> (Amos 5:21-24; 6:12b)

Due to the limitations of time and space we must now make a rapid transition from the 16th to the 20th century. Suffice it to say that Luther
impacted Christianity's story in ways that we are still discovering. By
consecration, worship, service, and mission, the priesthood—born of water
and the Spirit, bound by the eschatological promise of eternal life, and
committed to the universal task of spreading the gospel—is revealed to
all. Mission was the focus of Christianity during these four centuries. Just
as in the early part of the Middle Ages, when nations began to explore

and "conquer" the world, missionaries went hand-in-hand with the government representatives of the Europeans, and the colonialization which occurred encompassed both church and state. This was, in an ironic fashion, exactly what Luther had hoped would occur. But the integrity of the church was again called into question. Colonialism brought with it not simply the working together of church and state, but also the collusion of church and state in oppressing all people who were not of European ancestry and descent.

The largest blot in the recent story of Christianity is its legitimization of chattel slavery. The story of Christianity would not be authentic and faithful without the telling of this part, however demonic and hateful the story may be. Contrary to popular opinion, the continent of Africa was not inhabited by pagans and heathens waiting to be converted by the European missionaries. During the period of the early church, Christianity had already spread to areas of North and West Africa. As we have already noted, a number of the early church "fathers" were of African origin, which disproves one of the most influential presuppositions of European Christianity. Christianity in Africa was certainly tempered by traditional African religion, but it was never assimilated and never synchronized. The gospel always speaks for itself and, as such, is the basic, universal tenet of Christianity.

When the slave trade was prospering, the European presupposition (again erroneous), was that Africans were ignorant and primitive. But they were ignorant only if European culture was the yardstick by which to measure education, and primitive only if European culture was the standard by which to determine civilization. For the record, native Americans were perceived as ignorant and primitive for the same reasons. The importation of slaves from Africa into the New World began after native American slaves had been decimated by disease, and other native American populations had been reduced by war or had run off into the impenetrable hills and forests, from whence they participated in guerilla warfare against the European usurpers. The enslavement of Africans seemed a much better way of handling the problem of plantation and household labor, because the Africans were displaced from country and culture; they couldn't simply run home. As long as the Africans were kept uneducated and prevented from forming permanent relationships with other Africans, the source of slave labor remained intact.

The effects of chattel slavery on African-Americans has had a significant part to play in who and what we are and are not as a community today.

The mark of slavery still lives on in our relationships. More than 20 years ago Cyril Eastwood wrote:

> Why must the Gospel be proclaimed to all nations and what lies behind this sense of compulsion which has existed in every age? It is not now sufficient to present the Gospel of love merely as an antidote to the threat of eternal damnation nor is it any longer tenable to identify the Christian religion with European civilization, with the accompanying implication that this type of civilization is the panacea for all ills.[21]

I believe that Eastwood himself was not fully aware of what he was saying in these sentences. African-Americans today must go back to the gospel in its universal context of the doctrine of the priesthood of all believers in order to erase the mark left on our spirits by chattel slavery and slavery's unholy progeny: white racism. The integrity of the black community is at stake as it has never been before. Those of us who are black and Lutheran have a dual heritage of liberation second to none. We now turn to the contemporary situation for clarity.

## The Contemporary African-American Context

*Community Destruction*

> Seek me and live;
>     but do not seek Bethel,
> and do not enter into Gilgal
>     or cross over to Beersheba;
> for Gilgal will surely go into exile,
>     and Bethel shall come to nought.
> Seek the Lord and live,
>     lest he break out like fire in the house of Joseph,
>     and it devour, with none to quench it for Bethel, . . .
> Seek good and not evil,
>     that you may live;
> and so the Lord, the God of hosts,
>         will be with you,
>     as you have said.
> Hate evil, and love good,
>     and establish justice in the gate;
> it may be that the Lord, the God of hosts,
>     will be gracious to the remnant of Joseph.
>
> (Amos 5:4b-6, 14-15).

The black community in the United States is on a collision course with annihilation (genocide?). The problems are numerous, too numerous to deal with totally in this context. In order to be faithful, however, I will posit three major categories and discuss each.

(1) Our sin of idolatry
(2) Our sin of covetousness
(3) Our sin of dishonesty

Some would argue that sin is too strong a word. I will argue that anything which we *allow* to separate us from God is sin. I could have said anything which comes between God and us is sinful, but my point is to emphasize our part in committing sin. That item which makes us so human—free choice—is the very thing which gets us into trouble with God. We freely choose to place our egos first. At times there doesn't seem to be much of a choice, so we appear to be forced to cooperate with the demonic. It is my position that we are always inclined to choose the easy way, not necessarily the godly one, and these choices pull the African-American communities into the rapid whirlpools of sin, moving ever faster and deeper, and from which there is only one way out. I am here discussing only the African-American community, although other ethnic and racial communities may find this analysis compatible with their experience.

The sin of idolatry simply means worshiping other gods before Yahweh. Our story in the United States, for the most part, is one of idolatry. We have consistently worshiped the European-American community, to our demise. At first, during the period of slavery, we resisted and were successful in that resistance. But the demonic was stronger than we were, and, in an effort to become accepted, we gave up our God-given uniqueness. We have come to dress, speak, eat, and desire what European-Americans have told us, to the point where their issues have become our issues—not realizing that our own African-American issues have yet to be resolved. To illustrate this example I will use the present male–female struggle.

Much press has been given to the myth of the strong, castrating, black matriarchy. On the male side the rhetoric includes strong accusations that the female won't let the male lead; that all males are characterized negatively (i.e., *For Colored Girls . . . , The Color Purple*); that women got the jobs when men couldn't, and wouldn't let them (the men) forget it; and that the women expect too much from the men (expect them to be supermen). The rhetoric on the female side includes accusations that black men are only after one thing—sex; that black men are for the most part immature; that they won't include black women when important decisions and community issues are at stake; that they have no backbone and are sexist. We seem to have come to an impasse. We no longer appear to respect or love one another; instead we attack each other and seem to enjoy putting one another down. We don't listen to one another and we no longer converse or encourage one another. We quickly reject people because of the way they dress or look or where they live or went to school.

The best analysis of this is by Clyde Franklin and Walter Pillow, who refer to "The Black Male's Acceptance of the Prince Charming Ideal," the flip side of what Colette Dowling called *The Cinderella Complex*. According to them, two basic assumptions lie at the root of the problem: first, "present day Black women only *appear* to be more independent than are white women and Black men due to their historically imposed independent subsistence relative to" black men.[22] Because this is in appearance only, black females are in reality as dependent upon black men as white women are upon white men. "A second assumption is that Black men presently are socialized into the Prince Charming Ideal to *the same extent* as are white males with one exception—they do not receive either the means or the societal support by which to approximate the ideal as do their white counterparts."[23] The Cinderella Complex assumes that, psychologically and emotionally, women have been programmed to desire being cared for. The Prince Charming Ideal compliments the Cinderella Complex in providing a philosophical basis for men, in providing a protective, patriarchal role with all women in general and one's female partner in particular.

The Prince Charming Ideal has grown especially in the late 1970s and early 1980s. The male responses to the ideal are twofold: one on an internalization level and the other on a noninternalization level. Male responses fall into one of four categories (as indicated by the chart on the top of p. 188).

The researchers concluded that "both the Prince Charming Ideal and the Cinderella Complex lock persons into social roles which may be difficult to fulfill . . . approaching a particular (situation) from the framework presented . . . may improve the . . . problem resolution between Black males and Black females. This undoubtedly will contribute to the unification of Black men and Black women in America."[24] Why do I use this to illustrate sin? Where is the sin? It is in our desire to emulate the behavior of the white male–female relationship. Franklin and Pillow clearly state the way to eliminate these complex psychological longings: total rejection of the values and standards of acceptability among the European-American community. God's values and standards have receded. If we are to be at one with God and the universe, if we are the holy priesthood of all believers, we must confess our sin of idolatry and seek God's forgiveness.

|  | Internalization | Noninternalization |
|---|---|---|
| Action | —typically middle class<br>—consistent behavior<br>—positive interaction with<br>black females (same<br>expectation as black males) | —middle class (?)<br>—resents role<br>—likely to discard role<br>—conflictual and superficial<br>fulfillment of role<br>—demands full black female<br>participation |
| Nonaction | —lower class<br>—self-destructive and<br>antisocial behavior<br>inconsistent with ideal<br>(likely to be physically<br>abusive)<br>—poor self-esteem<br>—cannot deal with<br>expectations of black<br>females<br>—lack of respect for black<br>females | —any class<br>—sexist and/or very<br>independent behavior<br>—may act contrary to ideal<br>and have no female<br>relationships<br>—may have very responsible<br>and stable relationships |

The sin of covetousness is directly connected to that of idolatry. My understanding of this sin is to choose to emulate other cultural standards and values to an extent where a denial of one's God-givenness is very apparent. In other words, we reject God's gift of self and try to become totally other. This is also a direct consequence of colonialism and slavery. When the society sets up implicit standards of acceptability that exclude an array of God's people, they are also involved in practicing idolatry. The legacy of colonialism and slavery goes much deeper than the male and female roles discussed above. It also includes values such as language, hairstyles, food, symbols of success, education, employment, health, and legal practices, and all those other items which constitute culture, including the philosophical underpinnings. Because we have already begun using the example of gender roles, we will continue to do so in the examples that follow.

During slavery, black people were intentionally kept ignorant. In their extreme desire to maintain the less-than-human posture of the slave, the slavemasters and mistresses passed on those very ideals which would make the slaves "acceptable." The white woman was seen as aloof, pure, virginal; the black woman was seen as approachable, promiscuous, sensual. While the white man loved the white woman he pursued sexual fulfillment (his own, of course) with the black woman. Both white and black women were confused, although white women rationalized that sexual intimacy was distasteful so it was all right for the white men to exploit and mistreat black women. Slowly white women came to realize that sexual intimacy could be a good sensual experience and they came off what Calvin Hernton alludes to as the pedestal of "sacred white womanhood." [25] The irony of this initial step toward liberation was that the very taboos which protected the institution of slavery led to the preoccupation of white women with black men: not only were white women curious about the sexual potency of black men, but they also actively sought out black men for sexual relationships. Black men and white women tend to gravitate toward each other predominantly for sexual reasons, then, to the exclusion of black women.

> The myth of Negro sexuality . . . (has) affected American white women to the extent that many of them secretly envy or despise Negro females. The Negro woman . . . according to the myth of Negro sexhood . . . is endowed with an irresistible sexual attraction and enjoys the sex act more than any other creature on earth. . . . White women accept (these myths) as fact. Some not only envy Negro females but actually want to be black. [26]

Because black men have forged such a peculiar alliance with white women, black women have come to believe that the only way they can be attractive to black men again is to become as white as possible. The practical aspects of this transition have included straightening hair, speaking "the Queen's English," dressing in a European way, bleaching skin, and the creation of a color-caste system within the black community. How we have believed that the white European culture was the way out of all our problems—our salvation! How we desire to be the people God did not create us to be! How we covet ideas and ideals which are alien to our tradition and heritage! Once again our identity as a people is distorted and our Christian integrity is compromised! How much easier it would be for us to be created in the European white male image than in God's image! Where is the priesthood of all believers if we believe the premise of white-being-right more than we believe God's promise of one body, many members? The sin of desire, of covetousness, has, at its base, the sin of idolatry and the negation of the doctrine of the priesthood of all believers.

The sin of dishonesty, of lying to ourselves and to one another, builds on these other two and manifests itself in very demonic ways. We lie to ourselves and to one another when we think that we have "made it" to the exclusion of the rest of the community; when we escape from the reality of suffering in God's servanthood to suffering from drug addiction, alcoholism, attenuation, suicide, domestic violence, use of handguns (and other weapons), cerebral and spiritual atrophy; when we choose to forget the needs of the community and fulfill only private selfish needs; when we treat one another in the same selfish and self-serving ways that others have treated our communities; when we put aside our moral mandate from God and take on the immoral mandate of the society. We lie to ourselves when our congregations reject the black religious tradition which has ensured our spiritual and psychological survival and espouse European ways of worshiping. We lie to ourselves when black men and black women continue to put each other down in subtle, insidious ways that will, ultimately, see the extinction of the African-American family. We lie to ourselves when we believe and act as if European-American culture and Lutheranism are the way, the truth, and the life. The black community is in its death throes when our children (our future) are savagely, brutally, and systemically taken from us through the various masks of death: murder, drugs, kidnapping, child molestation, health-related problems, educationally related problems, and spiritually related problems.

## Community Building

> Therefore, if any one is in Christ, he is a new creation; the old has passed away, behold, the new has come. All this is from God, who through Christ reconciled us to himself and gave us the ministry of reconciliation; that is, in Christ God was reconciling the world to himself, not counting their trespasses against them, and entrusting to us the message of reconciliation. So we are ambassadors for Christ, God making his appeal through us. We beseech you on behalf of Christ, be reconciled to God.
>
> (2 Cor. 5:17-20)

The genius of Martin Luther King Jr. was his God-given gift of bringing the church out of buildings and institutions and into the world. The church is above all a fellowship of believers and as such a worldly religion. Believers are in the world and it is in the midst of worldly problems and issues that priesthood is fulfilled. "Relevant Christianity requires the healing of the inhabited world of men [sic], and this demands a new priesthood: a priesthood that believes in the redemption of the world."[27] Denominationalism to the exclusion of the universality of Christianity is also a sin of idolatry. The good news, the gospel, has been revealed to Christians who are not Lutheran. Yet there is much that Lutheranism has to contribute to the ongoing struggle for liberation among black Americans. Martin Luther's words in the 16th century began the process of bringing the church back into the world. Much backsliding has gone on since then. Martin

Luther King Jr. added his voice and gave his life in order that the church might get back on God's track. Our African heritage, the black church tradition, and the Lutheran reformation legacy can help us all get back on God's track.

The rift between black men and women must be bridged. Part of the inheritance we have received from slavery is the inextricable connection between racism and sex. Black men have taken the lead from white men and now attempt to oppress black women with sexism. In an attempt to come to grips with the double portion of oppression that they must carry all their lives, black women attempt to align themselves with white women in fighting sexism, and alienate themselves from black men. To be sure, there are some points at which no woman is liberated until all women are liberated, but the question with which black women must grapple is: At what expense? My dear sisters, whom I love with all my heart, are so busy fighting sexism, ageism, classism, and racism that the black community is losing them, their dedication to God, and the zeal with which they carry the Christian message. My beloved brothers are so busy fighting racism (as it affects the black male) and climbing to the top that they seem to be oblivious to the hurt and pain which the sisters are experiencing. This analysis, of course, does not intend to alienate those persons who are striving for justice and hungering after righteousness in ways that are Spirit-guided and directed because of their liberation in Jesus Christ.

The African-American community has, to a large extent, moved farther and farther away from the black church. They have lost faith because of the hustlers, the charlatans, and the hypocrites who exploited the community for self-serving reasons. Their faith in sacred places and people had been misplaced and, once disappointed, they refuse to trust any church person again. The problem is that there was never a priesthood that they felt fully a part of, that they put too much faith in the preacher and the people and not enough in Jesus Christ, the great high priest, and the miracle of Jesus' death for each and every one of us. At the other extreme are those African-Americans whose God has seen them through all manner of suffering and brought them this far by faith. The problem they have is with the world: everything is evil. So they worship the church: a particular congregation or building. They, too, have forgotten that Jesus Christ went into the world with love and forgiveness in his heart. Both of these groups of people and all the ones between these polarities are the priesthood.

How does the black community come to be so polarized, spiritually and psychologically? By no stretch of the imagination is our divisiveness an accident or a mistake. Dr. Andrew Billingsly in his book *Black Families in White America* posits that our sicknesses as a community are all due to the conflictual psychological state of living in two completely separate environments. White people receive their nurture and sustenance from the white community, but black people receive only their nurture from the black community; their sustenance comes from the white community. This is what creates schizophrenic people who are very likely to take their workplace frustrations out on those from whom they receive love and positive strokes at home. W. E. B. DuBois discussed the same issue at the turn of the century in terms of "double-consciousness":

> The Negro is a sort of seventh son, born with a veil, and gifted with second-sight in this American world, a world which yields him no true self-consciousness, but only lets him see himself through the revelation of the other world. It is a peculiar sensation, this double consciousness, this sense of always looking at one's self through the eyes of others, of measuring one's soul by the tape of a world that looks on in contempt and pity. One never forgets his twoness—an American, a Negro; two souls, two thoughts, two unreconciled strivings; two warring ideals in one dark body, whose dogged strength alone keeps it from being torn asunder. The history of the American Negro is the history of this strife.[28]

Given this background, how can members of the African-American community be priests to one another?

Black brothers and sisters are *equally* part of God's created people. The drug pushers, the schizophrenics, the physical and psychological abusers, the rapists, the murderers, the pimps, the prostitutes—all were born members of the priesthood. We don't always want to acknowledge that God created everyone, however. We don't always remember that our great high priest went out into the alleys and byways, bringing love and reconciliation with him. We don't always understand that our ministry is to go and do likewise, because we have not accepted in faith the greatest high priest of all, our brother Jesus Christ. We have selected pastors and priests to take over our responsibility in the world through the authority of a set-apart office. The responsibilities of the priesthood include the exercise of priestly powers by calling preachers and teachers to be the servants, the stewards of God's mysteries in the local congregation, by being priests in their family settings, and by declaring God's love, forgiveness, and reconciliation in the world as witnesses and missionaries. Each human being relates to others as priest, and as a consequence carries the church wherever he or she is.

The historical black church triggers in us the memories of pain, of struggle, of sacrifice, of survival against the odds, of love and acceptance when self-worth and self-esteem could not be found in society, of sanctuary and safety, of the promise of equality in another place at another time, of the consistency of God in a world where inconsistency and hypocrisy was the order of the day. These memories are as important for the black community as remembering the exodus from Egypt was and is for the Israelites. We remember in order to be at one with God, in order not ever again to put ourselves in a position of enslavement to false gods, and in order to be God's ambassadors of reconciliation in the world.

## Conclusion

How is the priesthood of all believers recognized today? The priesthood is recognized by the timeless ministries of learning, service, support, worship, and witness. Integrity, justice, humility, empowerment, and self-development are words which describe the attributes of this priesthood. God calls us back into wholeness with the rest of the universe that we might be priests to one another in our daily lives. Love between black persons is an expression of the priesthood in the African-American context. Being proud of our curly hair, our broad noses and wide lips, and our dark skins and our history, and being proud of how God created us is being the priesthood of all believers, the incarnation of Christian integrity.

Who are the priests in the African-American context today? They are Desmond Tutu and one of my nephews, Desmond Lee; they are Jesse Jackson and a pastor in Philadelphia, Jesse Brown; they are Winnie Mandela and a young member of my former congregation, Winnila White: their names are Ambrose, Albert, Will, Josiah, Simon, Earlean, Rudy, Maxine, Gaynell, Peter, Richard and Teresa, Craig, Maurice, James, and the multitude of other saints who remain nameless in this space but whose names are already recorded in God's book of life. These are the saints who maintain their Christian integrity at all costs in the face of the demonic. In the final analysis, we are all the priests who during our short sojourn in this world:

> Maintain good conduct among the Gentiles, so that in case they speak against you as wrongdoers, they may see your good deeds and glorify God on the day of visitation.
>
> (2 Peter 2:12)

# 12

# THEOLOGICAL EDUCATION AND PREPARATION FOR MINISTRY IN AFRICA

# VIVIAN V. MSOMI

I am going to tell part of a story. It is about Lutheran theological education and preparation for ministry in Africa. To attempt to present a comprehensive picture of a whole continent is presumptuous. Africa is big and diverse. Even within the Lutheran family such diversity is a reality. If one considers the different countries, their social and political conditions, she or he realizes that generalizations are difficult. Lutherans are in these different nations. Our story is complicated further by the various "brands" of mission societies which historically are related to these churches. Missionaries from the numerous Lutheran mission societies came to Africa from western and northern Europe and North America. Their different missionary methods tended to differ one from another, and so our churches have different emphases and methods.

While we have significant diversity in our backgrounds and present situations, we have much in common. We are able, therefore, to relate quickly to one another's experiences and find that sharing mutually beneficial. Still, political boundaries and limited fiscal resources have limited such sharing and fellowship. As a result, we often work in isolation.

The story of theological education and preparation for ministry within our Lutheran churches is complex and challenging. The first issue is whether the coupling of "theological education" and "preparation for ministry" is taken for granted. Does theological education go hand in hand with preparation for ministry? Is it justifiable to say that anyone who is theologically literate is automatically prepared for the ministry of the church? Nevertheless, are there specific theological areas which need to be covered and mastered by a person in order for the person to be adequately equipped for ministry? An even more difficult topic is to be clear about the type of pastors which we need to be preparing for ministry in contemporary Africa. The Lutheran family living in Africa must work toward having a clear picture on that one! I suspect that Lutheran tutors and church administrators have not done their homework well enough in this regard. In order to avoid frustrations by all parties concerned, we must strive to make our objectives clear.

Theological education is a key means through which the reservoir of our Christian heritage is made available to others. In most cases, those engaged in this form of education are preparing to be pastors of God's people. Yet how is the Christian legacy shared with all God's people, the *laos?* Our achievements in the latter area leave much to be desired.

The subjects considered in this volume include some of the pillars of the Lutheran portion of the Christian heritage. These pillars surely have definite implications for Lutheran theological education all over the world. It seems to me that we have not explored sufficiently the practical implications of these doctrinal statements for theological education and for the Christian life in general. Since our continent is diverse and African Lutherans share that variety, I shall consider southern Africa as a case study which may illumine other contexts.

Two factors stand out as we begin. The first is illustrated by a jocular observation enjoyed by African Lutherans. We say that if a Lutheran who has gone through confirmation class subsequently joins an African independent church, the Lutheran soon becomes a bishop! This points up the deserved reputation that the Lutheran churches have for taking Christian education seriously. In Africa this concern for Christian education is part and parcel of our Lutheran legacy. There is danger, of course, in miniaturizing that education into a smug package, as in the pastor who reportedly claimed, "All theology is summed up in Luther's *Small Catechism*." Second, there is the factor of the mission background of our Lutheran churches. The foreign mission societies' main objective was to extend the kingdom of God to the far corners of the earth. They understood themselves as ambassadors and custodians of the gospel's light to "dark" Africa. The custodian mentality made it difficult, even for the most astute among them, to perceive that soon the Africans would be ready to take full leadership in African churches. In 1945 a gifted Zulu pastor, preaching in Zululand, South Africa, said,

> We need missionaries. Without them we would be like orphaned children, and much good work done in love, blood and tears would come to nothing. But in spite of all this, we would not be very happy if the Mother Church is going to send out a great number of new missionaries, because this would hinder Zulu pastors from becoming district superintendents. . . . Fathers, let this be the last great gift out of your goodness. Let not everything remain static as in former times. Therefore, Fathers, we speak openly; we are not your enemies, we are co-builders with you, we do not fight. But we speak to you as a child speaks to his father at home. We do not force you nor do we want to leave you.[1]

The results of the mission society's paternalistic treatment is painfully clear through the speech and might have been camouflaged to make the content of the Zulu pastor's point acceptable to the missionaries. It is also clear that an African is claiming the right for Africans to full leadership in the African church. The missionary reluctance to give over the work of ministry and the positions of leadership to Africans is replicated in the story of theological education and preparation for ministry.

## A Historical Perspective

The evolution of the pattern of theological education in Africa needs to be viewed in the context of the growth of the so-called "younger churches." These churches have moved from their origins as mission synods to full autonomy today. For the latter part of the 19th century and the early 20th century, theological education in southern Africa was rudimentary. The focus was on training catechists and evangelists, not pastors. Missionaries regarded the catechists as their helpers to reach areas beyond the immediate reach of the mission stations. Devoted and dedicated catechists could be found in many Christian communities. They were persons who had very limited educations, but because they came from the local villages and were part of their communities, they were able to approach their people effectively with the message of the gospel. Their success is reminiscent of the success of the African independent churches, a phenomenon which baffles and perhaps intimidates many an African leader in the so-called "mainline churches."

The first phase of theological education can be called the "Missionary Era" because it was dependent and centered upon the European or American missionary. Initially, the intention was to train catechists. Each mission society devised its own plans and procedures for carrying out that training.

Numerous problems cropped up. All instruction had to be in the vernacular, but at that time there was no written literature available in the African languages. The missionaries themselves were scarcely masters of the local languages and dialects. There are many unsung heroes, both catechists and missionaries, in the account of how they communicated the message of Christianity to each other in order to carry on the work of conversion and establish worshiping communities. Eventually some of the mission societies decided to cooperate in training catechists. In South Africa a combined evangelical school was started. From these beginnings until 1912, the purpose uppermost in the minds of the missionaries and their supporters in Europe and North America was the raising up of Africans to help the missionaries in the proclamation of the gospel. In 1912 the missionaries opened a theological seminary to provide evangelists as well as catechists. The establishment of the seminary coupled with the subsequent growth of the Lutheran Christian communities reflected and also prompted the need for resident pastors in those communities. The shortest and quickest route to obtain such pastors was to upgrade the education of gifted evangelists to the point where they could be ordained. At first this was done by having missionaries give the evangelists private tutoring. Soon, however, the need for a more structured theological education was recognized. As is apparent, the origin of Lutheran theological education in Africa for Africans was prompted by pragmatic concerns: to provide helpers for the missionaries and to tend the congregations which still were under the control of the mission societies and their representatives.

Candidly, one may find the same purposes for theological education within Lutheran circles today. Many a Lutheran still thinks that a seminary exists solely for the job of adequately training men and women for serving parishes. There seems to be little expectation that the educated leaders of the church should also be thoroughly prepared to face the sociopolitical realities and risks of our societies as well. On the whole, most Lutheran pastors have been educated and have tended to follow in this traditional, pragmatic model.

Staffing theological seminaries was particularly difficult. Sometimes a seminary would have a faculty consisting of one missionary/pastor, teaching alone. Most were persons of outstanding talents and stamina who were versatile enough to span several theological disciplines. While we appreciate and respect their labors and dedication, still the educational limitations of such arrangements are self-evident. Bengt Sundkler, on the basis of a contigent-wide survey, wrote about these one-teacher schools,

The main problem is already implied in the somewhat generous use of the term "faculty." For the typical situation is that one single missionary, some-times assisted for practical theology by an African pastor, had to carry the whole teaching load, besides caring for the college administration and personal problems of the students and the field work.[2]

In this elementary and missionary-centered phase, the sparse human resources made it impossible to develop and offer a balanced program of theological education. In Southern Africa, especially after 1950, the situation improved to the point that several persons could be appointed to theological faculties and were enabled to teach subjects in which they were particularly competent.

The next of several periods can be termed the "Theological Certificate Phase." Only in the early 1960s did Africans become instructors in theological schools in Southern Africa. Pastors L. E. Dlamini and D. L. Makhathini had studied at Luther Seminary in St. Paul, Minnesota. We surmise (but do not yet have hard evidence to confirm it) that the first African joined the faculty of Makumira Seminary in Tanzania somewhat earlier in the 1960s than in Southern Africa. These appointments marked the dawning of a new era in African Lutheran theological education. Indigenous persons were increasingly seen to be a significant resource and force in our theological education. It is regrettable that the pace of development of African theological educators has been hampered by lack of personnel and insufficient funds, even to this day.

The present period may be termed the "Higher Theological Diploma-Degree Phase." We are now offering advanced degrees which require collegiate and graduate-level preparation. To be sure, these programs strain our resources even further. Today our theological education operates on two levels. The first is the Diploma level, which requires four to five years in what Americans might understand as a somewhat extended secondary school level. The second is the Bachelor of Theology degree, which corresponds roughly to the American collegiate to masters degree experience. Normally a person would be in such a program for four years or longer, including one year of internship. In some African nations the curriculum is ecumenical and the examinations are prepared by the Joint Board of Southern Africa, a body external to the institutions. Lutherans, as might be anticipated, take care of their denominational particularity through a number of courses in the curriculum.

The deepening and extending of theological education was prompted at least in part by the growth of educational opportunities in secular fields and professions. The need to upgrade our theological education originated within the Lutheran churches themselves as well as from outside stimuli. We realized that we needed to prepare persons more fully and adequately to meet the changes and problems of African societies so that they would be able to minister more competently and relevantly in our contexts. The external prod came from heightened standards in African professional education generally. Our fellow Africans expected us to improve along with them. A combination of these factors may be seen in the inauguration of a postseminary program in Marangu (Tanzania) during the 1950s. It was a direct response to the need to develop new leaders for the church who would take their places in African society as independence came to former colonial territories. I have not been able to pinpoint the factors which led to the later demise of this program.

Two other ventures must be mentioned, if only in passing. We are realizing the importance and vitality of carrying on theological education ecumenically. In Southern Africa our ecumenical attempts began when theological instructors from several different denominational seminaries met and discovered how much they had in common as church persons and educators. The first ecumenical staff institute, sponsored by the Fund for Theological Education, was held in January 1963. One concrete result was the formation of the Association of Southern African Theological Institutions. It in turn formed the Joint Board for the Diploma in Theology. I am bold enough to claim that in Africa we have achieved significant ecumenical cooperation and venturing in theological education that our American colleagues may find instructive. The second venture is Theological Education by Extension (TEE). The Lutheran Church in Southern Africa is one of the founding members of the African group which is advancing TEE, and I am pleased to report that the TEE College is doing important theological educational work in Africa. Again, some of our experiences may be helpful for Lutherans in America to study.

## Some Brief Evaluative Comments

It is therapeutic for us to assert to ourselves that we have moved beyond the foreign missionary phase in our theological education. The ball is now in our court as Africans to steer the course which will benefit Christians and all persons in our continent. Before we can do that, we need to be clear about where we are coming from, what ought be discarded, and what is to be promoted.

I will cite just some of the items, con and pro, that are current among us. For too long we have tended to promote the catechist-training mentality.

Other tendencies have been to prepare persons primarily for positions as parish workers and to be custodians of Lutheran doctrines. We have not adequately prepared people to think and labor in the ecumenical context which is typical of African Christianity. And we must search our souls to discover why Lutheran leaders in general are reluctant to be leaders in sociopolitical issues. Not only do we need to become concerned with sociopolitical issues, but we must also be found among the national leaders; we have the potential to bring uniquely Christian understandings to those issues.

We have done reasonably well in teaching Lutheran doctrines. Still, I have the nagging question as to whether we have moved any further than passing over the doctrines as if we are reciting lessons learned but which are not really part of our beings. We are up to the challenge to spell out clearly the implications and make the appropriate applications of Lutheran positions for life and faith in our part of God's world. For instance, early in students' theological education, we need to be specific in engaging them and ourselves in the meanings of justification by faith, priesthood of all believers, theology of the cross, doctrine of the two kingdoms, etc., for Christian discipleship and mission in present-day Africa.

Next is the whole area of worship. Our liturgy and hymns are still oriented toward European and American models and contributions simply translated into our languages. There is too much uncritical adoption of Western tunes. Some African Christians still think that it is un-Christian to use hymns with African poetry, rhythm, and music. I suspect that countries north of Southern Africa are more creative and advanced in the Africanization of worship. We have all experienced criticism and even resistance from the older generation as we attempt to introduce needed changes. Theological education and leadership will be vital in effecting liturgical and musical changes.

Ecumenism is a pressing and legitimate issue on our present and future agendas. At times one has the impression that we cherish our Lutheran heritage to the detriment of taking ecumenism seriously, even in just learning about the views of other Christians. In almost all African nations Lutherans are in the minority among the mainline churches and the African independent churches. Future Lutheran pastors cannot afford to be uninformed about them. We must be able to identify and then make needed contributions in ecumenical dialogues. Christians cannot be smug within their own denominational families or even in the wider universal church. We are, after all, a minority in the world. Knowledge of and openness toward one another is not a luxury but a necessity.

How we teach and what we model in our attitudes as teachers is a critical concern. If we want our students to grow as theologians, we need to be conscious that they will be theologians who are ministers of the gospel. The sometimes elusive "pastoral formation" stands ahead of us as a goal toward which we strive. Intentional emphasis on prayer, worship, and counseling as community events are to be woven through our courses and relationships in our schools.

And that brings me to one of the most important of these important concerns. We are Africans. We have a God-given and God-blessed heritage. That African heritage must be stressed in our theological enterprise. I regret that our seminary students sometimes are taught as if they will be pastors in Western churches. Our people's wholistic view of religion and life, their deep appreciation of their ancestral heritage, their identification with their places of birth and its very soil, their definition of the person in terms of relationships with others such as family, community, nation and humanity— all these are so rich and so often neglected. Theological educators and the churches for which education is undertaken need to support and cultivate further efforts that are being made in this direction. After all, our education and our theological efforts have African congregations as their central focus.

These brief evaluative comments indicate that there is much for us to do and to share with one another and our brothers and sisters in Christ, even across oceans. I am convinced that we can carry out these proposals and more within the contexts of being African and being Lutheran. We are not ashamed to be Lutherans. That heritage, too, needs to be brought further into the limelight. The implications of Lutheran positions for the African people can be drawn out more fully through the help of conscientious and effective theological education.

## New Horizons

If our efforts in theological education in Africa are to be worthwhile, there are some areas which we need to look toward and to which we must attend.

First, the matter of Africanization. While we shall continue to take the long-established Western theological tradition seriously, we know that Lutheran theology is largely the product of the German mind at work on the substance of the Christian tradition. Are the results to be applied *in toto* to Africa? That was the missionary mentality. We have moved far beyond it in so many ways that we can do so while retaining its distinctive contributions to understanding and living the gospel. As theological teachers, we must be liberated enough to affirm that God is in Africa, too. We can be bold enough to be totally free in sharing our story of discerning God's will for us as the relevant theology for Africa.

Second, centers of theological learning in Africa, whether they are seminaries, universities, etc., must clearly reflect that they are in this continent. It hurts many of us in South Africa that frequently these centers operate as if they were in Europe or North America. The issues at the top of our African agendas must occupy the top spots on the curricula agendas of our African educational institutions. That is the way of sound education. Yes, there is universality in knowledge and in the gospel, but genuine universality does not turn people into zombies who appreciate only the creative efforts of others but remain spectators themselves.

Third, our theological education must value and make accommodation for the positive qualities of our African heritage. Bluntly, these values which emphasize the wholeness of the human person are often neglected in the West. Unfortunately, our theological education frequently is fragmented between having African students and a Western style and model of life. We have absorbed enough of the Western approach as to be too comfortable with abstract intellectual matters. We struggle hard to deal with the spiritual guidance, pastoral formation, and emotional development of future pastors. We are in need of a wholistic—an African—model for theological education.

Fourth, we need to pay attention to work that has already been undertaken and to consider carefully the suggestions offered. The Lutheran World Federation Advisory Committee on Theological Education in Africa, during its five-year mandate, held several meetings in which keen insights were shared.[3] The crucial question I raise here is whether these have been shared with all Lutheran theological education centers in Africa. Have some of the practical suggestions been implemented? Let me mention some of them:

   a. The issue of contextuality is raised persistently and pointedly and the questions are asked about how the seminaries are being assisted and moved toward putting Lutheran theology in an African context. There will have to be research and experimentation, and that will take money, time, and personnel sympathetic to their own roots.
   b. The assistance to some theological education centers to upgrade them for advanced theological study seems to be under way.
   c. The concept of the "spectrum" of ministry has been considered at length. It needs to be implemented in our theological education. That will entail broadening our programs beyond preparing persons for

parish ministry. It includes equipping the people of God for diverse ministries. Our seminaries will then become places where our congregations will feel nourished and challenged. African theological education has to avoid an elitist mentality, and we have to come to grips with the rapidly growing independent churches. These factors point to the importance of understanding and empowering the priesthood of all believers.

d. The LWF interest in infrastructures, i.e., strengthening institutions of theological education and leadership development and the understanding of ministry in African societies, must be translated into practical terms. Each African seminary must be encouraged to develop programs which are strategies to challenge future pastors to be contextual in their theological and pastoral studies.

e. The role of Martin Luther as pastor is too often missing from theological education. His deep concern for the freedom of the individual and the dignity of the laity as well as his dynamic *Seelsorge* (care of souls) is inadequately explored. Luther's pastoral concern permeates all his theological works and there is a strong person-centered dimension in our Lutheran heritage. Our seminaries ought be called upon to develop this further in the pastoral attitudes of students. In our context, Clinical Pastoral Education and Industrial Mission Programs are necessities. The skill-related development in ministry includes equipping pastors to be catalysts for change and enablers of those engaged in other ministries of the church.

■

The story of Lutheran theological education in Africa is one of increasing Africanization. We are acutely aware of the riches of both our Lutheran and our African heritages. Those heritages are being brought into dynamic relationships with each other in a process which may at times generate some heat but will spread the light of the gospel here and elsewhere in God's world. The present scene is a bridge to the future. We are expected to capture the vision of future theological education in our continent. We can expect very rich discoveries for pastoral studies in Africa. There is a lot of exciting exploration ahead of us—and we will keep telling the story.

# 13

# BLACK AND LUTHERAN THEOLOGICAL EDUCATION FOR MINISTERIAL FORMATION IN AMERICA

# CRAIG J. LEWIS

C onfusion. That describes theological education today. Does anyone agree on what it is or is supposed to do, where it takes place, and how to do it? Laity and clergy, professionals and amateurs, churched and unchurched, might start their answers well enough, but soon all of us lose clarity and coherence.

Chances are we begin by saying that theological education aims at equipping and mobilizing persons to be leaders, and they will then mobilize and equip the rest of the whole people of God for the Lord's ministry and mission. We know that theological education is neither strictly an academic pursuit nor simply a job training program. We recognize that theological education, like all education, is a communal endeavor. By that I mean education engages the whole community in shaping and guiding itself and its individual members, while at the same time the community makes a statement about itself in relation to the world. Education is never simply or primarily the transmission of facts nor the effort to narrow the sphere of the unknown so as to broaden the sphere of the known. Education involves passing on the traditions, attitudes, values, and visions the community has of its destiny to future generations.

Still, when we try to get more specific about theological education, confusion creeps in. Confusion has its place. If Dr. King talked about "creative tension" to achieve justice, then Lutherans can consider "creative confusion" in putting together understandings about theological education.

To sort through issues in theological education, to begin to point toward a responsible future, and to put the black experience within Lutheran theological education, I suggest that we take a wholistic view. My focus will be on the persons who are being educated theologically for ministry and mission, what personal growth and maturity have to do with ministry and mission, and how their spiritual gifts and commitments to serve God relate to pastoral skills.

Some comments about black and white relations in the United States may shed some light on the situation in my country. Obviously and bluntly, in America blacks and whites live in separate communities. Despite the civil rights movement of the 1950s and 1960s, and the social experiments with racial integration, blacks and whites live at great cultural distances from one other. How, in the context of such racial/cultural isolation, can the two races strive for consensus in the church on the difficult subject of theological education for ministerial formation?

This is a critical question for black American Lutherans. We number less than 2% of the membership of the Lutheran church. Black theological education for ministerial formation is not only in confusion, it is in a state of crisis. Let me be candid. We are not attracting adequate numbers of black candidates for pastoral or lay professional ministries. A number of the persons who seek to prepare for those ministries do not seem to be as qualified as we desire. Lutherans have not provided the specific theological educational resources necessary to build competencies for leadership in black Lutheran congregations as well as in black and poor communities. And let's face the fact that we are a long way from the day when black candidates and clergy will be called as pastors and lay ministry leaders in the vast majority of predominantly white congregations. There simply are no specific programs in Lutheran seminaries to develop black Lutheran ministerial leadership. Curiously, one seminary has a program to assist black leaders in and for ministry, but it was created to serve bivocational or dual occupational pastors in the historic black churches. Black Lutherans preparing for professional ministry are not encouraged to use that program.

The truth is that Lutherans have not explored the potential of synthesizing our black cultural identity with the Lutheran heritage as a foundation for theological education. The need to do so is urgent if we are to overcome the current crisis in preparing black persons to be Lutheran pastors in the United States. I believe that the best strategy for improving theological education for black persons will combine the resources of Lutheran seminaries and colleges with those of black seminaries along with programs of black studies at particular non-Lutheran seminaries. The purpose ought be kept clearly in front of us: to meet the specific needs of black Lutherans in the mission and ministry God has for the church.

While the focus is on theological education and ministerial formation for the predominantly black Lutheran congregations and the whole black community, our concerns are inclusive. All Lutheran theological education needs to be liberated from its tight monocultural bonds. The challenge is to transform our theological education from a monocultural mode to a multicultural mode.

By multicultural theological education I mean processes of education in the church which seek to shape Christian witness for the multicultural, diverse realities of American and world societies. Multicultural theological education attempts to discern the unity within the diversity of cultures. It is essential for the church to have leaders in public ministries who demonstrate understanding of and the capacity to minister in the real world, a world marked by diversities and pluralisms, yet a world ruled and loved by God. Such a style of theological education is vital because we seek to mobilize and equip persons not so much for the church as it now is, but for the church in the world as it can and must be in the future. We need leaders who will transcend their own cultures for the purpose of bringing the meaning and joy of the gospel to people of other cultures.

## Theological Education: A Lutheran Approach

Lutheran churches in the United States use the term "theological education" mostly to refer to the professional academic preparation of persons who will serve as ordained ministers. More recently, "theological education" has come to include the professional and academic education of professional layworkers in the church, such as directors of religious education. Theological education could also include ongoing education engaged in by persons already ordained or certified for ministry. For our purposes, however, I will concentrate on theological education directed toward those preparing to enter the public ministries of the church and will reflect mostly the patterns that existed in the Lutheran Church in America.

With some exceptions, the procedures in the American Lutheran Church and the Association of Evangelical Lutheran Churches were quite similar. (These three church bodies formed the Evangelical Lutheran Church in America, which came into existence in January 1988.)

While theological education occurs in a variety of settings, including hospitals, colleges, social service centers, and congregations, the locus for most of it is in Lutheran seminaries. In fact, it has been expected that normally candidates for ordained ministry will hold the Master of Divinity from a Lutheran seminary or have spent at least one year in residence at such a seminary. Some exceptions have been made, at the discretion of the candidates' synods, for persons who graduate from accredited seminaries which are related to other denominations or are ecumenical. Lutheran theological education conceives of itself to be different from the more neutral academic programs of religious studies in schools of religion, and more denominationally specific than the programs in nondenominational divinity schools. Our theological education frankly concentrates on the mission of the Lutheran church and seeks to undergird it.

There have been different procedures for persons who are older than 30 and who do not have seminary degrees as well as those who have been ordained previously by another denomination. In those cases, a seminary faculty panel would examine the potential candidates and make recommendations about possible further theological education to the persons and to the synods. Candidates for lay professional ministries could prepare at any appropriately accredited institution, but those who prepared in Lutheran colleges and certainly those who completed masters-level degree programs at a Lutheran seminary were highly regarded as future church leaders.

Again, the three uniting Lutheran churches had different patterns, but each of them, in some way, endorsed or authorized a candidate to proceed into and to continue in the Master of Divinity program. Normally a person went through interviews, psychological testing, and other evaluative and counseling procedures. In the Lutheran Church in America, these steps were not under the jurisdiction of the seminaries but the synods. There was also a pastorally oriented examination for candidates, developed on a churchwide basis and suggested for synodical use, which was part of the final evaluation process. Ordination was not guaranteed by a seminary diploma, but depended upon the person's completion of the degree, fulfilling the church's evaluative procedures, and receiving and accepting a call, usually to a congregation. Given the close cooperation of the expressions of the church from congregation to synod and through churchwide agencies, it was logical for them to look to each other for support and to be responsible to each other.

For the most part we regard theological education to be of graduate level, that is, beyond the baccalaureate degree, and to be scholarly, even technical, in the areas of biblical, historical, systematic, and practical (sometimes termed "contextual") theology. We expect our seminaries to have educational programs which are aimed at providing students with a knowledge content and a skill content. The knowledge content includes:

(a) knowledge of the canonical Scriptures including the meaning of the biblical revelation, together with an understanding of the cultural, historical, and religious settings of the biblical texts and a basic understanding of hermeneutics;

(b) knowledge of New Testament Greek sufficient to do exegesis, and a lexical knowledge of biblical Hebrew;

(c) knowledge of the major doctrines of the Christian faith in terms of their biblical roots, historical developments, and conflicting facets of the tradition, together with current implications;

(d) knowledge of the Reformation and its ecumenical implications, the life and teachings of Martin Luther, *The Book of Concord*, the continuing development of the Lutheran tradition, and viable interpretations of that tradition today;

(e) knowledge of the theology and rites of the church, especially the sacraments, including attention to local traditions;

(f) knowledge of the periods, movements, personalities, and issues in the growth of the worldwide Christian church and the thought and life of the church in relation to the world;

(g) knowledge of the main types of Christian ethics as developed historically and in modern scholarship together with understanding methodological issues in ethical reflection today;

(h) knowledge of the biblical and theological foundation for God's mission throughout the world; and

(i) knowledge of the beliefs and practices of world religions and their relationships to the church's mission, plus understanding the Christian gospel in relation to religious and secular alternatives.

The skills content of our theological education focuses on the professional leadership needs of Lutheran congregations. Among the skills important for parish ministry are:

*(a)* skill in the use of written and spoken English;
*(b)* skill in communication;
*(c)* skills in interpersonal relationships and leadership;
*(d)* skills in counseling and providing pastoral care;
*(e)* skills in personal and group witness;
*(f)* skills in teaching;
*(g)* skills in providing effective and efficient administration; and
*(h)* skills in worship, music, and art.

The typical pattern of a Lutheran seminary program leading to ordination involves two years of full-time course work in the traditional theological disciplines, during which time a student is often engaged in some form of field work in a congregation. The great majority of students are enrolled on a full time basis, although increasingly they are persons in their later twenties and older. Either in the summer between the first and second year or after the second year, it is normal for the student to spend three months in supervised Clinical Pastoral Education (CPE). With few exceptions, CPE is undertaken in a hospital or similar setting. The third year is a 9- to 12-month internship in which a candidate serves on a full-time basis and under the supervision of an experienced pastor in a congregation. A committee of congregational members assists the seminarian through giving constructive advice about the person's performance, and a seminary faculty member is in regular contact with the seminarian and the supervising pastor. The fourth year is a return to the seminary for course work undertaken in the light of the internship year and the knowledge-skills contents. Lectures are the usual mode in the classroom but methodologies vary among and within seminaries.

The "knowledge content" approach in Lutheran theological education supposes that no matter who the students are or what methods are employed, students will arrive at the same answers, and those answers will coincide with what Lutherans have always believed, taught, and confessed. Regardless of method or personal stance, Lutheran seminary professors are expected to lead students to the predictable Lutheran answers to theological questions. On the other hand, emphasis on the "skill content" moves in the direction of the increased professionalization of theological education. The prevalent model for ministry in Lutheran and other "mainline" Protestant denominations is based on ministry as a profession with certain competencies and skills at the expense of both "knowledge content" and personal involvement. The delicate balance among knowledge, skill, and personality are being threatened in the seminary curriculum and in the formation of persons for ministry. The enumeration of "knowledge content" indicates that persons are being prepared to know and interact with society as a whole, while "skill content" puts at the forefront the ministry within serving, administering, and giving oversight to Lutheran congregations and church bodies. We seem to be moving in two worthy directions simultaneously. No wonder the much desired coherence and unity in Lutheran theological education is so elusive.

Theological educators struggle to integrate the theological disciplines and the "contents" of knowledge and skill through constant curricular change. Most of the changes, however, seem to fix on the sequencing of courses. There is little movement in the direction of interdisciplinary offerings. For all practical purposes, the nearly year-long internship and the three-month CPE remain the only major ways in which experiential learning is made part of the curriculum, and in both cases the student is away from campus and in contact with very few faculty.

Recent concern on the part of students about increasing spirituality in their seminary education and community life has pushed faculty and administrators to consider the person who is being educated as well as the contents being proffered in education. The emerging task is to consider how to integrate the student rather than integrate the subjects of the curriculum as a matter of high priority. This step will require extended reexamination of the curriculum, methods, and contexts of theological education. While the rise of such concerns from within the seminary communities is welcomed, there are other factors which shove us toward dealing creatively with confusion.

The greatest pressures for change in Lutheran theological education come from American culture. Challenges are being issued by the intellectual, cultural, and religious dimensions of contemporary America in several ways. Some critics characterize these trends as paganization, others as secularism, and still others as pluralism. Regardless of the terms used, Lutheran seminary faculty and administrators simply have to realize that for the first time in the church's history in the United States, we are defining our proper context not as Europe but as America. Lutherans are recognizing, often with reluctance and even pain, that the whole of American society is the proper context for our mission. The ministry of the Lutheran churches is expanding to address the individual and collective needs of a society which is already and is becoming increasingly pluralistic in composition and attitudes.

As the Lutheran churches seek to meet the challenges presented by racism, sexism, ageism, and classism, we need to be intentional in modeling new forms of the new life together in the body of Christ. Clearly, such an overall challenge and response will call on theological educators to recognize that for the most part our present processes used for ministerial formation are monocultural. It comes as a jolt to many to realize how outdated and inadequate is the "one world" ideological thesis which suggests that there is only one Christian family, and hence only one Christian story.

In the past five years considerable effort has been given to broadening the theological education program to equip the leadership of the church for ministry among the many different peoples who constitute the American multicultural context. Christian identity and cultural identification are being explored in new ways in our seminaries. A number of programs have been developed for Hispanic ministry. One seminary has developed a first professional degree program with a concentration in cross-cultural studies. Each seminary has at least one required course in multicultural concerns, and growing numbers of students are participating in study-travel seminars in Central and South America, Asia, and Africa.

As commendable as these efforts may be, they do not address directly the need to prepare persons for ministry in predominantly black congregations and communities. Just for starters, we need more attention, resources, and participation in internships in black congregations, black-oriented communities, and black-based hospitals and clinical settings. There is a pressing need for students to engage seriously and experientially in understanding liberation theology, ecclesiology from black perspectives, and black survival skills in predominantly white settings. While that might muddy the waters of theological education even more, I think we have the capacity to bring clarity and new structures into being. As we think about the prospects, a brief description of black theological education in the United States may be helpful.

## The State of Black Theological Education

"Black theological education" in this context refers to the processes aimed at developing leaders for the "black church." And by "black church," I mean black Christian communities of many denominations. Nearly nine of every ten American black Christians worship within all-black congregations. The 17.5 million black Christians belong to a constellation of 25 denominations, most of which are part of what is called the "historic black churches." [1] Many of the other black Christians, including Lutherans, who belong to racially mixed denominations or congregations also feel that they are part of the black church even though their membership is not officially with a historically black body. They feel kinship and identity with the black church because they are rooted socially in the black community, and feel accountable to the power and presence of the black church in that community. C. Eric Lincoln reminds us,

> To understand the power of the Black church it must first be understood that there is no distinction between the Black church and the Black community. The church is the spiritual face of the Black community, and whether one is a "church member" or not is beside the point in the assessment of the importance and meaning of the Black church. . . . The Black church, then, is in some sense a "universal church" claiming and representing all Blacks out of a long tradition that looks back to the time when there was only the Black church to bear witness to "who" or "what" a man was as he stood at the bar of his community. The church still accepts a broad gauge responsibility for the Black community inside and outside its formal communion. No one can die "outside the Black church" if he is Black. No matter how notorious one's life on earth, the church claims its own at death—and with appropriate ceremony. [2]

Because of more than two centuries of racial isolation, Christian belief and practice among blacks and whites in the United States differ significantly. Blacks in predominantly white denominations or congregations may discover that they share core beliefs and prefer practices more in keeping with the historic black churches than with those of the denominations in which they hold membership. Perhaps Gayraud Wilmore explains this paradox when he observes that the black church is "the last bastion of ethnic particularity of the Afro-American community in the United States, combining in a variegated tapestry of older and newer beliefs, ideologies, mythologies, attenuated cultural symbols, and social roles, perceptions of reality and patterns of behavior, those elements which add up to what it means to be Black—that indefinable quality of Black Christianity that is the same and yet so different from the standard brand of Christianity in America." [3]

Black theological education, then, is a distinct, perhaps unique enterprise insofar as it pursues the particular goal of preparing persons for the black church regardless of the similarities it may have to white theological education. In fact, the term "theological education" itself does not capture the full meaning of preparation for ordained ministry much less for lay professional ministries in the black church. The normal process of ministerial formation in the black church would include a generous combination of the following:

*(a)* service as a junior deacon;
*(b)* service as a deacon;
*(c)* a dramatic call by the Holy Spirit to ministry;
*(d)* proven record as a lay congregational leader;
*(e)* evidence of personal maturity and sound moral judgment;
*(f)* license to preach;
*(g)* ordination; and
*(h)* some education in a Bible college.

That is a significantly different route to ordination than the standard Lutheran procedure! Generally, graduate-level theological education in a seminary or divinity school is a normal requirement for ordination in middle-class black denominations. As might be anticipated, the black church has devoted only a small portion of its financial resources to graduate-level theological education, for, when specified, educational standards for ministry usually do not include receiving the Master of Divinity or equivalent degrees. The whole notion of academic theological education is viewed somewhat circumspectly. Are educated preachers really believers, the black church asks of the "God of our weary years and silent tears"? Can educated preachers lead in the manner which has been forged and tempered in the cauldrons of the experience of the black poor? Will educated black preachers be threatened by the emotional freedom of the black masses or the games brothers and sisters play in black congregations? Can the educated black preacher bring learning to ministry without imposing white culture on the community through the pulpit? Does the education of black pastors, especially in institutions and/or fields dominated by white ideology, distance them from the black community? Obviously, the questions have to deal with the resonances and the shared life between the black minister and the black community.

James Cone summarizes the challenge presented by the black church to theological education when he says, "The absence of a creative theological consciousness has had its impact on theological education in the Black church. Most Black churches do not support their theological schools, because they do not regard theology as essential to their mission. As they see it, their task is to preach the gospel without critically asking, what is the gospel and how is it related to Black life? Black churches tend to assume that everybody knows what the gospel is, even without asking about its primary meaning."[4] Among the prices which the black church is paying for not attending to critical theological reflection and growing theological consciousness, the black church has almost forgotten its historical and theological identity. Black church life and theological education have not focused on issues which are important to the black church such as its sociopolitical identity or the relationship of the American black Christian tradition to whatever is meant by the apostolic tradition or to African Christian traditions or to other Christian churches in the world.

Despite the black church's neglect of graduate-level theological education, there are several outstanding predominantly black seminaries in the United States, including the Howard University Divinity School, Interdenominational Theological Center, Virginia Union University of Theology, Hood Theological Seminary, and Payne Theological Seminary. These institutions are vitally important to the development of ordained leaders for the black church. But the number of seminaries needs to be placed in relation to the number of black persons preparing for ordained ministry. From 1970 to 1985 there was a dramatic increase in the number of persons in the U.S. seminaries. In 1970 there were only 808 black students enrolled in seminary-level programs leading to ordination, but by 1984 there had been a 261% increase to 2,917 persons. That huge jump was largely in the black-oriented seminaries, for the increase of black candidates in predominantly white institutions increased from 2.6% to 5.2% of total enrollments.[5] But white schools tend to be much larger than black institutions. The majority of black candidates for the Master of Divinity degree (76.8% or 2,272 in 1985) are at predominantly white seminaries and divinity schools, while 677 (23.2%) are in black schools. The gross numbers disclose that a significant majority of black leaders are being educated in nonblack environments, through curricula which allow scant, if any, room for black identity, multicultural concerns, and black ministry.

How do the statistics correlate to the needs? The number of black students in degree programs is troublingly few when we see those needs. The 1982-83 *Factbook of the Association of Theological Schools* puts the situation this way: "The 1980 census [of the United States] estimated that Blacks were 11.7% of the U.S. population. If theological schools enrolled this proportion there would be 6,156 Black students rather than the 2,576 registered in 1982."[6]

Some further notes need to be sounded. One is that a disproportionate number of black seminarians are enrolled as "special" or "unclassified" students. Often that indicates they are not taking a full-time course load and are working to support themselves and their families, and/or that they have not obtained the necessary church endorsements required by some denominations, such as the Lutheran bodies. Frankly, many of these candidates do not complete their degree programs. Second, an increasing number of women, both black and white, are entering seminary. That is fine and to be encouraged, but we need to ask about the results, particularly for black persons. In 1972, for example, there were 89 women enrolled in programs leading to ordination. By 1984 the number multiplied to 735 or 25.2% of all black students. Yet despite a critical need for better prepared leadership in the black churches (and their predominantly white counterparts), the ordination of black women has proceeded with the painful "deliberate speed" we know only too well.

Black seminary curricula are similar to those in white seminaries. The overall pattern of studies includes an introduction to biblical studies, church history, and theology. There is, as indicated, less emphasis on the historical rootage of the black church or black liberation theology that one might expect or hope for. The real core is on practical or applied theology. While liberation theology may have a limited role in the formal structure of the curriculum, it is taught cognitively and experientially in the form of the Christian faith as appropriated by ordinary black folk over the generations. The black seminary classroom is a laboratory for the black Christian experience in which the findings of daily life are brought together with the stuff of academic training. The content of the black community's faith is regarded less as a deposit or quantity to be acquired or learned and more of a style of living together in harmony.

Most black American pastors are bivocational or dual occupational. That is, they have full-time ministerial responsibilities in a congregation and a full-time secular job. It is to be expected that the majority of students in black seminaries are pastors of small congregations and may hold jobs as well as attend classes. Black theological education becomes a matter of education through participation in leadership instead of education as a preparation to begin a leadership position after graduation. That makes black theological education more learner-oriented based on the needs expressed by the student who is already in the context of leadership than it does on a "knowledge-skill content" to be applied at a later date. Black educational philosophy tends to rest on the pillars of self-knowledge and mutual understanding. Our methodology is not naturally that of the lecture-monolog but of the sharing dialog in which professor and seminarian learn together. The black style of theological education is encouraging, nurturing, and supportive of the students' needs and experience. In that way, our educational method bears a close resemblance to the style of black church life. Also consistent with the black church is the emphasis on preaching. Black theological education gives the art of preaching a higher priority than it gives critical reflection on philosophical-theological issues.

Beyond their educational roles, the black seminaries often have symbolic significance. They are the assembling points for black religious elders, the *shamans* of black Christianity. The institutions are or have been "homes" for respected persons such as Howard Thurman, Mordecai Johnson, Lawrence Jones, C. Eric Lincoln, Charles Copher, Major Jones, Henry Mitchell, Harry V. Richardson, Charles Shelby Rooks, Cain Felder, and many others. While there has been a drain of outstanding black religious scholars and educators from black seminaries, all contemporary black religious leaders recognize the significance of the theological education which takes place in those institutions.

I can only point toward some factors which I see as making major impacts on black seminaries. First, the seminaries bear heavy responsibilities in providing continuing education to a large number of black religious leaders, many of whom have little formal education. Faculty resources are thereby severely overextended. Second, there is a scarcity of faculty necessary to provide advanced graduate study in theology in such programs as those leading to the Doctor of Ministry, second-profession masters levels, and Doctor of Philosophy. Third, and in logical harmony with the first two, there is a lack of adequate human and fiscal resources, especially those which might be generated from the historic black churches. Given these factors, it is no surprise to recall that the majority of black persons studying in degree programs leading to ordination are enrolled in predominantly white schools. (A few of these schools, incidentally, are related to denominations with sizable black memberships, e.g., the United Methodist Church and the American Baptist Church, and others are either only loosely related or unrelated to church bodies, e.g., Union Theological Seminary [New York], Yale Divinity School, and Harvard Divinity School.) Some of these seminaries and divinity schools have developed programs of black studies which are intended to prepare leaders with specific and necessary competencies for leadership in the black church and its wider community. Many outstanding black scholars teach in these institutions, e.g., James Cone, Cornel West, Leon Watts, Preston Williams, J. Deotis Roberts, Vincent Harding, Albert Robateau, Gayraud Wilmore, William Wately, Luther Smith, Herbert O. Edwards, Henry Young, Peter Nash, and Peter Paris.

Those who teach in predominantly white institutions assume a special responsibility in that they help their schools to adjust resources to meet the needs of the black students, black church, and black community. Through their teaching, writing, and example, they are building bridges between white and black approaches to ministerial formation.

What about Lutherans? In 1985 there were 109 black students enrolled in the seminaries of the ELCA. Look at the figure again, because of those 109 persons, the majority (66) were not preparing for ordained ministry in any of the Lutheran churches. So there were only 43 black women and men who were seeking to be Lutheran pastors. And faculty members? The score is no better: four black scholars are on the faculties of Lutheran seminaries at this point.[7] Perhaps my comment about black theological education in Lutheran circles as being in a state of crisis as well as confusion was ridiculously mild. The processes of black theological education in predominantly white, and that includes Lutheran American, institutions, has been hampered by some of the following elements:

(a) the lack of a reasonable number of black students, faculty and administrators who could make an impact on all aspects of seminary life;

(b) the lack of consistent attention to the spiritual and personal formation of black students together with assistance in helping them shape and/or maintain their primary black identity and culture;

(c) the lack of a curriculum which makes adequate use of or even recognizes the black church and the black poor community as a context for theological education and praxis;

(d) the failure of the teaching methodologies and perhaps the traditional structures of the theological disciplines as handled in the predominantly white institutions to help students understand how such study may contribute directly to the liberation of oppressed people and how to minister to them; and

(e) the existence of personal racial prejudice and discriminatory behavior on the parts of influential persons in the seminary communities.

## Black Components in Ministry

So far I have laid out some issues, reviewed procedures, and cited some aspects about Lutheran, white, and black theological educations. Before I can open the way to possible points of synthesis and creative results from the confusion, we need to examine some distinctively black components in ministry. Within the whole people of God there are at least three discrete yet interrelated models which impact our approach to theological education for ministerial formation. The three models are so closely interrelated that they can be compared to the overlapping circles in one of the traditional symbols for the Trinity. The models are *priest, prophet,* and *civic leader.* Consider *priest* first. Of course, the concept has a biblical basis, rooted in the Old Testament's holy nation and royal priesthood, the one who comes from out of that community to stand before God on behalf of the people. The priest gathers the anxieties and hopes, the brokenness and aspirations of the community and even the world, offering them to the Lord for healing and wholeness. The New Testament vision of Jesus as the Lamb of God and the High Priest, the church as the royal priesthood, and its leaders as commissioned by Christ's Spirit to proclaim the message of reconciliation to the world gives us a Christ-centered priesthood. Now, what is a contemporary model for black Christians for a minister as priest? The priestly minister is a sacramental person with sacral authority possessing a existential knowledge, that is, the wisdom of God. The priest serves the community of the faithful by exemplifying a commitment to God and the faith which transcends empirical reality. Further, the priest is a Christian leader who is steeped in the nonrational, intuitive, and transcendent aspects of the Christian religion, and is able to inspire and be inspired by the sorrows and joys of God's people. Perhaps we could summarize the priestly circle by saying that it suggests the vertical dimension of ministry.

*Prophet* is the second model. Biblically, the prophet is the forth-teller, the speaker of the Word of the Lord to those inside and outside of the community of faith, addressing them in their own language about the issues of daily life, of justice and righteousness, of the impact of God's will and vision on human affairs. The message may be as direct and tough as Amos's, as compassionate and yearning as Hosea's, as energizing and promising as Deutero-Isaiah's. Jesus, obviously, is the prophet-preacher, forth-teller, the prophetic messenger and message of God. The New Testament congregations recognized prophet-preachers as charismatic, Spirit-gifted announcers of God's justice, mercy, and kingdom. In contemporary terms, the minister as prophet is recognized by the faithful to have charismatic authority and the power of the Spirit to speak the Word of God with judgment and grace so as to move the hearts, minds, and hands of women and men. That makes the prophetic minister an agent engaged in the liberation of the oppressed and oppressors from the bondages to the distortions of power. The black prophet-minister announces the will of God, names the slaveries and the pharaohs, points toward the results of defying God, and the promises of reconciling peace in Christ. Our prophet-preachers break the silence of those shoved to the margins of society. They are the voices of the voiceless, speaking for them and to them, and being spoken to by the people as only a black congregation can urge the preacher to tell God's truth. The prophet circle suggests the horizontal dimensions of ministry reaching into the congregations and the wider society.

The minister as *community-civic leader,* the third circle in the black models, is the one least understood by whites. Its biblical roots combine several factors. One element derives from some of the prophets. Elisha, Proto-Isaiah, and Jeremiah are among those who were public figures in conjunction with their roles as prophets, yet who were also recognized as advocates and advisors on policy and practice. Elisha criticized and aided kings, Isaiah warned Ahaz and helped Hezekiah; Jeremiah did the same for Zedekiah and Gedaliah. They were not only nay-sayers but active members of the social structure who spoke forthrightly, putting their reputations and lives on the line for justice. A second element is that of the "sage." The wise in Israel were those who discerned the will and ways of God in the ways of nature, history, and institutional structures. They could be counselors to kings, teachers to officials, or righteous spokespersons who rendered practical insights to society. Since the "fear of the Lord is the beginning of wisdom" (Prov. 9:10), the sage is a profoundly religious figure who opens the way for involved persons to see the will of God within situations. Witness is another biblical factor in the function of the black ministry leader. The word carries the double-edged meaning of being visible and being martyred. Remember Daniel and his companions, the post-resurrection stand of Peter, James and John, Paul before Festus and Jason in front of the Ephesian mob? Jesus is the model, too. After all, he spoke eloquently in parables, laid bare the signs of the coming kingdom, and is the faithful witness-martyr. And we know right well how the circle of civic leader-ministers fit into the black church. Just hear the names: Adam Clayton Powell, Jesse Jackson, Hosea Williams, Martin Luther King Jr. The civic leader-minister combines a thorough knowledge of the ways in which society operates, a theological approach to political-economic power structures, and courage to speak God's will in public arenas, derives nourishment and support from the black church; uses adroitly the means of communication in society; and liberates men and women to see and do God's justice in God's world.

The three circles of black ministry are authorized by the faith, history, and hopes of black Christians. We look for persons who relate the sacred and secular disciplines so as to manifest the whole message of God to the whole world, a message that deals with daily bread and work along with eternal peace and everlasting life. Black Christians empower such leaders to exercise the ministry of the whole people of God, yet who are accountable to the faithful. In return, the royal priesthood gives spiritual and material support, patience and encouragement to its ordained and lay leaders. I am convinced that such a black understanding of ministry is a gift which we can share with the rest of the holy, catholic, and apostolic church, and that theological education of black persons and white persons ought to include those circles. And that brings us to synthesis.

## Black and Lutheran Theological Education: Toward Synthesis

Let's begin to put the pieces together. The church stands today as it always has: in a changing world. The 16th and 17th centuries are long since gone, yet we need both to keep and to change the heritages which we have gained from those years and those ancestors. In the midst of change the church's constant mission is to interpret the event of Jesus Christ to the world and to intercede in his name for a world that is materially and spiritually in need. While our seminary faculties duly affirm in principle a relationship between Christian theology and the life of the church, academic theology in our seminaries tends to view the ministries of warm-bodied, living, ordinary Christians as mere addenda to the really interesting and important stuff of advanced, technical scholarship. The ministry of the whole people of God in the world which cries out for the grace of God is ignored or demeaned. Both black and Lutheran theological education prize theology. Theology is our formal confessional outlook which determines the direction of the curriculum and its programs. As goes the theological interpretation of our stance before God and the world, so goes the pattern for theological education.

In a changing world a theology which is responsible to God and to its own content will give increasing attention to making life more human. Plainly, the patterns of theological education ought to follow that trend. That is to say, theological education needs to be informed by the cries of the oppressed throughout the world. If you think that I am saying that theological education itself needs to be liberated from its own bondage and must be part of God's liberating message, you are right. For Lutherans, that will be tough to accept. Part of the difficulty is that Lutherans can no longer afford just to talk in high-sounding terms; our theological education must become intentionally ecumenical and incorporate indigenous understandings of the historical and contemporary church. And if you think that I am saying that Lutherans have to incorporate and value the religious experiences of people of color, you are right again.

Dare we think that the black Christian tradition is a significant resource for the redevelopment of theological education? Our sojourn in Africa and America has been marked by suffering, pain, and yet more suffering. While we fully affirm and share the concern of our white sisters and brothers for the spiritual dimension of the gospel, we say that is but one dimension of the good news. Are not black Christians among the growing majority of Christians prepared by the realities of our existence and our reading of the Bible to recognize the material dimension of the gospel? We have long lived by a wholistic gospel in order to match the sufferings of our race. Protest as well as healing, liberation as well as reconciliation are inherent in our personal faith and in the witness of the church.

Dare we think that God may have prepared the black churches of Africa and America through the sufferings of our ancestors and contemporaries in order to make a redemptive witness at this time? When we black folk excavate our African roots, we participate in a wholistic view of reality. When we are at home with ourselves and our culture, when we stop trying to be other than we are in order to blend in, then we are able to be whole in faith and action. When we come to that African, black-based unity, then we may even say that we are liberated. Such an awareness is the particular gift of the black laity. As the old saying goes, "I know I got a home in heaven, but I ain't homesick yet."

Dare we affirm the black genius? I think we must for ourselves, the church, and the world.

The black genius affirms life as a whole, both body and spirit. The splits between sacred and secular, holy and profane, piety and activism are unnatural, foreign for us.

The black genius, when liberated from our contemporary social environment, places the value of human life over property, and chooses community-building over community-manipulation.

The black genius has the ability and the experience to transmute personal and group suffering into moral victories. We know the meaning of the theology of the cross!

The black genius has led the members of the black community to surround one another with love and the blessed ties that bind in tough, even impossibly hard times. Our tragic history has led us to choose community and life over isolating despair and death.

I put all this together and claim that black people have a cultural, God-given sense of priorities which can enrich theological education for ministerial formation which preserves and also transcends our identity and unique place in God's eternal will.

To synthesize traditional black and traditional Lutheran approaches in theological education is more necessary than it is difficult. Black Lutherans have feet planted firmly in both our black Christian tradition and our Lutheran confessional heritage. While cultural transcendence and full inclusiveness in the body of Christ are meaningful goals, the immediate future will continue the racial isolation of blacks from whites. Synthesis will be difficult because the anthropology and educational theory of the black Christian community and the white Lutheran community are, at least in part, distinctly different. Traditional Lutheran anthropology and educational theory emphasize sin as a hostility and rebellion against God which corrupts all human intentions and actions. Only massive divine intervention can savingly change the human condition. That intervention takes the form of the Word of God as revealed in Scripture, incarnated in Jesus, and sustained through the power of the Holy Spirit. The goal of traditional Lutheran education is to achieve doctrinal clarity about the "pure teaching" of the Word. So Lutherans stress authoritative instruction based on the Scripture, interpreted and taught by officially recognized and accountable leaders. In fact, Lutherans tend to elevate Martin Luther (and some of his associates), the *Book of Concord,* and a cluster of doctrines seen almost solely through Lutheran lenses (e.g., justification, law/gospel, and two kingdoms) to the level of being even greater authorities than the Scripture.

Black Lutherans share with white Lutherans some of the same approaches to education, but there are differences. A black Christian world view is depicted most adequately in the biblical doctrine of the parenthood of God and the kinship of all peoples. Black Christians ground themselves in a biblical anthropology which affirms the equality of all people under God's just and loving rule, regardless of race or other natural conditions. Perhaps it may be somewhat exaggerated, but there is truth in saying that white Lutherans see all humans as equal sinners, while black Lutherans see humans as equal participants in being in the image and likeness of God. Consequently, education in the black community deals less with getting the right answers than with the quest for human freedom and justice in order to realize that God-based equality for all people. So we are theologically serious in struggling to overcome the sin of dehumanizing, God-denying, white racism.

It is significant that black Lutherans, situated at the margins of a predominantly white communion, have espoused no radical doctrine of sin that implicates blacks and whites in the same way. Black Christianity distinguishes the "sins" of black people from the "sin" of white racism, and states that the latter is far more wretched. Black folk theology, we can say, is a theological ethic or a political theology which begins with concern for liberation and ends with reconciliation. From a black Christian perspective, racism in America has created "a climate between Blacks and Whites in which Whites cannot forgive. Yet there can be no liberation for Blacks or Whites unless Whites repent of the sin of racism—both personal and social. There can be no reconciliation between Blacks and Whites unless Blacks forgive."[8] Black Lutherans need to work out correlations between the black theological ethic and the traditional Lutheran view of sin if meaningful dialog is to begin between white and black Lutherans. While Lutheran theological education seeks to develop leaders who possess certain forms of knowledge and who have certain skills, black theological education is concerned primarily with the development of the person's spirit, personality, and capacity to make informed, inspired decisions. Lutheran theological education prepares leaders with highly developed senses of accountability to the institutional structures beyond the congregation and local community, while black theological education recognizes and often might celebrate charismatic leadership which can defy the power structures which congregations and communities experience as oppressive.

The task of synthesizing black and Lutheran approaches in theological education calls for more formal research and plenty of soul-searching, but I think Lutherans in the United States are ready to take four programmatic initiatives:

1. Lutheran seminaries should attempt to develop cooperative programs with predominantly black seminaries. The latter can serve as theological resource centers for ministerial formation by sharing faculty members, and in bringing the Lutherans into collegial contacts with black churches and denominations in which the Lutherans are the learners. We should be clear that the effort is not intended to lure black candidates for ministry into the Lutheran church.

2. Lutheran churches in the United States should develop at least one resource center for black theological education and mission outreach. That center should provide such services as theological education by extension, internship supervision, parish-based Clinical Pastoral Education, urban and rural residencies, short-term lay theological education, and forums for interdisciplinary approaches to black ministry. This center is intended not

to segregate blacks and black ministry, but to provide focus and depth, to be a resource to the whole church.

3. Lutheran churches should develop a program for older, second-career black persons who are mature Christians with indigenous leadership qualities. The program should not require a bachelor's degree for admission, nor should certification for ministry be based on the persons' receiving the master of divinity degree. We already have such an option, but the ways through the maze to get to the goal are complex and discouraging.

4. Lutheran churches in the United States should develop a program of global theological education which will facilitate sharing between African and African-American Lutherans for the purpose of critical reflection and planning for mission.

These are just four achievable steps which can start us on the way to synthesis not only in theological education, but for liberation and reconciliation among black and white Lutherans.

## Principles for a Black and Lutheran Theological Education for Ministerial Formation

In order to have a synthesis and a future which has integrity for black and white Lutheran Christians, I propose that we consider some principles with which we may undergird our theological education for ministerial formation. I am still working out ideas, and suggest that we might consider an old-fashioned Christian-Lutheran-black-white idea for understanding ministry: *calling*. A real challenge theologically, socially, personally, and racially is the need to probe deeply into the meaning of vocation. But that might be the subject of another whole book! Keep vocation in mind, however, as I just enumerate eight principles for black and Lutheran theological education for further consideration in ministerial formation:

1. *Analysis and Synthesis:* A black and Lutheran theological education will require effective analysis and synthesis of our African and African-American cultural identity with our Lutheran heritage, thereby demonstrating that our church tradition and our culture provide some unique resources for the identity of personhood and the subsequent tasks of Christian witness.

2. *Liberation:* A black and Lutheran theological education will seek to liberate the processes of ministerial formation from overdependence on European-American theology and white theologians by increasing the identification, recruitment, preparation, and deployment of black scholars in our seminaries.

3. *Affirmation of Identity:* A black and Lutheran theological education will help learners and teachers explore their identities as children of God and members of the body of Christ. An understanding of the priesthood of believers which is operative in the black community needs to be discerned, lifted up, and related to theological education and later ministry.

4. *Consciencization:* A black and Lutheran theological education will help learners and teachers perceive the reality of social, political, economic, and religious oppression not as a world with no exits for its victims, but as a limiting situation which they can transform with the power of God. Such consciencization must become the motivating force for liberating action in the church and in the world.

5. *Contextualization:* A black and Lutheran theological education will reject any approach to the gospel which stresses universality apart from particularity. The Word of God as law must be related to the context of the people so that the gospel can free them to live as God's people in that context. Contextualization recognizes that God's self-disclosure is communicated through finite, fallible, human understandings. Thus the eventual locus of divine revelation is our personal, social, cultural, and ethnic existence. Black and Lutheran theological education will lead learners and teachers to proclaim truthfully the eternal message of God's redemptive revelation and action while reexamining and reinterpreting the vital issues of the Christian faith for the diverse situations in which people of different social, economic, and cultural circumstances live.

6. *Social Analysis:* A black and Lutheran theological education will develop the learners' and teachers' abilities to understand and challenge the economic and political structures of the world as well as the educational and theological structure of the church. Participants in such an education will confront the underlying rationalizations and powers used to justify those structures. Such a theological education will encourage the learners and teachers to develop their sociological imaginations to see that healing is mediated through social processes and structures. That approach will enable them to envision how they might use such disciplines as political science, economics, human relations, psychology, and professions such as law, medicine, social life, and political office in interdisciplinary and interprofessional manners.

7. *Pastoral Habitus:* A black and Lutheran theological education will seek to develop the learners' and teachers' understandings of a pastoral habitus which connects the heart, soul, and mind. Personality, theological stance, and pastoral style will be brought into a congruent whole. The impulse to minister will be connected with the gifts for ministry in response

to the needs of the world. Pastoral candidates will be helped to discover their own dominant spirituality and to identify ways to use their particular gifts in ministry.

8.    *Leadership Develooment:* A black and Lutheran theological education will seek to develop leaders who are priests-prophets-community figures motivated by service to the neighbor rather than ambition, upward mobility, or professional status. Leaders raised up by the Spirit and empowered by the believing community will respect and support their ministering colleagues and join with brothers and sisters in Christ to bring the reality of Christ's mighty love to the world. In turn, they will be models and inspirers for future generations of leaders.

## Far from the Last Word

*Confusion. Crisis.* These may be words which characterize theological education in general and black Lutheran theological education in particular. But we have learned that confusion and crisis are not strangers to black people. Theological education is important for the vision we have for the future. We have been able to use confusion and crisis creatively, and with God's help to make new that which others thought was worn out. We have come this far by the grace of God and are summoned to move on in faith. We intend to take that journey to the kingdom with the whole multicolored family of God, in justice and in love.

# 14
# WORSHIP AND THEOLOGY IN THE BLACK CONTEXT

# ALBERT PERO

## Worship/Witness and Theology in Contextual Correlation

**W**orship and theology are contextual, that is, they are shaped by the context within which they emerge. In America there are many factors that contribute to their contextuality; racial, ethnic, and sexual, to name a few. In this essay I will attempt to investigate and discover ways in which the Christian in a pluralistic society may come to affirm and participate in varied contextual forms of worship. Although the African-American experience with liberation theology will be the paradigm used, readers are encouraged to investigate the contextual arenas that are of primary interest to them.

The inscription inside the Statue of Liberty, entitled "The New Colossus," refers to America as the "Mother of Exiles." It concludes with these moving words:

> *"Keep ancient lands, your storied pomp!"*
> *Cries she*
> *With silent lips. "Give me your tired,*
> *your Poor,*
> *Your huddled masses yearning to breathe free.*
> *The wretched refuse of your teeming shore.*
> *Send these, the homeless, tempest-tossed to me,*
> *I lift my lamp beside the Golden Door!"*

This poem focuses on the linked problems of identity and power which have been so tragically played out on the stage of this nation's history. "Mother of Exiles" and "The New Colossus"—these symbols capture both the variety of groups and experiences out of which this nation has been hammered, and the fervent hope of many early Americans that in this land the world would see a new and more humane use of power, dedicated to the proposition that all persons are created equal.

We remind Americans that in our beginnings we were all exiles, strangers sojourning in an unfamiliar land. Even the first black persons who set foot on these shores came, as did most white persons, in the role of pilgrims, not as slaves.

However, if America became a "Mother of Exiles" for white people, she became at the same time a cruel system of bondage and inhumanity to black people. Far from finding in her a maternal acceptance, her black sons and daughters were thrust into the depth of despair, at times so hopeless that it wrung from their lips the sorrow song: "Sometimes I feel like a motherless child." What anguish is keener, what rejection more complete, or what alienation more poignant than this experience which called forth the metaphor, "motherless child"?

But that is only part of our story. For somewhere in the depth of their experiences within this great land those same black men and women found a ground of faith and hope on which to stand. Never accepting on the inside the identity forced upon them by a brutalizing white power, they also sang—even prior to emancipation—"Before I'll be a slave, I'll be buried in my grave and go home to my Lord and be free." A faith of this quality and integrity remains alive today.

There is, to be sure, a continuing dilemma of "crisis of commitment" in our country. But it is not the quarrels among blacks over the existence of God, or the debate about black power. The crisis is what it has always been since shortly after the first black Americans set foot upon these shores. It is not a crisis rooted in the black community. It is a "crisis of commitment" among white Americans who have consistently taken two steps forward toward becoming mature men and women on racial matters and one-and-a-half steps backward at the same time. The power of "The New Colossus" has never been fully committed to eliminating this monstrous racism from the life of the American people.

Though white men and women suppressed every attempt on the part of black people to be free, they failed to listen to the slaves' songs or the philosophy wrapped up in those songs. Black people not only sang to make their 15–16 hour work days easier, they sang with hope about their miseries, and gained metaphysical and eschatological insights which were impossible for most white people of that time. Consider the words of these black spirituals:

- *Didn't my Lord deliver Daniel*
  *And why not every man?*
  *He deliver'd Daniel from the lion's den,*
  *Jonah from the belly of the whale,*
  *And the Hebrew children from the fiery furnace,*
  *And why not every man?*

- *Nobody knows the trouble I've seen,*
  *Nobody knows but Jesus.*

- *Swing low, sweet chariot,*
  *Coming for to carry me home.*

- *Go down Moses*
  *Way down in Egyptland.*
  *Tell old Pharaoh*
  *To let my people go.*

- *Thro' many dangers, toils, and snares,*
  *I have already come;*
  *'Twas grace hath bro't me safe thus far,*
  *And grace will lead me home.*

  *The Lord has promised good to me,*
  *His word my hope secures;*
  *He will my shield and portion be*
  *As long as life endures.*

These lines, says Ruby Johnston, typify what the Christian religion has meant to the African-American. Authenticity cannot apply itself to the true function of black churches without taking into serious discussion their disenchantment, the destruction of all family ties, their dehumanization, rebellion, struggle for emancipation, and unique ability to commune with God through song. Their inception into "Christian America" produced this bitter and sweet fruit.

Church integration has always been a one-way street. Everything black was subordinate and inferior and would have to be given up for everything white. The white church, in its accommodation to white, middle-class society, attempted to make over black persons and their church in its own image. It also tried to force the black community into the mold of the white society to which the white church had always been in bondage and which it conceived to be the nearest thing on earth to the kingdom of God in heaven.

The black churches, which were "exiled" from the white Lutheran, Methodist, and Baptist denominations in the latter part of the 18th and early 19th centuries, borrowed heavily from the white churches which had first evangelized them and ordained their clergy. However, these black churches were able to develop their own styles of life and their own institutions. An authentic black culture and religion were germinated. Whatever may be said of the deficiencies or excesses of their preaching and brand of churchmanship, they were the preeminent expressions of the yearning for freedom and dignity by a people who had been introduced to a religion, but excluded from all but the most demanding aspect of the cultural mold of that religion.

On the other hand, the black churches which remained a part of the mainline white denominations were exiled from participation in the mainline culture. They were obliged to substitute whatever they held of their own for a system of white cultural and religion values. Thus a system developed in the black church and community that could only be a poor facsimile of the "real" thing—a second-class culture for second-class Christians.

Despite the fact that the white denominations have made a lasting contribution to these churches and to their communities by establishing hundreds of churches, schools, and colleges throughout the nation (and especially in the South), it must nevertheless be conceded that as long as these institutions remain under white control they remain unable to penetrate the white cultural accretion with a distinctive black ingredient as a viable component of the American ethos. At best, blacks have been the objects of a benevolent paternalism and have either atrophied or smothered to death in the avid embrace of the great white father. In such a situation it was inevitable that a kind of cynicism would develop on both sides.

The problem of the "whitenized" black churches today is finding how to recover their own self-respect by demythologizing the white cultural "bag" through which the faith was transmitted to them and in which they have curled themselves up so comfortably. In so doing they may discover that the essence of the Christian faith not only ultimately transcends the ethnocentric culture of white people, but that of the blacks as well; that this Christ, in whom there is neither Jew nor Greek, bond nor free, male nor female, is also neither black nor white.

Indeed, in liberating itself from the mythology of white Christianity and standing over against the suburban captivity of the white church (as it were), the "whitenized" black churches may be able to illuminate a theme from the left wing of the Protestant Reformation that the American experience has increasingly made opaque: while the church is not permitted to create its own culture alongside the secular, it does stand in a dialectical relationship to culture—more often in opposition than accommodation—as its most severe critic and reformer rather than its champion and celebrant.

This possibility rests upon what may at first appear to be a contradictory position, but is in fact a necessary concession to the perverted reality of the black religious situation in America. Before the "whitenized" black churches can immerse themselves into the mainstream of the church and perform their critical and reformatory role in relationship to the total culture, these churches must immerse themselves in a black theology and a black worship, both of which they have repudiated in the past, but for which they, nevertheless, have a peculiar responsibility.

Is this to say that the Christian faith as viewed through the black liturgical model is but another expression of an ethnocentric religion of culture? To this question we must today give a qualified affirmative answer. Qualified, because what we are seeking in the posture of black religion is temporary and transitional—a way of correcting the errors of the past and preparing the ground for the future. But we must insist that if the Christian church is to become a dynamic influence in the black community, which will continue to be beleaguered by white racism, it must become not only a religious institution, but a community organization. It must develop and embrace a theology not only as a defense against the racism of the white church and white culture, but as a necessary alternative to black worship in a flight from the dehumanizing effects of whiteness. Is it any wonder that black Christians are resisting easy and unexamined black and white relationships?

This is a hard saying that will not be readily accepted by our white Christian brethren. But the time has come when we who have accepted from their hands a religion devoid of an ethic relevant to our real situation and a culture in which we were never permitted to participate on equal terms must stand back from them to reassess our relationship to our own people and to the hostile society to which the white church continues in servile accommodation and for whose sake white Christians have betrayed us—their black brothers and sisters in Jesus Christ. We must stand back and be in a strategic exodus from this unequal engagement, this degrading, debilitating embrace, until we have recovered our own sense of identity, our true relationship to the people we serve, and until the white church is ready to enter into that partnership of life and mission which is able to renew the whole church of Christ.

There is need, then, for Christian theology to address itself to the experiences of black people, a black theology. Black theology is "that theology which arises out of the need to articulate the significance of black presence in a hostile white world. It is black people reflecting religiously on black experience, attempting to redefine the relevance of the Christian gospel for their lives."[1]

More specifically, black theology is the "theological explication of the blackness of black people" (see James Cone, *A Black Theology of Liberation,* Orbis, 1986, pp. 1-20). It explains in a religious content what it is to be black in a white world, and what black people should do about this situation. The study of black theology shows black people that Christ himself was for the liberation of the oppressed (a concept that many white theologians have omitted).

From these definitions, would one say black theology is necessary? When white people studied theology, they wrote under the assumption that blacks did not exist as a people; they were property. Reuben Sheares states, "The role or status of Blacks in relation to the Gospel or white theology was that of an outsider, perhaps lower than that of a heathen or an infidel."[2] Maybe it can be explained that the white man's theology justified the oppression of black people. They propagated the idea that God created blacks to be inferior to whites.

In the days of slavery, blacks were placed beyond or outside of white theology. They were not accepted in the fullness of the faith. Therefore in order for religion to be significant to them, blacks withdrew from the theology and the church which served to transform or convert them into sub-beings. "The independent black church emerged as a protest—a protest against the racist theology and the racist ecclesiology of the church in America."[3] The church of the slave era was an institution. Blacks were in a hostile land surrounded by a hostile people, with no way out. The church gave them hope of a better day (heaven) and a place to release the anxieties of the preceding week. "It enabled black people to survive, to function, to maintain some degree of sanity and hope; to preserve some semblance of pride and of self; to protest in the midst of a hostile environment until, in the fullness of time, alternatives, options, and strategies for dealing with the questions of freedom, justice and survival became feasible."[4]

Now blacks are emphasizing freedom on earth, and not in the hereafter. Today the black church emphasizes liberation. Is liberation today as important as survival was in the slave era? James Cone says, "The biblical God is the God who is involved in the historical process for the purpose of human liberation, and to know Him is to know what He is doing in historical events as they are related to liberation of the oppressed."[5] "The purpose of black theology is to place the actions of black people toward liberation in the Christian perspective, showing that Christ himself is participating in the black struggle for freedom."[6] It also deals with the fact that God is the liberator of the oppressed. Therefore, the importance of black theology is apparent.

The greatest movement of black liberation should come out of the church, for that is where one finds the majority of black people who still believe that one can do all things with the support of God. Thus the black church and black theology are unifying factors for the accomplishment of black liberation.

Black theology is significant not first because it is black or imaginative or ingenious, but because it is biblically, historically, and theologically authentic. Properly understood, the powerful impact of contemporary black theology, together with an appreciation of the meaning of the black experience in American history, provides one with a model for a theological revolution in this time.

Briefly stated, black theology insists that God intends for people to be free and whole, and that Jesus participated in the life of an oppressed people to help free those people and to affirm God's identification with his own suffering creation. Black theology contends that God exists where people hurt—and the meaning of hurt, oppression, and injustice has been experienced to an inordinate degree by those people in this country and the world who are not white.

Black theology is not new. When Richard Allen led blacks out of St. George's Church in Philadelphia after repeated indignities against them and formed the black Bethel Church in 1787, he was acting theologically. The black churches were theological when they risked everything to form solid links in the Underground Railroad to freedom. This theology has been conceived and transmitted in the life of black people and the black church in a largely oral tradition; what is new is its relatively recent articulation by a number of mostly young black theologians.

James H. Cone insists that his material is first of all a theology of liberation, committed to freeing God's people from oppression—and that blackness is both a concrete instance of *and* an ontological symbol for the condition of oppression. That such an understanding is not wishful racial thinking but is authoritatively biblical is illustrated in Cone's discussion of the primacy of the liberation theme in both the Old and New Testaments:

> In the Old Testament, the Liberation theme stands at the center of the Hebrew view of God. Throughout Israelite history, God is known as He who acts in history for the purpose of Israel's liberation from oppression. This is the meaning of the Exodus from Egypt, the Covenant at Sinai, the conquest and settlement of Palestine, the United Kingdom and its division, and the rise of the great prophets and the second exodus from Babylon. . . . Israel's savior is God himself, whose sovereign rule is guiding the course of human history, liberating the oppressed from the oppressors.
>
> The theme of liberation in the New Testament is present in the appearance of Jesus Christ, the Incarnate One who takes upon Himself the oppressed condition so that all men may be what God created them to be. He is the Liberator par excellence, who reveals not only who God is and what He is doing, but also who we are and what we must do about human oppression. It is not possible to encounter this man and still remain content with human captivity. . . . The Christian Gospel is the good news of the liberation of the oppressed from earthly bondage.[7]

Black theology is angry and urgent in ways hardly congenial to the Anglo-Teutonic theological idiom, but quite at home with the urgency of the Hebrew prophets and of Jesus Christ. It is particular and concrete and political in the very best and broadest sense of those words. It deals with the human situation right at the moment—in Memphis, in Harlem, in rural Alabama—and it identifies the oppressors by name. This happens in ways that make white people uncomfortable, but again in a tradition well known to us from the prophetic ministries of Amos and Hosea and Jesus of Nazareth.

The black experience provides a compelling analogy to the early Christian community—small, persecuted, existing in a hostile environment, racially and religiously oppressed but radically committed to freedom and human wholeness. When Jesus came to the Jews and Gentiles, when Paul went later to the Greeks, both were proclaiming to nations held under the powerful domination of the Roman empire that human liberation was nevertheless possible. In the centuries immediately following the life of Christ, the struggles of the early church in Rome—urban, hidden, scorned, persecuted—formed an experience for which the black church is a contemporary theological model.

In spite of centuries of suffering, three qualities of the black religious tradition have persisted in affirming life in the face of death and demonstrate what the church as a whole ought to be and do. These qualities are expressed by the church in its roles as *liberator, celebrant,* and *servant.*

In his article "The Genius of the Black Church," William B. McClain suggests the ways in which the black church performs these roles. First, he says, is its genuine and persistent efforts toward humanizing the social order and its refusal to accept a Christian message that does not contribute directly toward that end. Second is the free and responsive character of the black worship service, exhibiting a profound joy and a genuine commitment to life instead of death. Finally, in the black church there is no priestly-prophetic dichotomy—that is, the prophetic judgment over the institutions of society has never given way completely to a purely priestly, soul-saving function. McClain concludes:

> The genius of the black church is that it has brought a people through the torture chamber of the past two centuries. It has sustained black people throughout the history of the black man in this nation with a Gospel that has been interpreted without a dichotomy of social-religious, soul-body, priestly-prophetic categories. It declares that God's humanizing activity in the world is the tearing down of old systems that dehumanize and enslave and the building up of new structures and institutions to make the ordering of life more just, peaceful, and human. Such structures and institutions must be responsive to the human needs of the dispossessed, the disinherited and the powerless, and accountable under God to all whom they exist to serve.[8]

The black church has not always had the concept of liberation as its watchword. A common view is that the church served merely as a source of survival for blacks in the era when nothing more could be hoped for and that it wrongly diverted imagination from this world's struggles to rewards in the world to come.

The Reverend James Lawson, however, insists that even during that earlier period the black church was extremely ingenious and creative in the methods it used for survival. In the context of black worship, a code language was developed, so that "Steal Away to Jesus" was both a folk spiritual *and* a political exhortation to steal away from slavery to freedom. The central place of black Christians, both slave and free, in the Underground Railroad and the abolition of slavery—long neglected or ignored—is beginning to be acknowledged. Even though the period from about 1880 to 1940 was largely a period of accommodation by the black church to white society, there were nevertheless many exceptions, and it was during this time that the black church served as the basis upon which many mutual benevolent societies, fraternal organizations, and cultural activities, so necessary to survival, were established.

Now, however, the option of liberation—always a dear and distant hope—is possible and real, and the black church conceives of its mission accordingly. The Reverend Reuben Sheares II articulates this perspective:

As the Black church chooses to move beyond white theology, it also becomes necessary for it to move beyond a strategy or a theology of survival. The time is already here when to survive *per se* is not enough. The future well-being of black people in America requires liberation beyond survival; survival plus a quality of life and being—fullness of life for every man. Certainly it is recognized that survival can be a rather passive or drab affair, for all of its life-sustaining validity. . . . One can survive in life, without actualizing life or even having the opportunity to actualize life and self. Black people have survived. But the struggle for liberation is now upon us. The theology of survival must now flow into a theology of liberation, beyond white theology.[9]

That the liberation movement itself defines the Christian church is expressed best by the Reverend Albert Cleage Jr., minister of the Shrine of the Black Madonna in Detroit: "I address my remarks to those who believe in the movement but do not understand that the movement is the Christian Church in the twentieth century and that the Christian Church cannot truly be the church until it also becomes the movement."[10]

God has always been a God of liberation. The truth of that was understood by the ancient Hebrews and has been experienced and proclaimed once again by black Christians in America.

The celebrative style of the black religious experience is undoubtedly rooted in its African past, where all things were mythical, musical, and close to the gods. This past, of course, is unique and cannot be duplicated by white Christians. However, to the extent that the joy expressed in the black church against impossible odds is an affirmation of God's love in spite of all, the black church serves as a theological model for white Christians.

Part of the genius of the black church has always been its centrality in the lives of its people. Where the worship service is the central experience of the week rather than a polite observance at the end of it, there God is fully present and celebrated in the lives of his creatures.

Only the church that becomes a servant, however, can liberate its people and celebrate God's love. As Jesus was a "man for others," so the church must assume a servant role if it is to be the church.

The black church has served the real needs of its people in a sacrificial way from the very beginning. More recently and more visibly, it has been the focus first of the civil rights movements, then of broader-based coalitions in the struggle for economic empowerment, educational and employment opportunities, and a fair share in the decision-making processes.

From the perspective of the "brown" Christian, Cesar Chavez exemplifies this servanthood in a powerful way. His gentle, loving, and utterly determined persistence in seeking a fuller, more human life for migrant farm workers demonstrates the force of a Christian community committed to freedom. Says a close associate of Chavez:

> I think that the farm worker giving himself for his community comes about as close as you can get to real discipleship. You can't just sit around and enjoy Christ's sacrifice. Yet how many Christians have joined the church prepared to learn how to sacrifice themselves for others?
> The church could be carrying on Jesus' work as a community able to serve others. I don't mean individuals acting as people who want to serve, I mean *being servants*—placing yourself in the service of the oppressed.[11]

Liberation, celebration, servanthood—these are the cornerstones of any theology worthy of the Christian faith, and the model for their realization comes to us more clearly from a nonwhite perspective than from a white perspective.

The question of whether or not black theology can save the white church is a question for white Christians, not black ones. Blacks have little time for and less interest in such speculation, and in the final analysis only white Christians can answer it anyway.

Several black theologians nevertheless allude to the possibility of redemption for the white church, though most often in an oblique and rather doubtful way. C. Eric Lincoln writes:

> White theology suffers mortally from the sin of omission. It has sent its theologians to study in Europe where the problem isn't; or imported the best European theologians to bring us the light—but not for *our* darkness. In consequence, American theology has had few words to speak to *our* condition. White theology has not done anything for black people except to ignore them.[12]

Professor William B. McClain points out that "The white church was closed for black Christians, special services were held for them, or they were placed in 'nigger balconies'. It is a strange turn of history that the descendants of those who were seated in the 'nigger balconies' must now be the saviors (if in fact salvation is possible) for the descendants of those who created the balconies."[13] And he concludes: "The black church affirms the unity of life in the midst of seeming contradictions. When properly understood, it could lend the universality the church needs for renewal. But can niggers from the balconies become messiahs?"[14]

In writing of the National Committee of Black Churchmen, Leon W. Watts II raises the same question and the same possibility: "The National Committee of Black Churchmen is not an ecumenical organization alongside others. It is a movement of black churchmen committed first to the church of Jesus the Christ, then to the liberation of the black community. It may save Christianity in the western world by giving it back to the people." [15]

Finally, Reuben Sheares states the task facing white Christians as well as black:

> Black people and the black church exist and function beyond white theology out of necessity and as a matter of choice. But isn't it also imperative for white churchmen and the white church to move beyond white theology? The issues of survival and the liberation of man and the world confront the white church as well as the black church. It, too, shall need to disengage itself, to become a movement committed to the release of captives and the setting at liberty of those who are oppressed. For the future well being of black people, white people and all America lies beyond historic white theology. [16]

Dietrich Bonhoeffer wrote: "We are not Christ, but if we want to be Christians, we must have some share in Christ's large-heartedness by acting with responsibility and in freedom when the hour of danger comes, and by showing real sympathy that springs, not from the rear but from the liberating and redeeming love of Christ for all who suffer." [17] That may be extended to say that whites are not black (that is, oppressed), but because they are Christ's they can and must share fully in the suffering of those who are. It is at that point of redeeming love that liberation becomes possible for everyone.

We will not conclude that the black church can save the white church. That may be too much to hope for. There may be some small possibility, however, that a profound identification with the suffering and celebration expressed in the black religious experience can be of assistance to Lutherans in their attempts to correlate the kerygma to the black situation.

Indigenous churches have been in existence for centuries and they are increasing. In Africa alone there are some 6000 indigenous churches. [18] In America since the 18th century they have been integrated into European forms of religion, while others continue in traditional African ways. Many have adopted ideas from other parts of the world, or created their own free style of religion.

In spite of wide variations among black indigenous churches in America, they are in many ways similar. Minimal research will demonstrate attributes peculiar to indigenous churches: they are led by blacks, supported by blacks, and directed toward black religious concerns. This might be one of the many givens which accounts for the fact that Christianity is the fastest-growing religion among Africans, with over one-sixth of Africa's people Christian. [19] Even during slavery in the United States, black people usually worshiped separately, in their own manner and with their own black preachers.

As we have seen, the oldest independent churches began in the late 18th century as protests by educated freedmen against white churches' snobbery in the northern cities. While these churches can be categorized as indigenous, they nonetheless are similar to the white churches from which they were exiled.

After the Civil War they expanded rapidly to include masses of liberated slaves. The national Baptist conventions and the black Methodist Churches have always been loose affiliations, and since the Civil War, especially in southern states, local congregations have often been much closer to the religious ethos of Africa than are the national organizations. Even more independent are the hundreds of tiny black churches outside the major black denominations. Most of these stem from the Baptist tradition, the holiness movement, or Pentecostalism. Mass migration from the southern countryside to the northern cities in this country swelled not only the large, sophisticated, urban churches, but also produced a proliferation of radically indigenous, innovative, lower-class "storefront" churches. These comparatively new, urban "storefront" groups have been completely free of paternalistic white supervision and have sometimes returned to beliefs and practices typical of the religious underground of the West Indies. Among blacks in the United States, storefront churches tend to be most like African and West Indian indigenous churches.[20]

In the American culture, subjugation of black people came early and brutally, but Africa remained mostly self-governing until the late 19th century. Christianity was not widely accepted in Africa until well into the 20th century.

Most obviously, the worship of black indigenous churches around the world is distinctive. Whether in Africa, the West Indies, or the United States, most black worship is more exuberant and more physical than most white worship. The services of black indigenous churches tend to be long, joyful celebrations, like the traditional all-day festivals of shrines and villages in Africa. A black church usually starts when folks arrive, which means that some of the parishioners are clapping and singing long before the main service begins. Three- or four-hour services are not unusual, and worshipers try to have a "good time."

Everybody present gets involved in black worship. Black churches tend to be small, so that members can be friends. It is typical of black churches that individuals stand to "testify" to the Lord's blessings—perhaps a miracle, more often simply God's continued protection and the privilege of worship. There are plenty of official positions within the typical black church, in order to give task and status to as many members as possible. Small congregations are divided into even smaller, more intimate fellow-ships—committees, choirs, ushers, and other groups—to make sure every-body has a place in church where he or she can "feel at home."[21]

*Pageantry* is a popular element of black worship. Black church leaders are expert at using elaborate gestures, movements, robes, and other litur-gical paraphernalia to create an atmosphere of awe. Many of the worshipers in a typical church are robed. On a Sunday morning in Africa or the United States, black women can be seen hurrying to church in their white uniforms.

*Physical touch* is also integral to black worship. Among black Protes-tants, Baptism has often had special importance, partly due to their Eu-ropean Baptist heritage, but also because of the water symbolism in much African religion.[22] Communion and other orthodox sacraments tend to be replaced in black churches by novel sacraments: anointing, sprinkling, holy articles to be touched.

*Music,* both vocal and instrumental, is the staple of black worship. The songs are short, quickly mastered, and lustily sung. They are constantly revised. They carry the enthusiasm of worship: inspiring the congregation, enlivening the sermon, enabling whatever healing or ecstasy the Spirit gives. Black music is noted for its intricate rhythms, blue notes, and dis-tinctive tones and harmonies. Happy hand-clapping and foot-tapping almost invariably accompany singing, and often there is dancing, although usually quite restrained and dignified.[23]

United States spirituals are famous for their eloquence in expressing the uncanny hope of suffering black people. In Africa, too, little-known com-posers are writing thousands of spirituals. Studies of new hymn collections in West Africa have shown that most of them shout praises to God for his saving power, even though most of the people who sing them are in church because they have some critical need. They celebrate God's victorious might, even though they are still waiting to experience it.[24] This sensuous vitality despite objective misery is typified by the United States spiritual:

*Oh, nobody knows de trouble I've seen;*
  *Glory Hallelujah!*
*Sometimes I'm up, sometimes I'm down,*

*Oh, yes, Lord,*
*Sometimes I'm almost to de groun',*
*Oh, yes, Lord,*
*Oh, nobody knows de trouble I've seen,*
*Glory Hallelujah!*

*Black preaching* is drama. The black preacher is a storyteller; the "Amens" and "Praise the Lords" he evokes from the congregation remind some observers of the call and response of African storytelling.[25] Preachers usually begin in a low key, explicating Scripture verse by verse, then slowly gather their own emotions with those of their listeners, until their encouragements pass into ecstasy. James Baldwin, who was a boy preacher, described it:

> There is no music like that music, no drama like the drama of the saints rejoicing, the sinners moaning, the tambourines racing, and all those voices come together and crying holy unto the Lord. There is still for me, no pathos like the pathos of the multi-colored, worn, somehow triumphant and transfigured faces, speaking from the depths of a visible, tangible, continuing despair of the goodness of the Lord. I have never seen anything to equal the fire and excitement that sometimes, without waning, fills a church, causing the church, as Leadbelly and so many others have testified, to "rock." Nothing that has happened to me since equals the power and the glory that I sometimes felt when, in the middle of a sermon, I knew that I was somehow, by some miracle, really carrying, as they said, "the word"—when the church and I were one. Their pain and their joy were mine, and mine was theirs—they surrendered their pain and joy to me, I surrendered mine to them—and their cries of "Amen" and "Hallelujah" sustained and whipped on my soles until we all became equal, wringing wet, singing and dancing, in anguish and rejoicing, at the foot of the altar.[26]

The vital ethos of African Christianity is now being preserved and written as a theology. Black theology is very complex and not at all easy for whites and even some blacks to understand, but it is essential to the correlation of the kerygma to the black situation. There are doctrines, revelation, soteriology, and eschatology to be developed from a law/gospel Lutheran perspective, since blacks can be found in the Lutheran church. Cone's brief study is only the beginning of a necessary correlation of the kerygma to the black situation in formal theological expression.

The last part of this essay has two sections. The first is a short reflection on what seem to be the most salient aspects of black worship. The second section is more methodological in that it will correlate the "applicability" or "transferability" factor inherent in the ecumenical and interracial attempt to cross-fertilize divergent traditions.

## Some Correlational Aspects of Contexual Black Worship

*Liturgy, life and liberation.*  One can sum up the definition of the distinctiveness of the black Lutheran experience of worship in the word *liberation*. James Cone, in his important book on spirituals, says virtually the same thing:

> The slave's view of God embraced the whole in life—his joys and hopes, his sorrows and disappointments; and his basic belief was that God had not left him alone, and that his God would set him free from bondage. That is the central theological idea in black slave religion as reflected in the spirituals.[27]

Describing the liturgical meaning of this central theme he says, "Instead of testing God, they (black slaves) *ritualized* him in song and sermon."[28]

This insight suggests that many black Lutheran churches approach the traditional and basic liturgical question of relevance, the "liturgy and life" discussion, in a way diametrically opposed to mainline, white denominations. Whereas the latter churches struggle to make worship "relevant" to the rest of the week's work and play, the black experience is to make the week's work and play and struggle the stuff of worship. Put more simply: Where white Christians try to take something away with them from worship (such as "inspiration," or sermon ideas, or warm memories of moving experiences), black Lutheran Christians should be able to render that need unnecessary by what they *bring* to worship. Unquestionably any dispassionate comparison of personal anticipations and expectations concerning "going to church" on any given Sunday would reveal a vast difference between black and white. In all likelihood white Lutheran Christians would be found to go to worship with a mixture of mild interest and some strong expectation of boredom, whereas blacks would be found to approach the occasion with a high level of excitement and expectation of sharing much joy and sorrow in the context of praise. (And if it be pointed out that this may not be so true of younger, more militant blacks, it must be acknowledged for the sake of the argument that the same is true of their white counterparts.)

Another way to portray this difference is to contrast the generally active character of black worship with the more passive character of white worship. Of course this relates to the matter of spontaneity and order. But the roots of participation are not simply in the freedom of the liturgical moment. They spring from a deep commitment to bringing life to the Lord. That commitment is for the sake of the liberation of life. Again, to draw a contrast, whereas white worshipers tend to think of the relevance of worship in terms of its power to "uplift" or inspire or produce higher morals and serious discipline (all of which are finally more constricting and guilt-producing), black worshipers think of worship as an opportunity to be freed from guilt, repression, and frustration.

The most obvious implication of this set of contrasts is for the structure and style of white worship: how can life be "let in" to the liturgy? This is precisely the question that much of the so-called "celebrative" or informal, experimental worship of today is trying to answer. This is the aim of much that is nonstructured, sensitivity-oriented, folklike in terms of music, and led by the laity, in contemporary worship. The prior question, however, is how fully these techniques can translate "black" worship into white experience. That will be taken up in this essay's second main section.

*Spontaneity and the Spirit: The Role of Ritual.*    To a white spectator, one of the most obvious features of worship in the black church is its seemingly spontaneous character. This is most noticeable in the style of preaching and in the people's responsiveness to preaching and to prayer. This, in contrast to the highly structured solemn services of the white churches, has led many to suggest that what white worship needs today is a healthy dose of black freedom. Insofar as this would undoubtedly help white worship to approximate more fully the Pauline dialectic of freedom and order (1 Cor. 14:39-40), this makes considerable liturgical sense.

But black spontaneity probably needs a closer look if white Christians are properly to understand it and its liturgical functionality. For instance, such spontaneity is certainly not unexpected. In any given congregation it is probably possible to predict fairly regularly who will be spontaneous, when, and how. This is not to be cynical: the same can be said of a traditional Protestant revival or prayer meeting. This is to say, however, that as with all the gifts of the Spirit, there is an implicit order. The so-called freedom or spontaneity of black worship goes deeper than simply being permitted to shout out an "Amen." That is but a sign. What underlies it is identified by James Cone as he comments on spirituals and their relation to black worship:

> Through the song, black people were able to affirm that Spirit who was continuous with their existence as free beings; and they created a new style of religious worship. They shouted and they prayed; they preached and they sang, because *they had found something.* They encountered a new reality; a new God not enshrined in white churches and religious gatherings.[29]

The freedom that is going on in black worship is not one of its *aspects;* it is its *goal.* It is as ethical as it is liturgical. But now we can advance the discussion at least one step further.

This perspective illuminates the function of ritual or liturgy: it is to serve the order of the Spirit. It is not accidental that Paul's teachings on ethics, the gifts of the Spirit, and worship, all are to be found in the same set of chapters: 1 Corinthians 11–14. The order of the Spirit is basically a matter of communication, communion, and community. Predictably there are aspects of the Spirit's sense of order that do not look orderly to people (hence: "do not forbid speaking in tongues"—14:39), and conversely, people's disorder from time to time has to be corrected by the Spirit's order (hence my paraphrase: "everyone is in such a hurry to start his own supper . . ."—11:20). But the highest order is neither tongues nor supper, but love. Both the cultic and communal possibilities are transcended by the ethical (if we may use such distinctions). But cult and community are necessary as signs and instrumentalities. This is the meaning and importance of what seems to be spontaneity in black worship. It points to the freedom which for an oppressed people is the final truth and life. It makes possible the meeting and sharing without which love cannot function in a true and lively fashion.

If this line of reflection has merit, the question it raises for worship in the white church is the possibility that ritual and ceremony have come to function as an isolating, counterethical way, cutting worshipers off from one another and from the truth of their lives. It further suggests that even if this be the case, the answer does not lie solely in encouraging surface spontaneity (such as unplanned dialog sermons or sentence prayers), but in discovering the repressive or alternately liberating goal of worship: its ethical force. And once again, that is to speak not of its relevance but of its openness to the life that is brought into it: the life of men and women in the world and the life and presence of "God with us." That would be a vastly more important lesson to learn from black worship than how to be spontaneous, though these two levels are not unrelated.

*Poverty and Preaching.*   The thesis of this section is that the poverty of the black church has contributed to the richness of its preaching. This has happened in a number of ways.

In the first and most formal way, the relative poverty of black preachers has made them far more dependent on the Bible and on their people than those who have enjoyed the luxury of theological seminaries, courses in homiletics, and sermon-testing congregations. And this is not to say that black preaching is necessarily literalist or fundamentalist. Again, Cone says: "The Bible serves as a source for song and sermon ideas but not as an infallible authority equivalent with revelation itself."[30] It can never be forgotten by the American people how powerfully the biblical images and narratives of Martin Luther King's oratory stirred and united the black community. That was the result both of the acceptance which was his by virtue of his being a preacher and also of the deep relationship to the Bible which preaching in the black church has established.

Yet another way poverty has served biblical preaching is the relative freedom the black church has had with regard to the "distractions" of liturgical worship. In a sense, the Reformation's "centrality of the Word" in worship has been realized more effectively in the black church than in churches more lineally descended from the Reformation. This situation has freed black worship to find its source for prayer, praise, and preaching in the Bible. It is one of the more instructive phenomena of the present-day liturgical movement that it is "Catholic" churches that are, in a similar fashion, working most diligently to develop liturgical devices and resources wherein the language of the lessons gets refracted in all the texts, sung and spoken.

More important, however, is the simple fact that the poverty and oppression of the black community finds a truer mirror in the Bible, and therefore in preaching, than do opulence or even middle-class comfort. The well-known, but rarely appreciated fact that the early church (to say nothing of wandering Jewish exiles), was made up basically of poor people, has to be taken with considerable seriousness by anyone who would seek to understand an undoubted richness and effectiveness of black preaching. Just as was said in the previous section, the significance of the surface phenomena of shouting, responding, singing, crying, and laughter as homiletical possibilities, refers to a deeper reality: the congruence between the content of the biblical message and the life setting of the congregation.

*An Indigenous Music.*   The liturgical role of music is yet a further evidence of the liturgy/life, culture/religion unity that we find in the black church. Not only *is* there such a thing as black music, but that music has found its way into the church. Professor Cone's insistence on the unity between spirituals and blues, and on their common theme of liberation is suggestive as to why and how this ecclesiastical use of an indigenous music has come about. He acknowledges the fact that there is a legitimate debate as to how extensively spirituals and liberation can be linked. But corroboration for his thesis might lie closer at hand than is customarily thought. Any discussion of black, "soul," indigenous music sooner or later must come to grips with another set of experiences: the tendency of many black churches, especially middle-class ones, to borrow more classical, "white," ecclesiastical music.

The Rev. Charles G. Adams of Detroit has observed that though black churches feel free to use all styles of music, there are congregations which almost exclusively use "white" hymns and music. Such a congregation, he says, "has lost its flexibility in an overly anxious attempt to *identify wholly with white culture as a sign of emancipation.*" Aside from the fact that this is emancipation or liberation of a sort vastly different from our previous use of that term, or Cone's, the significance of this fact may be to buttress Cone's linking of black ecclesiastical music to the liberation motif: when a black congregation no longer needs liberation from slavery, it then feels free to liberate itself from its indigenous music.

This raises another dimension of this question: *Ought* black churches to use white music (if indeed there be such a thing), and *dare* white churches use black music? Already we begin to anticipate the "transferability" problem. We come upon the separatist/integration battle at the point of song. Curiously enough, within the black community that issue doesn't always produce the expected musical results. Black indigenous churches do not necessarily sing spirituals (though they may sing blues). Much of this question may turn on the generation gap, and it significantly raises a question mark over the very use of the phrase "indigenous music" to describe products of a previous century. This does not necessarily rule spirituals out of a contemporary context, as rock music's use of black music proves, but it isolates a problem which is at least similar to that found in white churches, where traditional musical styles are having no easier time in finding acceptance.

Much more could be said about music in the black church, but perhaps the most relevant matter for white churches, and a result of this indigenous character of black ecclesiastical music, is the participatory quality of music in black churches. Whether the music is congregational or produced by a large, volunteer choir, there rarely seems to be the feeling of a concertlike "performance" which is so characteristic of mainline Protestant churches. Here again, a significant concern of the Reformation has been realized: the congregation as the true choir.

In closing this section it has to be noted that the way music functions in black worship is indicative of its true liturgical role: as providing a poetic vehicle for the person to transcend the limitations and frustrations of life and truly to celebrate the liberating power of the blessed community. Cone expressed both sides of this new, liberating reality: *"I am the blues* and *my life is a spiritual,"* [31] and, "The spiritual is the community in rhythm, swinging to the movement of life." [32]

How do realities like that get expressed in the worship of white Protestantism? Holy Communion does not seem to loom large in the worship of some black churches for the very fascinating reason that the entire experience of worship is an experience of communion. This has already surfaced in a number of the quotations cited already from James Cone's book. "Black music is unity music . . . [it] is unifying because it confronts the individual with the truth of black existence and affirms that black being is possible only in a communal context." [33]

At this juncture it will be helpful to recall our previous reflection on the communal aspects of the "order of the Spirit," and to contrast this aspect with the individualistic feeling of white worship. This will provide a new perspective on the liturgical efforts now being made at the "kiss of peace" or elsewhere in the liturgy, to symbolize this communal, corporate nature of worship. Interestingly enough, black churches seem to have no need of all the devices and even gimmicks that white churches are developing for this purpose. The "brothers and sisters" do not have to be coaxed into shaking hands!

## The Nonapplicability Factor

There are some cautions that should be observed in setting up a black/white dialog concerning worship and theology in correlational context. They are grouped here under the rubric of "nonapplicability." Just as the minority liberation movements with their emphasis on pluralism are insisting that it is neither necessary nor possible to harmonize all differences, so also in any comparison of worship styles across the black/white gap it is necessary to take seriously the limitations of exchanging styles and shapes of worship. There are bound to be factors in both the black and white churches which make unqualified sharing an impossibility—and for documentary evidence in this area, any study of this issue should include (which this essay does not) a review of how integrated congregations deal with the contrasts described herein.

Nevertheless, what are these factors which may make for nonapplicability?

*The European/African Background Difference.*   Now that black writers are emphasizing their African origins it becomes more vital than ever to be conscious of the European background of the major (white) Protestant bodies. Every major denomination with an African mission (and there is the first problem: Africa has always been seen as a mission station by Europe) is now realizing, especially at the liturgical point, what a gulf there is between these two cultures and their ways of celebrating and humanizing life. "Indigenization," with all its problems, is a suggestion of the intensity of the nonapplicability factor.

*The Ethnic Effect.*    Being a minority is a special gift. The white church is not (yet) an ethnic or racial body: it is either a consensus or the lowest common denominator. The ethnic possibility creates a very different set of instrumentalities to appropriate a given tradition, such as the Christian faith. Even as white European churches seem to have understood and appropriated something essential about the universality of the faith, so also black American Christianity has understood something equally essential about the particularity of the new Israel.

*Suffering and Oppression.*    Increasingly the history and nature of the black church are being read as the history of suffering and oppression. The other side of that coin—and this must be debated and discussed—is that the white church is complicitous with the architects of that suffering and oppression. The more gentle among us may wince at that charge, but it must be made, and met. Can the captors join in Israel's plaintive song in a strange land? Can the captives—even some generations later—participate in the forms of faith whereby they were enslaved in the name of the faith?

So there are discontinuities between black and white experiences of religion and worship. The sources of the unity of the church are not in our hands or of our making. Assimilation has its dangers. It may be that I have exaggerated these dangers and differences and have been insensitive to the common Christian assumptions shared by all. But the catholicity of the church has always been a marvelous patchwork quilt of historic, geographic, and ethnic diversity. Is not this part of the promise inherent in the determination of this presentation to prepare some liturgical suggestions shaped by the distinctive religious experiences and liturgical forms of black churches which will be useful to black and white Christians in this present period of multicultural dialog leading to an inclusive church?

# NOTES

This work contains numerous references to *Luther's Works*. 55 vols. Jaroslav Pelikan and Helmut T. Lehmann, general editors. St. Louis: Concordia; Philadelphia: Fortress, 1955–1986. References to these volumes are here abbreviated as *AE*, followed by volume and page number.

### Chapter 1:  Richard J. Perry, "Justification by Faith and Its Social Implications"

1. James Weldon Johnson, "Lift Ev'ry Voice and Sing," cited from *Lutheran Book of Worship* (Minneapolis: Augsburg, 1978), 562.
2. Henry Mitchell, *Black Preaching* (San Francisco: Harper and Row, 1979), p. 27.
3. Ibid., p. 29.
4. "Preface to the Latin Writings," *AE* 34:336.
5. Henry Mitchell and Nicholas Cooper Lewter, *Soul Theology: The Heart of American Black Culture* (San Francisco: Harper and Row, 1986), p. 84.
6. *95 Theses*, Thesis 34, *AE* 31:28; "Sermon on Two Kinds of Righteousness," *AE* 31:297-306.
7. Theodore G. Tappert, ed. and trans., *The Book of Concord* (Philadelphia: Fortress, 1959), p. 30.
8. "Lectures on Galatians," *AE* 26:137.
9. *The Freedom of the Christian, AE* 31:361.
10. *Address to the Christian Nobility of the German Nation, AE* 44:138.
11. *Against the Robbing and Murdering Hordes of Peasants, AE* 46:49-55.
12. Charles W. Heathcote, *The Lutheran Church and the Civil War* (Burlington: The Lutheran Literary Board, 1919), especially chap. 3. Up to 1840 the only Lutheran synod to publically adopt antislavery resolutions was the Franckean Synod located in New York state. The same body was the first synod to ordain an African-American as a Lutheran pastor. The Rev. Dr. Daniel Alexander Payne was ordained in 1839. He eventually left the Lutheran church to join

the African Methodist Episcopal Church. He served that denomination as pastor, bishop, educator, historian, and college president.

13. Lerone Bennett Jr., *Before the Mayflower: A History of Black America*, 5th ed. (rev.) (Baltimore: Penguin Books, 1984), p. 35.
14. Ibid., p. 45.
15. Ibid., p. 46.
16. Julius Lester, *To Be a Slave* (New York: Dell Publishing Co., 1968), p. 77; Arna Bontemps and Langston Hughes, eds., *The Book of Negro Folklore* (New York: Dodd, Mead Co., 1959), p. 56.
17. Bert James Loewnberg and Ruth Bogin, eds., *Black Women in Nineteenth Century American Life: Their Thought, Their Feelings* (University Park: Pennsylvania State University Press, 1976), p. 235. Among other works on the involvement of black women in the struggle for freedom and justice are: Angela Davis, *Women, Race and Class* (New York: Vintage, 1981); Paula Giddings, *When and Where I Enter: The Impact of Black Women on Race and Sex in America* (New York: Bantam, 1984); Bell Hooks, *Ain't I A Woman: Black Women and Feminism* (Boston: South End Press, 1981).
18. Linda Brent, *Incidents in the Life of a Slave Girl* (San Diego: Harcourt Brace Jovanovich, 1973), p. 205.
19. Quoted from "Anthony Burns to the Baptist Church at Union Fauquier County, Virginia," in *The Mind of the Negro as Reflected in Letters Written During the Crisis, 1800–1860*, ed. Carter G. Woodson (New York: Russell and Russell, 1969), p. 660.
20. Mari Evans, "Who Can Be Born Black," from *I Am a Black Woman* (New York: William Morrow, 1970), p. 93.
21. Henry Mitchell, *Black Belief: Folk Beliefs of Blacks in America* (New York: Harper and Row, 1975), p. 130.
22. James H. Cone, *A Black Theology of Liberation*, 2nd ed. (New York: Orbis Books, 1986), pp. 94-95.
23. Edward P. and Anne Streaty Wimberly, *Liberation and Human Wholeness: The Conversion Experiences of Black People in Slavery and Freedom* (Nashville: Abingdon Press, 1986), p. 39.
24. Martin Luther King Jr., *Strength to Love*, 1981 ed. (Philadelphia: Fortress, 1963), p. 135.
25. Herbert Aptheker, *American Negro Slave Revolts* (New York: International Publishers, 1983), p. 163.
26. Wyatt Tee Walker, *Somebody's Calling My Name: Black Sacred Music and Social Change*, 2nd ed. (Valley Forge: Judson Press, 1982), p. 17.
27. Christa Dixon, *Negro Spirituals: From Bible to Folk Songs* (Philadelphia: Fortress, 1976), p. 111.
28. John Lovell, *Black Song: The Forge and the Flame* (New York: Macmillan, 1972), p. 16.
29. Mitchell and Lewter, *Soul Theology*, p. 33.
30. Lovell, *Black Song*, p. 340.
31. Ibid., p. 198. Lovell gives seven purposes for spirituals: to give the community a true, valid, and useful song; to keep the community invigorated; to inspire the uninspired individual; to enable the group to face its problems; to comment on the slave situation; to stir each member to personal solutions and to a sense

of belonging in the midst of a confusing and terrifying world; and to provide
a code language for emergency use.

32. Ibid., p. 225.
33. Albert Raboteau, *Slave Religion: The Invisible Institution in the Antebellum South* (New York: Oxford University Press, 1978), p. 127. On the "invisible" church, see especially chaps. 3–6.
34. John W. Blassingame, *The Slave Community: Plantation Life in the Antebellum South*, Revised and Enlarged Edition (New York: Oxford University Press, 1979), pp. 20-21.
35. Peter Paris, *The Social Teaching of the Black Church* (Philadelphia: Fortress, 1985), p. 5. The word "allow" is used advisedly. Paris states the slaves demonstrated careful deliberations and skillful diplomacy in negotiating the approval of their masters.
36. Olin P. Moyd, *Redemption in Black Theology* (Valley Forge: Judson Press, 1979), pp. 158-159.
37. See Gayraud Wilmore, *Black Religion and Black Radicalism* (New York: Orbis, 1983); and Mechal Sobel, *Tabelin' On: The Slave Journey to an Afro-Baptist Faith* (Westport: Greenwood, 1979).
38. Paris, *The Social Teaching of the Black Church*, p. 13.
39. See C. Eric Lincoln, *Race, Religion and the Continuing American Dilemma* (New York: Hill and Wang, 1984), chap. 3.
40. C. Eric Lincoln, "The Black Church Since Frazier," in *The Negro Church in America*, ed. E. Franklin Frazier (New York: Schocken Books, 1974), p. 116.
41. DuBois, *The Souls of Black Folks*, p. 141.
42. Wimberly and Wimberly, *Liberation and Human Wholeness*, p. 19.
43. Ibid., pp. 19-20.
44. Ibid., p. 27.
45. Ibid., p. 49.
46. Ibid., pp. 40-41.
47. King, *Strength to Love*, pp. 112-114
48. James H. Cone, "The Theology of Martin Luther King, Jr.," *The Union Seminary Quarterly*, XL: 4 (1986): 27-28. Cone quotes King's sermon, "Thou Fool," delivered August 27, 1967.
49. King, *Trumpet of Conscience* (New York: Harper and Row, 1967, 1968), p. 76.
50. John Hope Franklin and Isadore Starr, eds., *The Negro in Twentieth Century America: A Reader on the Struggle for Civil Rights* (New York: Vintage, 1967), p. 144.
51. King, *Strength to Love*, p. 150.
52. Lerone Bennett, *Pioneers in Protest* (Chicago: Johnson Publishing, 1968), p. 132.
53. Sarah Bradford, *Harriet Tubman: The Moses of Her People* (New York: Corinth Books, 1961), p. 33.
54. Ibid., pp. 24-25.
55. Wimberly and Wimberly, *Liberation and Human Wholeness*, p. 30.
56. John Hope Franklin, *From Slavery to Freedom: A History of Negro Americans* (New York: Vintage Books, 1969), p. 259.

57. James H. Cone, *For My People: Black Theology and the Black Church* (New York: Orbis, 1984), p. 148.
58. Gayraud S. Wilmore and James H. Cone, *Black Theology: A Documentary History, 1966–1979* (New York: Orbis Books, 1979), p. 539.
59. Mitchell and Lewter, *Soul Theology*, pp. 6, 162. (Italics added.)

**Chapter 3: Rudolph R. Featherstone, "The Theology of the Cross: The Perspective of an African in America"**

1. Kenneth Scott Latourette, *A History of Christianity* (New York: Harper and Row, 1953), pp. 90-93.
2. Jürgen Moltmann, *The Crucified God: The Cross of Christ as Foundation and Criticism of Christian Theology* (New York: Harper and Row, 1974), p. 325.
3. Douglas John Hall, *Has the Church a Future?* (Philadelphia: Westminster, 1980), p. 41.
4. Henry H. Mitchell, *Black Belief: Folk Beliefs of Blacks in America and West Africa* (New York: Harper and Row, 1975).
5. Alister E. McGrath, *Luther's Theology of the Cross: Martin Luther's Theological Breakthrough* (New York: Basil Blackwell, 1985), p. 7.
6. Ibid., p. 25. Emphasis in original.
7. Ibid., p. 10. McGrath cites the following when pointing to one Gasparo Contarini who faced a spiritual dilemma like Luther's, prior to Luther: "Even if I did all the penances possible, and many more besides, they would not be enough to atone for my past sins, let alone merit salvation. . . . [Christ's] passion is sufficient, and more than sufficient, as a satisfaction for sins committed, to which human weakness is prone. Through this thought, I changed from great fear and anguish to happiness. I began to turn with my whole heart to this greatest good which I saw, for love of me, on the cross, his arms open and his breast opened right up to his heart. Thus I—the wretch who lacked the courage to leave the world and do penance for the satisfaction of my sins!—turned to him, and asked him to allow me to share in the satisfaction which he, the sinless one, had performed for us. He was quick to accept me and to permit his Father to totally cancel the debt which I had contracted and which I was incapable of satisfying by myself.
   "Now, since I have such a one to pay my debt, shall I not sleep securely in the midst of the city, even though I have not satisfied the debt which I had contracted? Yes! I shall sleep and wake as securely as if I had spent my entire life in the hermitage!"
8. Ibid., p. 12.
9. Douglas John Hall, *Has the Church a Future?*, p. 47.
10. Martin Brecht, *Martin Luther: His Road to Reformation* (Philadelphia: Fortress, 1985), pp. 221-231. Brecht argues for a 1518 date for Luther's theological breakthrough. On the other hand, Alister McGrath suggests that 1515 is a more reasonable date. What is clear is that Luther scholars are vastly divided over the date.
11. Alister E. McGrath, *Luther's Theology of the Cross*, p. 146.
12. Ibid.
13. Ibid., p. 147.

14. James H. Cone, *A Black Theology of Liberation*, 2nd ed., (New York: Orbis Books, 1986), p. 110.

15. Ibid.

16. "Heidelberg Disputation, 1518," *AE* 31:40. It should be noted that the printed translation of Thesis 20 follows that of Alister McGrath. See *Luther's Theology of the Cross*, n. 3, pp. 148-149.

17. Carl E. Braaten, *The Apostolic Imperative: Nature and Aim of the Church's Mission and Ministry* (Minneapolis: Augsburg, 1985), p. 16. Italics added.

18. Walther von Loewenich, *Luther's Theology of the Cross* (Minneapolis: Augsburg, 1976).

19. James H. Cone, *God of the Oppressed* (New York: Seabury Press, 1975). See also Sharon H. Ringe, *Jesus, Liberation, and the Biblical Jubilee* (Philadelphia: Fortress, 1985).

20. James H. Cone, *A Black Theology of Liberation*, p. xxi.

21. Ibid.

22. Ibid.

23. Shirley C. Guthrie Jr., *Diversity in Faith—Unity in Christ* (Philadelphia: Westminster, 1986), p. 31. Italics in original.

24. James H. Cone, *God of the Oppressed*, p. 163.

25. I am deeply indebted to and appreciative of James H. Cone's *Speaking the Truth: Ecumenism, Liberation, and Black Theology* (Grand Rapids, Mich.: Eerdmans, 1986). In fact, what follows reflects a heavy reliance upon and use of Part II, pp. 81-110 of this work.

26. Gayraud S. Gilmore, *Black Religion and Black Radicalism*, 2nd ed., (New York: Orbis Books, 1986), p. 2.

27. James H. Cone, *Speaking the Truth: Ecumenism, Liberation, and Black Theology* (Grand Rapids, Mich.: Ecrdmanns, 1986), p. 88.

28. Lawrence Jones, "Black Churches in Historical Perspective," *Christianity in Crisis*, November 2 & 16, 1970, p. 228.

29. Walter Brueggeman, *Genesis, Interpretation: A Bible Commentary*, no. 1 (Atlanta: John Knox, 1982), p. 289.

30. Bruce C. Birch, *What Does the Lord Require? The Old Testament Call to Social Witness* (Philadelphia: Westminster, 1985), p. 38. Emphasis in original.

31. John MacQuarrie, *Principles of Christian Theology* (New York: Charles Scribner's Sons, 1966), p. 248.

### Chapter 4: Judah Kiwovele, "An African Perspective on the Priesthood of All Believers"

1. Heribert Bettscheider, *Das Problem einer Afrikanischen Theologie* (Steyler Verlag, 1978), p. 88.

2. Nathaniel Mnyalpe, *Recorder*, Lupembe (February 1986).

3. Ibid.

4. Josiah Msigwa, *Recorder*, Nganda-Njombe (February 1986).

5. Bettscheider, *Das Problem*, p. 82.

6. Ibid., p. 90.

7. Manas Buthelezi and Ilse Toedt, eds., *Theologie in Konflixtfeld in Suedafrika* (Stuttgart/Munchen, 1976), pp. 103, 391.

8. Heinz Brunotte and Otto Weber, eds., *Evangelisches Kirchen Lexikon*, vol. 3 (Göttingen Vandenhoeck und Ruprecht, 1959), pp. 333-334.
9. Ibid., p. 334.
10. Ibid., p. 335.
11. Ibid., p. 336.
12. Buthelezi and Toedt, *Theologie in Konflixtfeld*, p. 4.
13. Brunotte and Weber, *EKL*, p. 336.
14. Ibid.
15. Edmond Jacob, *Theology of the Old Testament* (New York: Harper and Row, 1955), p. 247.
16. Helmer Ringgren, *Faith of the Psalmists* (Philadelphia: Fortress, 1962), pp. 1-2.
17. Ibid., p. 27.
18. Brunotte and Weber, p. 327.

**Chapter 5: Ambrose M. Moyo, "A Time for an African Lutheran Theology"**

1. Augustine, Retractions, 1.13. Quoted by E. E. Evans-Protchard, *Theologies of Primitive Religion*. Oxford: Clarendon Press, 1965, p. 3.
2. For a brief study of the development of Christianity in Egypt, cf. C. P. Groves, *The Planting of Christianity in Africa*, vol. 1. (London/ Redhill: Lutterworth, 1948), pp. 34-46.
3. Cf. Groves, pp. 46-53.
4. See the statistics and projections given by David B. Barrett, *World Christian Encyclopedia: A Comparative Study of Churches and Religions in the Modern World* (Nairobi/New York: Oxford University Press, 1982).
5. For a brief summary of the history of Lutheran missions in Africa, cf. *The Encyclopedia of the Lutheran Church*, vol. 1, ed. Julius Bodensieck (Minneapolis: Augsburg, 1965), pp. 10-21.
6. Cf. J. M. Chirenje, "Portuguese Priests and Soldiers in Zimbabwe: Interplay between Evangelism and Trade," *International Journal of Historical Studies* 4 (1973): 36ff.; H. Bhila, "Trade and Early Missionaries in Southern Zimbabwe," in *Christianity South of the Zambezi*, vol. 2, ed. M. F. C. Bourdillion, (Gweru: Mambo Press, 1977), pp. 25-42.
7. Quoted in Chirenje, p. 40.
8. Ibid.
9. Ibid.
10. Quoted by C. J. M. Zvobgo, "The Influence of the Wesleyan Methodist Missions in Southern Rhodesia, 1891–1923," in *Christianity South of the Zambezi*, vol. 2, ed. J. A. Dachs, (Gweru: Mambo Press, 1973), p. 64.
11. Cf. Hugo Sodestrom, *God Gave Growth: A History of the Lutheran Church in Zimbabwe, 1903–1980* (Gweru: Mambo Press, 1985), p. 24.
12. Benjamin Ray, *African Religions: Symbol, Ritual, and Community* (Englewood Cliffs: Prentice-Hall, Inc., 1976), p. 24.
13. Ibid., p. 202.
14. See the "Preface" in the Communion liturgy as found in the Lutheran Hymnal (USA). See also L. D. Reed, *The Lutheran Liturgy* (Philadelphia: Fortress, 1947), p. 721.

15. Ibid., p. 720. Italics added.
16. *Christianity in Independent Africa*, ed. Edward Fashole-Luke, Richard Gray, Adrian Hastings, and Godwin Tasie (London: Rex Collins, 1978), p. 364.
17. T. Twesigye, *Common Ground: Christianity, African Religion and Philosophy* (New York: Peter Lang, 1987), p. 84.
18. On the role of the Mwari cult and spirit mediums during the first and the second *chimurega* (guerrilla) wars in Zimbabwe, cf. T. O. Ranger, *Revolt in Southern Rhodesia, 1896-97: A Study in African Resistance* (London: Heinemann, 1967); *Peasant Consciousness and Guerrilla War in Zimbabwe* (Berkeley and Los Angeles: University of California, 1985).
19. *What Is Contextual Theology? An Institute of Contextual Theology Publication* (Cape Town: Blackshows [Ltd]), p. 1.
20. A. I. Berglund, *Zulu Thought-Patterns and Symbolism* (Cape Town: David Philip, 1976), pp. 37-42.
21. Adrian Hastings, *African Christianity* (New York: Seabury Press, 1976), pp. 63-64.
22. Ibid., p. 64.
23. Ibid., p. 66.
24. Clive Dillon-Malone, "The Mutumwa Churches of Zambia: An Indigenous African Healing Movement," *Journal of Religion in Africa*, 14 (1983): 201.
25. Ibid.
26. Cf. E. E. Evans, *Nuer Religion* (New York/Oxford: Oxford University Press, 1956).
27. Cf. J. S. Mbiti, *African Religion and Philosophy* (New York: Preager, 1969), p. 188.
28. Cf. J. S. Pobee, *Toward an African Theology* (Nashville: Abingdon Press, 1979), pp. 134-135.

## Chapter 6: Simon S. Maimela, "The Twofold Kingdom–An African Perspective"

1. *Temporal Authority: To What Extent It Should Be Obeyed*, AE 45:88-91.
2. "Psalm 82," *AE* 13:53-59; "A Sermon on Keeping Children in School," *AE* 46:237.
3. "Psalm 101," *AE* 13:194.
4. Attributed to John de Gruchy by Charles Villa-Vicencio in "Theology in Politics in South Africa," *Journal of Theology for South Africa* 17 (December 1976): 28-29.
5. W. A. de Klerk, *The Puritans in Africa* (London: Rex Collins, 1975), p. 233 (see also pp. 216, 218).
6. Ibid., pp. 247, 262.
7. Ibid., p. 217.
8. Allan Boesak, *Farewell to Innocence* (New York: Orbis, 1977), p. 57.
9. The banning and its subsequent lifting on Dr. Manas Buthelezi, the bannings of Dr. Beyers Naude and other church leaders, the banning of the Christian Institute and its publication, *Pro Veritate*, in 1977, and the banning and continuous vilification of black theology essays are only a few examples of the state's attempts to silence the church's critical voice and to regard its prophetic ministry as seditious.

10. "Psalm 82," *AE* 13:44-49, 70-71; "Psalm 117," *AE* 14:14; "The Sermon on the Mount," *AE* 21:265-267; *Temporal Authority, AE* 45:119; *Whether Soldiers, Too, Can Be Saved, AE* 46:96; *On War Against the Turks, AE* 46:184; "A Sermon on Keeping Children in School," *AE* 46:227.
11. "Psalm 82," *AE* 13:47-50.
12. Ibid., 13:53-59.
13. "Psalm 101," *AE* 13:197; "A Sermon on Keeping Children in School," *AE* 46:237.
14. "Psalm 82," *AE* 13:58. See also *Temporal Authority, AE* 45:120, *Large Catechism,* Fourth Commandment.
15. "Psalm 82," *AE* 13:47-50.
16. Ibid., 13:49; "Sermon on the Mount," *AE* 21:265-267; *Temporal Authority, AE* 45:119; *On War Against the Turks, AE* 46:184.
17. *Temporal Authority, AE* 45:105-106, 109-113.

### Chapter 7: James Kenneth Echols, "The Two Kingdoms: A Black American Lutheran Perspective"

1. Carl Braaten, "The Future of God," in *Two Kingdoms and One World,* ed. Karl Hertz (Minneapolis: Augsburg, 1976), pp. 344-346.
2. James H. Cone, *For My People* (Maryknoll: Orbis, 1984), p. 182.
3. Carl Braaten, *Principles of Lutheran Theology* (Philadelphia: Fortress, 1983), p. 133.
4. Paul Althaus, *The Ethics of Martin Luther* (Philadelphia: Fortress, 1972), p. 43.
5. *Temporal Authority, AE* 45:83f.
6. *Whether Soldiers, Too, Can Be Saved, AE* 46:93ff. This treatise was not published until 1527.
7. Ulrich Duchrow and Heiner Hoffman, "Die Vorstellung von Zwei Reichen und Regimenten bis Luther," in *Two Kingdoms and One World,* ed. Karl Hertz (Minneapolis: Augsburg, 1976), p. 18.
8. Althaus, *The Ethics of Martin Luther,* p. 43.
9. Ibid., p. 51f.
10. "Temporal Authority," *AE* 45:85-87.
11. Ibid., 45:92.
12. Althaus, *The Ethics of Martin Luther,* pp. 60-61. Luther used "governments" and "kingdoms" interchangeably, according to Althaus.
13. "Temporal Authority," *AE* 45:95.
14. Ibid., 45:101.
15. "Treatise on Good Works, 1523," *AE* 44:93.
16. "Temporal Authority," *AE* 45:125.
17. Ibid., 45:111-112.
18. Edmund Schlink, *Theology of the Lutheran Confessions* (Philadelphia: Fortress, 1961), pp. 226-269.
19. Theodore G. Tappert, ed., *The Book of Concord* (Philadelphia: Fortress, 1959), pp. 37-38; see also pp. 81-94.
20. See E. Franklin Frazier, *The Negro Church in America* (New York: Schocken, 1974); Albert J. Raboteau, *Slave Religion* (New York: Oxford University,

1978); Joseph R. Washington, *Black Religion* (Boston: Beacon Press, 1964); and Gayraud Wilmore, *Black Religion and Black Radicalism,* 2nd ed. (Maryknoll: Orbis, 1983).

21. Henry Mitchell and Nicholas Cooper-Lewter, *Soul Theology* (San Francisco: Harper and Row, 1986), p. 19.

22. James H. Cone, *Black Theology and Black Power* (New York: Seabury, 1969), p. 33.

23. Lester Scherer, *Slavery and the Churches in America, 1619–1819* (Grand Rapids, Mich.: Eerdmans, 1975), p. 30.

24. Ibid., p. 32.

25. Richard Allen, *The Life Experience and Gospel Labors of the Rt. Rev. Richard Allen* (Nashville: Abingdon, 1960), p. 97.

26. James H. Cone, *The Spirituals and the Blues* (New York: Seabury, 1972), p. 97.

27. Mitchell and Cooper-Lewter, *Soul Theology,* p. 79.

28. Ibid., p. 66.

29. Latta R. Thomas, *Biblical Faith and the Black American* (Valley Forge: Judson Press, 1976), pp. 17-18.

30. Ibid., p. 105.

31. Cone, *Black Theology and Black Power,* pp. 35-36.

32. Idem., *The Spirituals and the Blues,* p. 92.

33. Ibid., p. 95.

34. *The Twelve Articles,* AE 46:8-16. The quotation is on pp. 9-10.

35. "Admonition to Peace: A Reply to the Twelve Articles of the Peasants in Swabia," AE 46:17-43.

36. Ibid., 46:20.

37. Ibid., 46:25-26.

38. Ibid., 46:29.

39. Hubert Kirchner, *Luther and the Peasants' War* (Philadelphia: Fortress, 1972), pp. 17-18.

40. *Against the Murdering and Robbing Hordes of Peasants,* AE 46:49-55. This treatise was written in May 1525 and provoked criticism against Luther. He responded, often using fragments of the earlier tract in his July 1525 *An Open Letter On the Harsh Book Against the Peasants,* AE 46:63-85. The quotation is from p. 73.

41. Kirchner, *Luther and the Peasants' War,* pp. 17-18.

42. Karl Hertz, ed., *Two Kingdoms and One World,* p. 68.

43. Quoted in ibid., p. 83f. from Luthard's *Die Ethik in ihren Grundzügen.*

44. Quoted in ibid., p. 87, from Sohm's "Der Christ im öffentlichem Leben."

45. Quoted in ibid., pp. 89-91, from Hermann's *Die Religion in Verhältnis zum Welterkennen und zur Sittlichkeit: Eine Grundlegung der systematischen Theologie.*

46. Quoted in ibid., p. 100, from "Hirtenbrief der Rheinischen Mission an die Herero-Christen." See also pp. 92-100.

47. Braaten, *Principles of Lutheran Theology,* p. 124.

48. Karl Hertz, ed., *Two Kingdoms and One World,* p. 238.

49. Wilmore, *Black Religion and Black Radicalism,* p. xiii.

50. Peter Paris, *The Social Teaching of the Black Churches* (Philadelphia: Fortress, 1985), pp. 3-4.
51. Ibid., p. 6.
52. Ibid., p. 15.
53. For a more thorough treatment of black American Christian activism, see Wilmore, *Black Religion and Black Radicalism*.
54. Allen, *The Life Experience and Gospel Labors of the Rt. Rev. Richard Allen*, pp. 23-25.
55. Monroe Fordham, *Major Themes in Northern Black Religious Thought, 1800–1860* (Hicksville: Exposition Press, 1975), pp. 111-143.
56. Raboteau, *Slave Religion*, p. 212.
57. Ibid., pp. 218-248
58. Ibid., p. 294.
59. Paris, *The Social Teaching of the Black Churches*, p. 111.
60. Wilmore, *Black Religion and Black Radicalism*, pp. 53-73.
61. Ibid., p. 64.
62. Henry Highland Garnet, "An Address to the Slaves of the United States of America," in *Black Nationalism in America*, John H. Bracey Jr., August Meier, and Elliot Rudnick, eds. (Indianapolis and New York: Bobbs Merrill, 1970), p. 70-71.
63. Ibid., p. 71.
64. Ibid., p. 76.
65. Cone, *Black Theology and Black Power*, p. 143.
66. Christa K. Dixon, *Negro Spirituals from Bible to Folksong* (Philadelphia: Fortress, 1976), p. 81.
67. Wilmore, *Black Religion and Black Radicalism*, p. 87.
68. Benjamin Quarles, *Black Abolitionists* (New York: Oxford University Press, 1969), pp. 3-4.
69. Ibid., p. 54.
70. Ibid., p. 20.
71. James M. Washington, ed., *A Testament of Hope: The Essential Writings of Martin Luther King Jr.* (San Francisco: Harper and Row, 1986), p. 219.
72. Ibid., p. 218.

**Chapter 8: John S. Pobee, "Relationships to Ideologies and Non-Christian Religions"**

1. David B. Barrett, "2000 A.D.: 350 Million Christians in Africa" in *International Review of Missions* 59 (1970): 39-54; A. F. Walls, "Toward Understanding 'Africa's Place in Christian History' " in *Religion in a Pluralistic Society*, ed. J. S. Pobee (Leiden: E. J. Brill, 1976), p. 82.
2. See J. S. Trimingham, *Islam in West Africa* (Oxford: Clarendon Press, 1959); Ivor Wills, *The Northern Factor in Ashanti History* (Lagon: University Institute of African Studies, 1961).
3. J. A. Essuah, "Bishop Essuah Speaks to Catholics" in *Standard National Catholic Weekly* 39/14 (3 April–10 April 1977).
4. C. G. Baeta, *Prophetism in Ghana* (London: S C M, 1962), p. 39; J. S. Pobee, "I Will Lift Up My Eyes unto Mozano," in *International Review of Missions*, vol. LXXV, no. 298 (April 1986): 126.

5. K. A. Busia, *Africa in Search of Democracy* (London: Routledge and Kegan Paul, 1967), p. 23.
6. J. S. Mbiti, *African Religions and Philosohy* (New York: Doubleday, 1970), p. 181.
7. J. S. Pobee, *The Word Became Flesh* (London: CAMEC, 1984).
8. P. K. Sarpong, "Christianity Should be Africanised, Not Africans Christianised" in *African Ecclesiastical Review,* vol. 17, no. 6, 1975; see also J. S. Pobee, *Toward an African Theology* (Nashville: Abingdon, 1979).
9. *Gold Star Leader,* 20th April 1907.
10. John Mensah Sarbah, *Fante National Constitution* (London: Clowes, 1906), p. 256.
11. K. Wiredu, *Philosophy and African Culture* (Cambridge: OUP, 1980), p. 53.
12. Lord Acton's statement in a letter to Bishop Mandell Creighton (1887), that "Power tends to corrupt; absolute power corrupts absolutely," has been verified time and again. Before Lord Acton, William Pitt, Earl of Chatam (1708–1778) had also observed that "unlimited power is apt to corrupt the minds of those who possess it" (Case of Wilkers, Speech, January 9, 1770).
13. Wiredu, *Philosophy and African Culture,* p. 52. See also J. Verkuyi, *Contemporary Missiology: An Introduction* (Grand Rapids: Ecrdmanns, 1978), p. 374.
14. R. A. Maricus, *Saeculum: History of Society in the Theology of St. Augustine* (Cambridge: OUP, 1970), pp. 146ff.
15. J. Lochman, *Reconciliation and Liberation* (Belfast: Christian Journal, Ltd., 1980), p. 16.
16. J. S. Pobee, "Creation, Faith, and Responsibility for the World" in *Journal of the Theology for Southern Africa* 50 (March 1985): 16-26, esp. p. 22.

## Chapter 9: Sibusiso M. Bengu, "A Social and Political Analysis of Apartheid/Racism from a Black Lutheran Perspective"

1. Cedric Mayson, *A Certain Sound: The Struggle for Liberation in South Africa* (London: Epworth Press, 1984), p. 39.
2. Ibid., p. 38.
3. Ibid., p. 47.
4. Report of the LWF-ELCT Consultation on the Root Causes of Socio-Economic and Political Injustice, 1982, pp. 18, 70.
5. LWF Report, Budapest, 1984 (Geneva: Lutheran World Federation, 1985), pp. 245-246.

## Chapter 10: Albert Pero, "On Being Black, Lutheran, and American in a Racist Society"

1. W. E. B. DuBois, *The Souls of Black Folk* (Greenwich, Conn.: Fawcett Premier Book, 1968), pp. 16, 17. Originally published in 1903.
2. James C. Cone represents the progenitor of this new method in black religious research and we are very much indebted to him for his pioneering works in this area.
3. William H. Grier and Price M. Cobbs, *Black Rage* (New York: Basic Books, Inc., 1968), p. 8.

4. Leronne Bennett, *The Challenge of Blackness* (Chicago: Johnson, 1972), p. 34.

5. Leon W. Chestang, "Character Development in a Hostile Environment," Occasional Paper No. 3 (November 1972), School of Social Service, n.p., p. 2.

6. K. H. Fishel Jr. and Benjamin Quarles, *The Negro American* (Glenview, Ill.: Scott, Foresmen and Co., 1967), pp. 204-205.

7. August Meier and Elliott Rudwick, eds. *Black Protest in the Sixties* (Chicago: Chicago Quadrangle Books, Inc., 1967), p. 130.

8. James H. Cone, *Black Theology and Black Power* (New York: The Seabury Press, 1969), p. 8.

9. W. P. Mueller and J. Jacobsen, "Samuel Beckett's Long Last Saturday: To Wait or Not to Wait" in *Man in Modern Theatre,* ed. Nathan Scott Jr. (Richmond, Va.: John Knox, 1965), p. 77.

10. Jean D. Gramps, "The Self-Concept: Basis for Reeducation of Negro Youth," *Negro Self-Concept: Implication for School Citizenship* (New York: McGraw-Hill, 1965), p. 41.

11. Gordon Allport, *The Nature of Prejudice,* (New York: Doubleday/Anchor Books, 1958), p. 142. This research is not specifically designed to analyze the problems of women, Spanish-speaking people, or Indians. This writer believes that they are vital areas to be concerned about and gives encouragement to those who are working in these areas. This research is concerned about correlating the kerygma to the black condition and if by solving the problem others who have had a similar experience take clues from it, well and good.

12. See Melville J. Herskovits, *The Myth of Negro Past* (Boston: Beacon Press, 1941), chap. 4, and also DuBois, *The Souls of Black Folk,* chaps. 4, 10.

13. Grier and Cobbs, *Black Rage,* p. 86.

14. Allison David and John Dolland, *Children of Bondage* (Washington, D.C.: American Council on Education, 1940), chap. 10.

15. Grier and Cobbs, *Black Rage,* p. 95.

16. Andrew Billingsley, *Black Families in White America* (New York: Prentice Hall, Inc., 1968). See esp. chap. 4.

17. Benjamin E. Mays, *The Negro's God* (New York: Atheneum, 1968).

18. See Albert J. Raboteau, "Ethiopia Shall Soon Stretch Forth Her Hands: Black Destiny in Nineteenth Century America," *The University* (Jan. 27, 1983). See also Adam C. Powell Jr., *Marching Blacks* (New York: Dial Press, 1945; rev. 1973), p. 194.

19. See Howard Thurman's writings: *Deep River* (1945), *Jesus and the Disinherited* (1949), et al.

20. See the influential works of B. E. Mays: *The Negro's Church* (1933), *The Negro's God* (1938), et al.

21. See the important black religious tradition in M. L. King's works.

22. Malcolm X, *The Autobiography of Malcolm X* (New York: Grove Press, 1965).

23. See the writings of James H. Cone and Gayraud S. Wilson.

**Chapter 11: Cheryl A. Stewart, "Integrity in the Priesthood of All Believers"**

1. Definitions from *Cassell's New Latin Dictionary,* ed. D. P. Simpson (New York: Funk and Wagnalls, 1960), p. 317.

2. *Random House College Dictionary*, rev. ed. (New York: Random House, 1979), p. 692.
3. Cyril Eastwood, *The Royal Priesthood of the Faithful* (Minneapolis: Augsburg, 1963), p. 3.
4. Ibid., p. 4.
5. Ibid., p. 23.
6. Hans Küng, *The Church* (Garden City, N. Y.: Doubleday, 1976), p. 467.
7. Ibid., p. 409.
8. Eastwood, *The Royal Priesthood*, p. 32.
9. Küng, *The Church*, pp. 476-488.
10. Eastwood, *The Royal Priesthood*, p. 87.
11. Ibid., p. 110.
12. Ibid., p. 137.
13. Ibid., p. 229.
14. Ewald M. Plass, *What Luther Says, An Anthology* (St. Louis, Mo.: Concordia, 1959), Vol. III, p. 1138, 1139-1140.
15. Martin Luther, "To the Christian Nobility of the German Nation," *AE* 44:126.
16. Ibid., 44:129-130.
17. Ibid., 44:134. Brackets added.
18. Ibid., 44:136.
19. Plass, *What Luther Says*, p. 1140. Parentheses added.
20. Ibid., pp. 1142-1143.
21. Eastwood, *The Royal Priesthood*, p. 241.
22. Clyde W. Franklin II, and Walter Pillow, "The Black Man's Acceptance of the Prince Charming Ideal," *Black Caucus, Journal of the National Association of Black Social Workers* (Spring 1982), p. 3.
23. Ibid., p. 3.
24. Ibid., p. 7. Parenthesis added.
25. Calvin C. Hernton, *Sex and Racism in America* (New York: Grove Press, 1965), p. 16.
26. Ibid., p. 50-51.
27. Carlyle Marney, *Priests to Each Other* (Valley Forge, Pa.: Judson Press, 1974), p. 9.
28. W. E. B. DuBois, *The Souls of Black Folk* (New York: The New American Library, 1969), p. 45. Sexist language not notated to retain author's thoughts.

### Chapter 12: Vivian V. Msomi, "Theological Education and Preparation for Ministry in Africa"

1. Bengt Sundkler, *Christian Ministry in Africa* (Uppsala: Swedish Institute of Missionary Research, 1960), pp. 180-181.
2. Ibid., p. 202.
3. See Lutheran World Federation, Department of Church Cooperation, Advisory Committee on Theological Education in Africa, minutes: 1. Zomba, Malawi (1982); 2. Yaounde, Cameroon (1983); and 3. Arushe, Tanzania (1985).

### Chapter 13: Craig J. Lewis, "Black and Lutheran Theological Education for Ministerial Formation in America"

1. *Factbook on Theological Education for the Academic Year 1982–83*, ed. William Baumgaertner, The Association of Theological Schools in the U.S. and Canada, P.O. Box 130, Vandalia, Ohio, 45377-0130.

2. C. Eric Lincoln, *The Black Church Since Frazier* (New York: Schocken Books, 1974), pp. 115-116.
3. Gayraud S. Wilmore, *Black and Presbyterian* (Philadelphia: Geneva Press, 1983), pp. 50-51.
4. James H. Cone, *My Soul Looks Back* (Maryknoll: Orbis Books, 1986), p. 90.
5. Statistics from *The Factbook on Theological Education*.
6. Ibid.
7. They are James Echols, Rudolph Featherstone, Albert Pero, and Winston Persaud.
8. James J. Gardiner and J. Deotis Roberts, eds., *Quest for a Black Theology* (Philadelphia: Pilgrim Press, 1971), p. 63.

## Chapter 14: Albert Pero, "Worship and Theology in the Black Context"

1. James H. Cone, "Black Consciousness and the Black Church," *Christianity and Crisis*, November 2 & 16, 1970, p. 247.
2. Reuben A. Sheares II, "Beyond White Theology," *Christianity and Crisis*, November 2 & 16, 1970, p. 229.
3. Ibid.
4. Ibid., pp. 230-231.
5. Cone, "Black Consciousness," p. 247.
6. Ibid.
7. Ibid., p. 246.
8. William B. McClain, "The Genius of the Black Church," *Christianity and Crisis*, November 2 & 16, 1970, p. 252.
9. Sheares, "Beyond White Theology," p. 233.
10. Albert B. Cleage Jr., *The Black Messiah* (New York: Sheed and Ward, 1968), p. 37.
11. Glen Germahl, "The Vision of Cesar Chavez," *Christianity and Crisis*, 21 (January 1971): 299.
12. C. Eric Lincoln, "Who's Listening?" *Christianity and Crisis*, November 2 & 16, 1970, pp. 225-226.
13. McClain, "The Genius of the Black Church," p. 250.
14. Ibid., p. 252.
15. Leon W. Watts II, "The National Committee of Black Churchmen," *Christianity and Crisis*, November 2 & 16, 1970, p. 243.
16. Sheares, "Beyond White Theology," p. 235.
17. Dietrich Bonhoeffer, *Letters and Papers from Prison* (New York: MacMillan, 1967), p. 14.
18. David B. Barrett, *Schism and Renewal in Africa* (London, 1968), p. 66.
19. Ibid., p. 79.
20. Frazier's *The Negro Church in America* (New York: Schocken, 1964) is still the best published outline of U.S. black church history. Its bias is contradicted by articles in the *Journal of Negro History*. Arthur Huff Fausset's *Black Gods of the Metropolis* (Philadelphia: University of Pennsylvania Press, 1944) is helpful when compared with similar descriptions of African and West Indies churches. In addition to my own experiences in the U.S., I have also used Arthur Piepkorn's files describing black denominations to write this paragraph on U.S. black churches.

21. E. B. Welbourne and B. A. Ogot, *A Place to Feel at Home: A Study of Two Independent Churches in Western Kenya* (London: Oxford University Press, 1966). They suggest this as a motive for indigenous East African churches.

22. Melville Jean Herskovits first pointed to this connection in *The Myth of the Negro Past* (New York: Harper & Brothers, 1941), pp. 232-233, but he weakened his case by adding his speculation that this water symbolism became more important in the new world because of many river priests who were deported as slaves.

23. This subject is treated in detail by LeRoi Jones, *Blues People: Negro Music in White America* (New York: William Morrow & Co., 1963), to my mind the best book on U.S. black culture published.

24. David Beckmann, "Trance: From Africa to Pentecostalism," *Concordia Theological Monthly* XLV (January 1974).11-26; Harold W. Turner, *African Independent Church: The Life and Faith of the Church of the Lord* (Aladura), II (Oxford: The London Press, 1967), pp. 301, 309.

25. Joseph R. Washington Jr., "How Black is Black Religion?" in *Quest for a Black Theology*, eds. James J. Gardiner and J. Deotis Roberts Sr. (Philadelphia: Pilgrim Press, 1971), pp. 22-43, is one of several who makes this comparison.

26. James Baldwin, *The Fire Next Time* (New York: Dial Press, 1963), pp. 47-48.

27. James H. Cone, *The Spirituals and the Blues* (New York: Seabury Press, 1972), p. 73.

28. Ibid.

29. Ibid., pp. 30-31.

30. Ibid., p. 40.

31. Ibid., p. 7.

32. Ibid., p. 33.

33. Ibid., p. 5.

# APPENDIX: A HARARE MESSAGE OF BLACK LUTHERANS

## I. An Introductory Overview

We, African and African-American theologians and church leaders of the Lutheran family of churches, have been holding a Conference of International Black Lutherans (CIBL) at the University of Zimbabwe, Harare, from September 4–12, 1986, to explore what it means for us to be both black and Lutheran, and to share our experiences of this doubly rich heritage. The participants comprised of Lutheran pastors, teachers, students, church officials, and bishops from the Lutheran churches in Africa and North America.

The choice of Harare as the venue of this conference was not entirely fortuitous. Zimbabwe has enormous significance for us as one of the Frontline states which border on South Africa, a country which symbolizes the denial of human rights and dignity to the people of color, especially of the African ancestry. Therefore, our conference, held in Harare at the heels and in the shadow of the eighth Summit of the Non-Aligned Movement (NAM), which focused on the economic problems between the North and South, and between the rich and poor countries, was intended to call the world's attention to South Africa as the embodiment of the plight and oppression of the people of color as well as of the hope of victory for blacks in their struggle to break the chains that hold them in bondage on the global level.

The conference brought together 39 African and African-American Lutherans to dialog with one another and to reflect together on the theme: "The Lutheran Heritage and the Black Experience in Africa and North America." Under the rubric of this general theme, a number of lectures were read on the topics: "Justification by Faith and Its Social Implications," "The Two Kingdoms Doctrine and Its Continuing Relevance," "The Theology of the Cross," "The Priesthood of All Believers," "Apartheid and

Racism," "Ecumenical Issues," "Relationships to Ideologies and Non-Christian Religions," "Liberation Theologies," "Theological Education and Preparation for Ministry," "Worship and Theology in the Black Context," and "Daily Bible Studies." These lectures were intended to stimulate discussions and thereby help us to speak to one another and to share our experiences as blacks and as Lutherans. In addition, these lectures were intended to help us achieve the following objectives:

*(a)* to dialog about our African and African-American experience, our identity, our relationships and mission as blacks and Lutherans;

*(b)* to develop our God-given potential for the continued passing on of our historical legacy through research, production, and publication of materials for theological education;

*(c)* to posit common solutions and to create new theological insights based on the black experience in order to enrich the Lutheran church in particular and the church catholic in general.

As we wrestled with our theme for the conference and what it means for us to be both black and Lutheran, we were struck by the fact that there was a general consensus that the Lutheran heritage and its doctrinal formulations continues to be a resource for us in our present situation. This, notwithstanding, we could not, however, help but sense that the manner in which this heritage has been appropriated by Lutherans in different historical contexts leaves much to be desired. In consequence, Lutherans have not been in the forefront of human struggles for sociopolitical and economic liberation. Our awareness of the contradictions between theory and praxis in Lutheranism with its detrimental consequences for black Lutherans has made us appreciate all the more the significance of our being both black and Lutheran, a significance that we would like to give a theological affirmation and interpretation, namely that:

*(a)* We are irrevocably black by divine act and therefore are a gift of God to the Church;

*(b)* We are Christians by miraculous divine intervention and through the work of the Holy Spirit;

*(c)* We are Lutherans by paradoxical circumstances reflecting the sinful human condition and the sin of denominationalism.

This twofold heritage of being both black and Lutheran should be understood as God's special gift to enrich the church. It challenges the Lutheran church to become more open to the excluded experiences and theological insights of its black constituents, so that the Lutheran portrayal of God's presence in and among humanity might yet become inclusive of all of human experience.

It is out of our appreciation of this divine gift of our twofold and rich heritage that we joyfully affirm our commitment to the continuing reformation of the church for the purpose of the salvation of humanity in all its spiritual and physical aspects, and for the transformation of our world and interpersonal relationships through our understanding and interpretation of the Holy Scriptures, the writings of Martin Luther, the Confessions, and our black heritage.

## II. A Black Critique of the Lutheran Heritage

As black Lutherans of Africa and North America, we both affirm and claim as our own the essence of the Lutheran heritage, which we understand to be the faithful confession, in every age, that Jesus Christ is the Son of God and the Savior of the world. We, however, wish to assert unequivocally that for Lutherans and Lutheranism to be faithful in the contemporary confession of Christ as Lord and Savior, the Christian faith must be understood, interpreted, and lived out in a theologically wholistic, ethnically inclusive, and culturally contextual manner. Therefore, we take issue with any and all expressions of Lutheranism which are less than faithful to its essence, the gospel. As such, we respectfully and charitably raise several issues with those of our European-American Lutheran sisters and brothers in Christ who, in our day, understand, interpret, and live out the Christian faith in theologically dichotomous, ethnically exclusive, and culturally monolithic, if not imperialistic, fashion. In so doing, we declare our commitment to join with them in the common struggle to be faithful to the gospel.

Specifically we take issue with that European-American understanding of justification that affirms and maintains a radical dichotomy between God's activity of justification and sanctification. As black Lutherans, we agree that the confession of Christ has profound significance for humanity in terms of God's love and unconditional acceptance of the repentant sinner in Christ and God's promise of eternal life. Yet we believe that the confession of Christ also extends to an understanding of the transformation (sanctification) of the believer which is rooted in the converting reality of justification. Hence, while acknowledging that Christians are simultaneously saints and sinners *(simul justus et peccator),* we also assert unequivocally that there is an inextricable link and relationship between who one is, namely a baptized and adopted child of God, and what one does, namely living and acting in conformity to the will of God. Given our black experience, characterized by racial oppression and which currently assumes the forms of apartheid, discrimination, and lingering effects of Western colonialism and cultural imperialism, and our understanding of the biblical witness, we declare that God is concerned about the whole of life, and that means that justification and justice must never be separated. For God's will for humanity is justice. In consequence, those who have God's mercy in Christ are called to seek after, work for, and engage themselves in those activities that will bring about justice to those who are oppressed. In the final analysis justification has to do with the right relationships, namely the reconciliation between God and alienated human beings, and between human beings themselves. In this regard, the message of the epistle of James with its emphasis upon the connection between faith and good works embodies an understanding of discipleship which is indispensable to the faithful confession of Christ.

Secondly, we take issue with what we consider to be Lutheranism's misinterpretation and misappropriation of the two kingdoms doctrine. From our perspective, there is an essential theological truth reflected in this formulation which provides the basis for Christian activism in the world. Yet scholars have persuasively pointed out that Lutheran quietism has been grounded in a dualistic interpretation of the two kingdoms doctrine, and we know from black experience that, in the face of racial, colonial, sexist, and class oppression, this tradition of political conservatism and quietism more often than not predominates.

Hence, with exceptions, Lutheranism proclaims the liberating message of the gospel in a way that dichotomizes reality, proclaiming spiritual liberation while ignoring the implications of that liberating message for those suffering under sociopolitical structures of oppression. Theologically we declare that our God is the God of both heaven and earth whose will extends to the totality of reality. Even as we recognize that some Lutherans have misappropriated the doctrine in a manner that has led to the tradition's legacy of quietism, we summon Lutheranism to understand, interpret, and live out the doctrine in accord with the injunctions of Matthew 7:21, Acts 5:29, and James 2:26, so as to faithfully confess Christ.

Thirdly, we take issue with the manner in which some Lutherans have articulated and institutionalized the ministry of the whole people of God (the priesthood of all believers). This theological insight has often been employed, in the life of the church, to give lip service to the calling and the ministry of the whole baptized community. Quite to the contrary, however, it has actually encouraged clericalism by effectively making the sacrament of Baptism a rite, while making the rite of ordination a sacrament. Thus the ministry of the whole people of God is vertically conceived, being grounded in clerical authority and prerogative. Yet both the biblical witness and our cultural experience confirm the fact that an understanding, interpretation, and embodiment of the ministry of the whole people of God should be horizontally oriented, emphasizing servanthood and communal cooperation in the utilization of God-given gifts for the sake of the gospel. In addition, to faithfully confess Christ with respect to both the whole people of God and the doctrine of justification is to be ethnically inclusive, rather than exclusive, since God's diverse humanity is present among all the baptized people of God.

Finally, we take issue with that European-American understanding of Lutheranism that imposes upon black Lutheranism a culturally monolithic expression of the tradition rather than culturally contextual and diverse expressions of the tradition. We consider to be culturally monolithic that approach to ecumenism which views it from the singular perspective of creedal theology. While valuing an exploration of creedal theology, our cultural experience and the biblical witness require us in our ecumenical contacts with all Christians to raise the issue of ethics or praxis in relationship to the concern for liberation, wholistically understood. We consider to be culturally monolithic that approach to theological education which exclusively emphasizes the Western theological tradition, a tradition that is to be grasped intellectually and mastered. While valuing intellectual reflection, our cultural experience and the biblical witness requires us as regards ministerial formation to insist upon the integration of all theological knowledge with professional skills and personal belief. And we consider to be culturally monolithic forms of worship which, while grounded in a particular culture, are claimed to be universal. While valuing all forms of worship through which God is praised, we are persuaded by the spirit of God and Luther's concern for indigenous worship, that the African and African-American cultures are gifts of God to us. Accordingly we declare our intention to embrace both our Lutheran heritage and our respective cultures in worship, to indigenize worship. Thus, as black Lutherans of Africa and the United States, we intend to commit ourselves to culturally contextualizing the Lutheran heritage we share in common with others.

## III. Contributions and Gifts of Black Lutherans

While there is much in the Lutheran heritage and its historical appropriation that deserve to be criticized, there is also much in this heritage which continues to be a resource in our present situation. Not wanting to throw out the baby with the bath water, black Lutherans have gathered in Harare to initiate a critical as well as constructive examination of Lutheran theology in the light of black experience and our understanding of biblical witness to the gospel of Jesus Christ, the Liberator. This initiative was undertaken in the belief that our unique historical experience which has given rise to a particular appropriation of the biblical and Lutheran heritage has much to offer the church which is at present dominated by a European-American theological and cultural outlook. This we herewith offer for discussion among the whole international family of the Lutheran church.

Out of the myriad of insightful theological concepts that were presented and discussed in the course of this conference, a number of general theological themes and statements may be drawn which point to the fundamental and distinctive theological contributions and innovations that African and African-American Lutherans may make to the Lutheran theological heritage, *inter alia:*

1. Justification by faith points to the intrinsic relationship that exists between faith and deeds, and between who one is, as a forgiven sinner and child of God, and what one does, in relation to one's neighbors and in fulfillment of God's will. But somewhat differently, justification by faith points to the effecting of reconciliation and restoration of broken relationships between God and humans, and between humans themselves who, as forgiven sinners and brothers and sisters in Christ, engage themselves in acts of love toward one another, thereby building up God's world.

   (a) This black insight enlarges the traditional emphasis on faith almost to the exclusion of good deeds. To the average Christian, traditional Lutheranism has been understood to teach a separation between justification and sanctification, and between Christian righteousness before God *(coram Deo)* and social righteousness before *our* fellows *(coram homonibus).*

   (b) To overcome this separation, black Lutherans are persuaded that Lutheranism would be greatly enriched if it were to embrace the epistle of James as the epistle of wholistic Christian power rather than an epistle of straw. For this epistle rightly asserts that faith and good deeds belong together, and that faith without works is useless and inauthentic.

2. The two kingdoms doctrine points to the better theological portrayal of God's twofold but mutually interpenetrable governance which, correctly understood, should lead to a healthy Christian activism that leads to the transformation of the world politically, socially, and economically without collapsing into one the realized and future kingdom of God.

3. The theology of the cross points to a methodology which challenges Lutheranism to synthesize our Christian symbols and pragmatic actions beyond mere methodology to become a way of life.

4. Priesthood of all believers points to a fundamental understanding of the nature of Christian ministry, one which is inclusive and emphasizes the servanthood of all the people of God, who must be horizontally oriented and cooperatively serve one another in the utilization of their God-given gifts for the sake of the gospel. In so doing, believers build up Christian community, edify one another, and develop solidarity among themselves. Therefore, this doctrine criticizes and proposes alternatives to the present clericalism and hierarchical church structures in the preoccupation with the ordained ministry.

5. Ecumenism points beyond the Western, European-American ethnocentricism of many Lutheran ecumenical ventures, particularly those that point to a recovery of (or return to) "catholic unity," especially between Lutherans and Roman Catholics and Anglicans. Black Lutherans assert that "catholic unity" is more than consensus on the Western creedal theology. We consider such a European-American understanding nothing but a culturally monolithic expression of the Western catholic tradition which is pursued at the expense of an authentic ecumenism which is culturally, ethnically, and contextually diverse in its expressions of the Christian faith. We commit ourselves to ecumenism that is more inclusive and culturally contextualized; it is a Christian unity whose vision is diverse and broad enough to include African and African-Americans and similar non-European cultural expressions of Christian faith. Our findings thus present a new vision of ecumenism.

6. Theological education points to a contextualization of the Lutheran curriculum so that we might produce leaders with a clearer proclamation of the gospel and more relevant ministry among black Lutherans.

7. Worship points to a contextualization of the liturgy as the work of the people. This must be one with and inseparable from the brothers and sisters around the world who struggle for liberation in a variety of ways.

We have initiated at this conference answers to the critical question of our Lord Jesus Christ: "Who do you [black Lutherans] say that I am?" We have begun the task of answering this question by rescuing theology from the hands of European-American Lutherans, from the shelves of the seminaries and universities and from arrogant absolutism, thereby allowing the Holy Spirit to direct our path toward wholeness.

Faith in Christ, active in love and justice, is the cure, the healing balm from Gilead.

# Contributors

SIBUSISO M. BENGU
Secretary for Research
Department of World Service
Lutheran World Federation
Geneva, Switzerland

JAMES KENNETH ECHOLS
Professor of Historical Theology
Lutheran Theological Seminary at Philadelphia

RUDOLPH R. FEATHERSTONE
Professor of Theology
Trinity Lutheran Seminary
Columbus, Ohio

JUDAH KIWOVELE
Bishop, Southern Diocese
Evangelical Lutheran Church in Tanzania

CRAIG J. LEWIS
Director
Commission for Multicultural Ministries
Evangelical Lutheran Church in America
Chicago, Illinois

SIMON S. MAIMELA
Professor of Systematic Theology
University of South Africa

AMBROSE M. MOYO
Senior Lecturer in Religious Studies
    and Head of the Department of Religious Studies,
    Classics, and Philosophy
University of Zimbabwe

VIVIAN V. MSOMI
Rector
Lutheran Theological College
Umpumulo on Natal, South Africa

ALBERT PERO
Professor of Systematic Theology and Culture
Lutheran School of Theology at Chicago

RICHARD J. PERRY
Director for Black Ministries
Commission for Multicultural Ministries
Evangelical Lutheran Church in America
Chicago, Illinois

JOHN S. POBEE
Associate Director
Program for Theological Education
World Council of Churches
Geneva, Switzerland

CHERYL A. STEWART
Coordinator of Crossings Campus Ministry
    for the City Colleges of Chicago
Chicago, Illinois